"I am delighted to recommend *How We Love* as a comprehensive guide for formation in celibate chastity. I believe this lucid and practical guide will be extremely useful in both seminaries and formation programs of religious men and women. Academicians as well as directors of initial and ongoing formation will appreciate the breath of research Brother John Mark Falkenhain, OSB, and his clear-eyed response to the contemporary challenges of preparing those called by the Lord to the commitment of celibacy. This book will help priests and religious continue to offer a joyful and mature witness to a life of celibacy as a free and generous self-gift to God and others."

> —Cardinal Joseph W. Tobin, CSsR
> Archdiocese of Newark, New Jersey

"*How We Love* provides significant insights for vocation and formation directors responsible for assessing candidates to religious life as well as readers who want to enhance their understanding of living vowed celibacy with integrity. Written with incredible depth, this essential resource focuses on answering two fundamental questions: 'How well-formed do we expect someone to be before entering our programs?' and 'Where do we expect them to be just before final profession or ordination?' Because vocation directors assess the personal characteristics of applicants for the capacity to learn the skills needed for vowed communal life, I highly recommend this book. It provides helpful and concise information for identifying the skills needed for cultivating healthy vowed celibacy."

> —Deborah Marie Borneman, SSCM
> Director of Member Relations and Services,
> National Religious Vocation Conference

"This timely work will prove to be an invaluable resource for human formation directors and for the seminarians with whom they work. A methodologically precise, well-researched, faith-filled and profoundly helpful process that maps the journey from self-knowledge to self-acceptance and into that inner freedom in Christ which alone allows the celibate to live dynamically and joyfully as self-gift for the sake of the Kingdom."

> —Tomás Surlis
> Pro-Rector of Saint Patrick's College, Maynooth, Ireland

D1474010

"Celibate chastity, like any other virtue, requires careful formation. *How We Love* offers young men and women a guide for pursuing this desire and is an excellent resource for formators, vocation directors, and spiritual directors to ensure the quality of Catholic vocations today."

—David Songy, OFM Cap
President of Saint Luke Institute

"Brother John Mark has created a model of formation that pulls together all the varied pieces needed to prepare someone for a life of celibacy. From his experience in working with numerous religious communities and in the seminary, he gives practical advice for addressing the full gamut of challenges to celibate living. His material is equally useful for both men and women celibates."

—Sr. Jane Becker, OSB, PhD
Monastery Immaculate Conception, Ferdinand, Indiana

"Br. John Mark's treatment is timely and grounded in his experience of doing celibacy formation. It is theologically balanced, psychologically up-to-date, and practical. A comprehensive guide for those involved in the ministry of formation as well as for those preparing to live a celibate life. Each chapter contains gems of wisdom."

—Donald Goergen, OP, author of *The Sexual Celibate*

"With his book, *How We Love*, Brother John Mark infuses the choice of a life of celibacy with new understanding and motivation. In addition to a welcome approach to how celibates can—and must—live an emotionally stable life in witness to the Gospel, he also provides the necessary framework for formators in religious communities and in seminaries to put their programs on a firm and measurable foundation. This book is a real service to the church in time of need."

—Justin DuVall, OSB
Vice-Rector of Bishop Simon Bruté College Seminary

How We Love

A Formation for the Celibate Life

John Mark Falkenhain, OSB

LITURGICAL PRESS
Collegeville, Minnesota

www.litpress.org

© 2019 by John Mark Falkenhain, OSB
Published by Liturgical Press, Collegeville, Minnesota. All rights reserved. No part of this book may be used or reproduced in any manner whatsoever, except brief quotations in reviews, without written permission of Liturgical Press, Saint John's Abbey, PO Box 7500, Collegeville, MN 56321-7500. Printed in the United States of America.

1	2	3	4	5	6	7	8	9

Library of Congress Cataloging-in-Publication Data

Names: Falkenhain, John Mark, author.
Title: How we love : a formation for the celibate life / John Mark Falkenhain, OSB.
Description: Collegeville : Liturgical Press, 2019. | Includes bibliographical references.
Identifiers: LCCN 2019000169 | ISBN 9780814687963 (pbk.)
Subjects: LCSH: Celibacy—Catholic Church. | Sexual abstinence—Religious aspects.—Catholic Church. | Chastity.
Classification: LCC BX1912.85 .F35 2019 | DDC 262/.1420865—dc23
LC record available at https://lccn.loc.gov/2019000169

CONTENTS

SECTION VI: FOR FORMATION PERSONNEL

Acknowledgments

Who knows how many people have had a hand in the writing of this book? One gathers ideas, questions, and points of view from the countless people with whom he lives, works, and has the privilege of serving in the classroom, the monastery, or the office. Still, there are a few without whom this project could never have come to fruition.

First, I wish to thank my monastic community at Saint Meinrad Archabbey who allowed me the time and freedom from other work to finally put down in writing what I have been teaching with their support and encouragement for the last fifteen years. I also wish to extend a note of thanks to the community of priest faculty members at Curley Hall at The Catholic University of America with whom I had the pleasure of living while I wrote this book. Their kindness, good company, and support were unforgettable. Of particular note among this group of scholars and gentlemen is Fr. Raymond Studzinski, OSB, a confrere of mine whose cheerful company and encouragement while working on this project led me to consider him not only a confrere, but a dear friend.

Beside the author, the person whose work and intelligence is most represented in this book is Beth Owen Davis, who served as initial editor for this volume. For the last several years, Beth has been a trusted colleague whose friendship and support on this and other projects has made my work not only more successful, but much more enjoyable. Thank you, Beth.

Finally, I wish to offer a special acknowledgment to my parents, Roland and Donna Falkenhain, whose wisdom and goodness overwhelm me. People of deep faith and integrity, they seem to know without formal training, what has taken me years of graduate education and clinical practice to learn about people and how they love. It is to them that this book is dedicated.

SECTION I

A NEW APPROACH
TO CELIBACY FORMATION

CHAPTER 1

INTRODUCTION

This book is a response to the need I have experienced in my own work for a careful and comprehensive book about formation for celibate chastity. I have spent the last fifteen years of my religious life involved in celibacy formation for diocesan seminarians and men and women religious. My formation for celibate chastity was fairly limited, partially because our community, like many men's communities, at the time relied on the seminary to carry out the task of celibacy formation. This left me, as a non-ordained monk, with relatively little preparation for what many would consider one of the most challenging aspects of the lives of consecrated religious or priests.

Aside from the obvious fact that not all consecrated religious attend seminary, there are additional important reasons why celibacy formation should be implemented with equal intentionality and skill in both religious formation programs and seminaries. The primary argument is that the celibate life of a religious man or woman differs in some important ways in theology, experience, and context from the celibate life of a diocesan priest. This insight is certainly important for religious men and women to consider, but it is also helpful for diocesan candidates to understand. An appreciation of the relative uniqueness of religious celibacy can help diocesan candidates to further articulate for themselves the charism of clerical celibacy.

If religious and seminary formation directors are a bit at a loss for how to proceed with formation for celibate chastity, it is not for lack of a good reason or even several reasons. None of us were trained for celibacy by our parents (although we might be able to look to our parents for training in chastity and fidelity), and most men and women charged with celibacy formation were themselves formed by religious and priests who experienced very little, if any, celibacy formation. Just as young parents often fall back on the methods and strategies for parenting they were raised with, formators also tend to rely primarily on their own formation experience in deciding how to go about their work. For the most part, this ensures a healthy sense of continuity and tradition within communities and presbyterates; however, just as we tend to pass on the wisdom, traditions, and successful methods for living the priestly and religious life, we also risk passing on limitations, ineffective strategies, and blind spots.

This book aims to offer a thorough, practical, and easily implemented program for celibacy formation—one that is adaptable to both seminary settings and formation programs in men's and women's religious communities. The background I bring to this work is that of a Benedictine monk, a clinical psychologist (including several years of experience working in the field of pediatric psychology), a researcher in the areas of clergy sexual offense and perseverance in religious life, and a lifelong Catholic. While my clinical background in pediatrics may seem a little disconnected from my research interests in clergy sexual offense and religious and priestly formation, both of these aspects of my professional life have come together nicely in the work of promoting celibacy formation.

A Developmental Perspective

Psychologists working with children and adolescents typically adopt a developmental perspective when approaching their work. A developmental perspective views individuals as moving along a particular trajectory of growth. Understanding how individuals have developed to their current point of maturity (or immaturity) is helpful in charting a path moving forward. This approach helps the psychologist establish short- and long-term goals for growth and helps identify a plan or path for moving in that direction.

"Formation" is a developmental word. Like pediatricians, psychologists, and other developmental professionals, formation directors must consider whether a candidate's current state of religious, spiritual, and psychosocial maturity is appropriate for his or her age and life experience, and whether the rate of maturing is adequate for the amount of formation the person has received and sufficient for reaching long-term goals. A developmentally informed approach to priestly and religious formation is guided by certain questions:

1. Where should young men or women be in their human and spiritual development before coming to the celibate life?

2. Where do we expect them to be by the end of initial formation?

3. What are the benchmarks that indicate the desired progress?

4. What will they need in order to continue growing in the celibate life once the period of initial formation is complete?

The Importance of Appropriate Development

The research on clergy sexual offense underscores the need for a strong developmental perspective when approaching celibacy formation. In an empirical analysis of child sexual offenders among clergy and religious brothers, the largest single group or subtype of offenders identified was one not marked by acute psychiatric disturbance or even chronic personality disorder, but rather poor psychosexual development.[1] Clergy offenders tended to score within the normal limits on measures of psychopathology (41%); however, examination of these subjects' subclinical profiles and collateral data indicated significant delays in their social, emotional, and sexual development. These men were described as being emotionally and sexually underdeveloped.

Avoiding the risk of clergy sexual offense, however, is not the only reason to pay close attention to the developmental progress of men and women in formation for celibate chastity. Poor emotional, social, and psychosexual development more often results in less criminal, but still problematic behaviors among priests and religious—behaviors and attitudes that ultimately affect parish and community life.

In a 2015 survey conducted in preparation for a national conference on celibacy formation, seminary and religious formation directors were

1. Marc A. Falkenhain and others, "Cluster Analysis of Child Sexual Offenders: A Validation with Roman Catholic Priests and Brothers," *Sexual Addiction & Compulsivity* 6, no. 3 (1999): 317–36.

asked to identify behaviors associated with unhealthy celibacy among priests or religious. [2] The most frequent responses included social isolationism (more typical among men); forming exclusive friendships or "coupling" (more typical among women religious); inability to relate to members of the opposite sex; denial of self as a sexual being; discomfort with self; inability to set appropriate boundaries; addictions; and immature and attention-seeking behaviors.

On the positive side, robust spiritual, emotional, and psychosexual development tends to predict adjustment, satisfaction, and perseverance among clergy and religious men and women. In his dissertation examining the psychological adjustment of diocesan priests, Nestor found that clergy who scored higher on measures of intimacy skills were likely to be more satisfied in their priestly vocation. [3] Two more recent investigations into factors contributing to priests and male religious leaving their vocations similarly found that, at least for men, social support and connectedness were important predictive factors affecting whether a priest or religious perseveres in his vocation in the first five to ten years post-ordination or final profession. [4]

The importance of attending to the spiritual, psychosocial, and psychosexual development of celibates is perhaps articulated no more beautifully than in Pope John Paul II's document on priestly formation, in which he writes: "[I]n order that his ministry may be humanly as credible and acceptable as possible, it is important that the priest should mould his

2. "Celibacy Formation in College Seminaries and Theologates, a 2015 report to the USCCB Secretariat of Clergy, Consecrated Life & Vocations," conducted by the Center for Applied Research in the Apostolate, last accessed April 21, 2017, https://www.sliconnect .org/wp-content/uploads/CARA-Survey-Summary-Report.pdf; "2015 Survey of Religious Communities' Celibacy Formation Programs," John Mark Falkenhain and Beth Owen Davis, last accessed April 21, 2017, https://www.sliconnect.org/wp-content/uploads/St. -Meinrad-SLI-Survey-Summary-Report.pdf.

3. Thomas Nestor, "Intimacy and Adjustment among Catholic Priests" (PhD diss., Loyola University, 1993).

4. Dean R. Hoge, *The First Five Years of the Priesthood: A Study of Newly Ordained Catholic Priests* (Collegeville, MN: Liturgical Press, 2002), 5–8; John Mark Falkenhain and Jane Becker, "The First Ten Years of Solemn Vows: Benedictine Monks on Reasons for Leaving and Remaining in Monastic Life," *The American Benedictine Review* 59, no. 2 (June 2008): 184–97.

human personality in such a way that it becomes a bridge and not an obstacle for others in their meeting with Jesus Christ the Redeemer of man."[5]

Although he is writing specifically on the topic of priestly formation in *Pastores Dabo Vobis*, Pope John Paul's statement could just as easily be applied to religious formation—both of men and women. Our basic human development, including our social, emotional, and sexual development, is foundational to fulfilling the purpose of our religious or priestly vocations: helping others see Christ and establishing God's kingdom in the world around us.

The Current State of Celibacy Formation in the United States

Exploration of celibacy formation programs in the United States suggests that we are making progress in our efforts to better prepare men and women for a life of celibate chastity. This is certainly evident given that many older priests and religious report having had very little or no formal training for celibacy in their years of initial formation. As recently as fifteen years ago, recently professed monks reported receiving very little formation for celibacy.[6] Catholics are not the only group that appears to have shied away from dealing with issues of sexuality and romantic attraction in preparing for ministry in the past. A survey of accredited Christian seminaries in the United States in the late 1990s indicated that, across several denominations, information related to sexuality and sexual integration was embedded in other courses (if included at all) rather than being offered in stand-alone courses or more intentionally designed formation programs.[7]

Celibacy formation has been more strongly emphasized in seminary and religious formation programs in the United States in recent years. In our 2015 survey of seminary and religious formation directors, 75% of graduate seminaries and 57% of college seminaries reported having

5. John Paul II, *Pastores Dabo Vobis: On the Formation of Priests in the Circumstances of the Present Day* (Washington, DC: United States Catholic Conference, 1999), 117.

6. Falkenhain and Becker, "The First Ten Years of Solemn Vows," 196.

7. Sarah C. Conklin, "Seminary Sexuality Education Survey: Current Efforts, Perceived Need and Readiness in Accredited Christian Institutions," *Journal of Sex Education and Therapy* 26, no. 4 (2001): 301–9.

celibacy formation programs that they considered "well established" (with clearly identified content and personnel), while an additional 22% and 42%, respectively, reported having programs they described as "in progress" (see Table 1). Among women's religious communities, 35% of those responding to our survey reported having "well established" celibacy formation programs with an additional 37% reporting programs "in progress." Men's religious communities reported slightly higher levels of organization than their female counterparts with 39% reporting "well established" programs and 48% reporting programs "in progress." A disappointing finding is that 3% of graduate seminaries and 28% and 13% of women's and men's religious communities respectively reported having "ad hoc" celibacy formation programs, or programs that have little consistency from year to year. [8]

Table 1. Organization of Initial Celibacy Formation Programs in US Seminaries and Religious Communities

"Which of the following most accurately describes your celibacy formation program?":

	"well-established"	*"in progress"*	*"ad hoc—having little yearly consistency"*
Theologates	75%	22%	3%
College Seminaries	57%	43%	0%
Women's Religious Communities	35%	37%	28%
Men's Religious Communities	39%	48%	13%

It is not surprising that among the three groups, seminaries report the highest levels of organization and stability with respect to celibacy formation programming. This makes sense given the more highly centralized organization of diocesan life, the availability of published formation documents for priestly formation, and the heightened focus on seminary

8. "Celibacy Formation in College Seminaries and Theologates," 7, 18; "Survey of Religious Communities' Celibacy Formation Programs," 3.

formation (and celibacy formation in seminaries in particular) in the wake of the clergy sexual abuse crisis. In general, seminaries also tend to enjoy greater stability with respect to staffing and, more important, with respect to numbers of young people in formation on an ongoing basis. Our research showed that, at least among women's religious communities, smaller communities and communities that did not currently have candidates in formation were less likely to report high levels of organization and stability in their celibacy formation programs. Common sense tells us that larger seminaries and larger religious communities are also more likely to have a greater pool of personnel and resources to draw from when addressing various topics within celibacy formation (i.e., theology of celibacy, sexual identity, internet pornography, addictions, etc.). With respect to ongoing formation, only 42% of men's religious communities and 14% of women's communities reported having formal ongoing formation programs for celibate chastity.

In terms of specific content of celibacy formation programs, most seminaries and religious communities reported that their programs include treatment of the following areas: theology and the meaning of chaste celibacy, affective maturity, human sexuality, dealing with loneliness, and appropriate boundaries. Graduate seminaries (75%) appear to address the issue of how to cope with the experience of falling in love more often than college seminaries (57%) and men's and women's religious communities (48% and 65%, respectively); and formation programs serving men (i.e., both seminary and men's religious communities) address issues related to internet pornography (68%–96%) much more frequently than formation programs in women's religious communities (28%). This latter finding bears some consideration in light of increasing rates of internet pornography use among women in the general population.

With respect to the different theological dimensions of celibacy emphasized in formation programs, a service-oriented theology of celibacy "for the sake of the kingdom" is by far the most popular theological dimension emphasized in seminaries and religious communities. Interestingly, seminaries were more likely also to advocate a spousal theology of celibacy (75% of graduate seminaries and 70% of college seminaries) compared to men's and women's religious communities (19% and 21%, respectively). This finding is somewhat ironic considering that the spousal theology is probably more traditionally associated with celibacy in the context of consecrated life. It is possible that there are ideological biases at play causing this dimension to be downplayed among men and women religious. It may also be that seminary programs, by nature of being schools of theology, are able to spend more time studying (and therefore studying more broadly) the various theological dimensions of celibate chastity compared to formation programs among religious communities.

Within the content area of human sexuality, internet pornography, sexual integration, sexual orientation, and masturbation are among the most commonly addressed topics in college and graduate seminary celibacy formation programs. Among formation programs in religious congregations, sexual integration, sexual orientation, dealing with sexual attraction, and pornography (particularly in men's communities) are the most frequent topics included. The physiology of sexuality is the least commonly emphasized aspect of human sexuality, except among formation programs in women's communities, among whom 45% endorsed this as a topic covered in their programs.

Existing Models for Celibacy Formation

Despite a relative abundance of writings on the theology, history, and spirituality of celibate chastity, a recent review of the literature uncovered few concrete and implementable models for celibacy formation. The two available are targeted exclusively at priestly formation.

The *Program of Priestly Formation* (PPF), fifth edition, offers a valuable list of qualities and skills recommended for candidates pursuing a life of clerical celibacy. [9] These include affective maturity; a solid understanding of the meaning of celibacy; care for others; modesty; vigilance; self-mastery; and the capacities for friendship, appropriate self-disclosure, boundary setting, solitude, and for giving and receiving love. The *Program of Priestly Formation* goes on to identify the delivery systems to accomplish this work in the life of the seminary, including instruction; personal reflection; community life and feedback; application to the tasks of seminary life; formation advisors, mentors, and directors; spiritual direction; and psychological counseling.

9. *Program of Priestly Formation,* 5th ed. (Washington, DC: United States Conference of Catholic Bishops, 2006).

Based in part on the previous edition of the *Program of Priestly Formation*, the National Catholic Education Association (NCEA) published a resource book for the celibacy formation of diocesan priests in 1999.[10] The NCEA document, written by Thomas Krenik, proposed seven guiding elements to be used in celibacy formation with graduate seminarians: internalization of presbyterial values; pattern of contemplative prayer; capacity for solitude; age-appropriate psychosexual development; capacity for intimacy in human friendships; experience of community support; and accountability to others. Although brief, the NCEA offering is helpful in recommending some specific content, resources, and guiding questions for addressing each of these guiding principles of priestly celibacy formation. No published models of celibacy formation for men and women religious were identified.

How We Love: Formation for the Celibate Life

This book aims to offer a comprehensive guide for formation in celibate chastity, usable in both seminary and religious formation programs (both men's and women's). The proposed program is comprised of objective, research-based recommendations drawn from a wide variety of sources, including Catholic Church teaching; official documents on priestly and religious formation; research on the state of celibacy formation in the US; research on factors contributing to perseverance in priesthood and religious life; research on factors contributing to clergy sexual offense; and thorough reviews of the scientific literature on issues related to sexuality and sexual identity. A particular contribution of this volume will be to provide formation directors and candidates with thorough, well-researched, and ideologically neutral information on issues related to human sexuality and sexual identity—an area in which formation directors often find themselves least prepared to offer instruction and guidance.

Because most of what has been written in the area of celibate chastity has focused on clerical celibacy and has been written primarily by men for men, this work also attempts to be sensitive to the needs and perspectives of consecrated religious and of women. It is my firm conviction that

10. Thomas W. Krenik, *Formation for Priestly Celibacy: A Resource Book* (Washington, DC: National Catholic Education Association, 1999).

by developing an approach that explores areas of overlap and distinction between men and women and between diocesan priesthood and various forms of consecrated life in the church, all groups are best served.

With this in mind, a number of heuristic values underlie the model upon which this text is built. They include

- providing a framework from which to begin constructing or continue organizing a program for celibacy formation

- providing a framework that is adaptable to both clerical and religious formation

- providing a framework that is consistent with the directives provided in the main formation documents for priestly formation—i.e., *Pastores Dabo Vobis* (John Paul II, 1996) and the *Program of Priestly Formation,* fifth edition (2006)

- providing a framework that can be used in both men's and women's communities

- providing a framework that accounts for individual differences among candidates

- providing a framework that helps inform screening of candidates and ongoing formation

This book may be used in a number of ways and in a variety of settings. One obvious application is the utilization of this volume as a guide for organizing a formal semester- or year-long course on celibacy formation within a larger seminary or religious formation program. This book can also be used on an individual basis. Men and women in formation undertaking some directed reading or self-study about celibacy formation are likely find this an excellent resource.

Newly appointed formation directors faced with the task of constructing a celibacy formation program from the ground up, or who simply wish to increase the level of structure and consistency in an existing program, are likely to find this a helpful resource for both program organization and content. Chapter 14, "Putting It Together," aims specifically to assist formation directors in identifying benchmarks and establishing a schedule of formation goals in each of the major content areas covered in this book.

Finally, directors of ongoing formation or already ordained and professed individuals engaging in their own ongoing formation in the area of celibate chastity will surely find this text rewarding and perhaps even challenging. Some sections will be worth returning to at many intervals in the lifespan of a vocation, as living the celibate life often reveals to us more of who we are as emotional, sexual, relational, and spiritual creatures over time.

CHAPTER 2

ESTABLISHING THE MODEL

In my work with men and women in formation for celibate chastity, I always begin by suggesting that when we make a promise or a vow of celibacy, we place ourselves in a box. Some react by suggesting that this seems confining, and I agree with them—it *is* confining. Celibacy is meant to limit us in important ways; however, we choose these limits and impose them on ourselves in order to gain certain freedoms and give a particular witness to the church and to the world.

Once we have placed ourselves in the "celibacy box," we encounter a bit of a paradox. On the one hand, the parameters of celibacy are very clear and apply universally to everyone who makes the vow of celibacy: we will refrain from marriage or exclusivity in relationships, and we will refrain from genital sexual expression. On the other hand, the actual experience of *living* celibacy varies greatly from person to person. Just as no two people will have the exact same experience of being married or of parenting, the experience of living a celibate life will differ from person to person. What accounts for these differences? And how do we prepare men and women for a life that will turn out to be unique to each person?

The experience of living the celibate life is unique to each individual due to a number of personal factors. Four stand out in particular: one's motives for choosing celibacy; one's theological understanding of celibacy and how he or she uses that theological understanding to inform and direct life as a celibate; one's sexual identity; and, finally, whatever skills (and limitations) one brings to and is able to acquire for living the celibate life.

In the illustration of celibacy as lived experience below, the solid outline represents the basic expectations that help to define the life of celibate chastity (i.e., refraining from marriage and refraining from genital sexual expression), and the factors within the box account for each person's unique experience of living out the celibate commitment.

Refrain from Marriage/Refrain from Genital Sexual Expression

- ◆ Motives for Celibacy
- ◆ Theological Dimensions
- ◆ Sexual Identity
- ◆ Skills and Limitations for Living the Celibate Life

Because these factors—motives, theological dimensions, sexual identity, and skills for living the celibate life—significantly influence the individual's lived experience of celibacy, we will designate these as the four main content areas around which to structure a celibacy formation program. This allows us to take individual differences into account while forming men and women for a common witness in the church. Now that the major content areas are established, it will be helpful to add one more overarching theme to our emerging model: self-knowledge and self-acceptance.

In the fifth edition of the *Program of Priestly Formation* (PPF), one of the church's primary documents on the formation of men for priesthood, the United States Conference of Catholic Bishops articulated a keen and helpful insight that can help us direct all of our efforts toward forming free and healthy celibates, for both priesthood and religious life. In the section of the PPF on human formation—which includes formation for celibacy—the bishops suggest the following: "In general, human formation happens in a threefold process *of self-knowledge, self-acceptance, and self-gift*—and all of this in faith" (emphases added).[1] This statement is well worth examining in detail.

If we were to attempt to summarize the goal of any Christian vocation (including the celibate vocation), we could probably do no better than to say that the goal of any Christian life is self-gift. The gospels remind us

---

1. *Program of Priestly Formation*, 5th ed. (Washington, DC: United States Conference of Catholic Bishops, 2006), 33.

that if we wish to save our lives, we must lose them, or as Christ himself admonishes us, we must lay down our lives for others in imitation of him. This is what it means to love.

As a specific approach to the Christian life, celibacy must also have self-gift as its ultimate goal. In fact, one could safely say that celibacy, like poverty and obedience, is pointless unless it steers us in the direction of self-gift: of being more loving, more capable of laying our life down for others. We will explore this notion of love as the theological end of celibacy in greater depth when we discuss the theological dimensions of celibate chastity; but for now, let it suffice to say that if celibacy takes as its aim self-gift, then let us follow the bishops' counsel and agree that it must be preceded by self-knowledge and self-acceptance. But, why?

We might better understand the importance self-knowledge and self-acceptance as precursors to self-gift if we first ask what kinds of things people must know and accept about themselves before making a final commitment to celibate chastity. If we return for a moment to the four main content areas of our emerging model for celibacy formation, we will quickly see that self-knowledge and self-acceptance in each of these major content areas results in greater freedom of choice. Individuals must have a clear understanding and acceptance of what is motivating them to adopt celibacy, for example, for their decision to be adequately discerned. An honest and accurate knowledge and acceptance of one's motives help reveal whether one is choosing to be celibate for healthy reasons and for reasons that are consistent with the church's vision for celibate men and women. Along the same lines, those embarking on the celibate life should also be knowledgeable of the theological underpinnings of celibate chastity and be able to accept and adopt for themselves strong theological and spiritual motives for pursuing celibacy as a way of life. Before making a final gift of oneself to celibate chastity, candidates must be able to say that they not only share but are inspired by the church's theological vision for their life as people who will forego marriage and genital sexual expression for the sake of the kingdom of God.

With respect to sexual identity, anyone who has given even minimal thought to the importance of psychosexual development relative to celibate chastity will recognize that candidates must have adequate and ongoing knowledge and acceptance of themselves as sexual individuals on the way to making a free and final choice of celibacy. If, as St. Thomas Aquinas suggests, "Grace builds on nature," then the grace of celibacy builds on our nature as sexual people. Consequently, people must approach the enterprise of the celibate life with an accurate understanding and an honest acceptance of who they are as sexual and romantic individuals so that their choice is not made on false pretenses or without adequate information.

Finally, given that persevering in a life of celibacy requires certain skills and the development of particular virtues, candidates must know and be able to accept whether or not they have or can develop the necessary skills for living the celibate life in ways that fulfill the church's vision for celibacy. As we will point out, some of these skills will have to be in place before a person approaches formation, while others may be taught, fostered, and facilitated by the formation process.

Returning, then, to the bishops' assertion that self-gift must be preceded by self-knowledge and self-acceptance, we can see that by increasing our self-knowledge and by growing in acceptance of ourselves as we truly are, the choice and the gift that is the celibate life is made freely. Freedom is the necessary condition promoted by growth in self-knowledge and self-acceptance. Note that when we speak of freedom in this context, we are not speaking of a freedom that involves having unlimited options or unbounded self-determination, but rather a condition that results from knowing who one is and what one is choosing for one's life. It is not the slavery of ignorance or naiveté, but the liberty to knowingly lay down one's life without fear of later regrets or the too-late discovery of things one should have known about oneself at the time of commitment.

If we superimpose these goals of growing in self-knowledge and self-acceptance onto our four major content areas of motives, theological dimensions, sexual identity, and skills for celibacy, our final model for initial and ongoing formation for celibacy emerges:

Refrain from Marriage/Refrain from Genital Sexual Expression

- ◆ Motives for Celibacy
- ◆ Theological Dimensions
- ◆ Sexual Identity
- ◆ Skills and Limitations for Living the Celibate Life

Self-Knowledge • Self-Acceptance • Self-Gift

Over the course of this book, our ultimate goal will be to grow in self-knowledge and self-acceptance in these four major areas on the way to making a permanent and free gift of self to a life of celibate chastity. Each chapter sets forth a conceptual framework and establishes a common vocabulary with which candidates can better understand their own experience and communicate who they are to those who will assist and join them in their formation for the celibate life: formation personnel, spiritual directors, peers in formation, counselors, and close friends.

An "Elegant" Model

In the fields of science and social science, a research or intervention model is considered "elegant" to the extent that it is able to explain much while remaining fairly simple. My aim has been to establish a similarly elegant model for celibacy formation. As we will discover, the proposed model is simple enough to be easily implemented and internalized, but comprehensive enough to be applied to a variety of formation settings. Consideration of the various theological dimensions to celibacy, for example, recognizes the differences between formation for religious life and diocesan priesthood. The inclusion of sexual identity—including the specific constructs of sex, gender, sexual orientation, history of sexual experiences, and attitudes and values regarding sexuality—is not only essential, but broadens its applicability to men and women as well as to individuals entering formation with a wide variety of romantic and sexual experiences, personality traits, and cultural influences. Because growth in self-knowledge, self-acceptance, and, above all, self-gift is a never-ending endeavor, this model is useful not only for initial formation, but also for ongoing formation programs in celibate chastity.

In the sections and chapters that follow, we will explore each of the four major content areas, articulate specific formation goals for each area, and begin to identify who is responsible for the work to be done. Chapters 3 and 4 will look at motives for the celibate life and underscore the importance of clarifying and evaluating motives in terms of how healthy and sustainable they are for a lifetime of fruitful celibate chastity consistent with the church's vision for this particular witness.

Chapters 5 and 6 will explore the various theological facets supporting celibacy in the contexts of diocesan life, apostolic religious life, monastic and contemplative life, and the missionary experience. A model for pursuing theological reflection on the celibate life as an important means of transformation, conversion, and perseverance is introduced and elaborated upon in chapter 6.

Chapter 7 provides a thorough and careful exploration of sexual identity as an important consideration for formation for the celibate life. Adhering both to the teaching of the Catholic Church and the scientific research literature, I will propose a multifactored model for sexual identity that includes our sex, gender, sexual orientation, history of sexual experiences, and the values and attitudes we hold regarding sexuality. Chapter 8 will use this model to explore three ways of approaching what it means to integrate one's sexuality into one's larger identity as a celibate man or woman.

Finally, chapters 9 through 13 explore five major skills necessary for living the celibate life: affective maturity, the establishment and maintenance of effective boundaries, community as a source of support and accountability, coping with romantic and sexual attraction, and the capacity for solitude.

The last two chapters of the book are directed more specifically to formation personnel and cover the special topics of structuring a formation program and addressing the need for ongoing formation. While these chapters are primarily written with formation directors and leadership in mind, they are likely to be helpful to men and women in initial formation as well, especially the chapter on ongoing formation. Chapter 15 will also be of interest to already ordained priests and professed religious who are utilizing this volume for the purpose of ongoing formation.

SECTION II

MOTIVES

CHAPTER 3

Exploring Motives for Celibacy

As we look at motives, let's begin with two questions for reflection. Spend a minute or two on the first one, and don't read any further until you have answered it:

1. *Why did you decide to become a (priest/sister/religious brother)?*

Now that you have an answer to the first question, spend a minute or two answering the second:

2. *Why did you decide to become a celibate?*

Which question did you find easier to answer? With every group I have worked with—priests, seminarians, monks, religious women, religious men—the consensus is always that the first question—why we chose to become a priest, sister, brother, etc.—is much easier to answer than the second. We get a little stuck with the second question: Why did you decide to become a celibate?

The most common answer I hear is: "I guess I decided to become a celibate because it came with the territory of priesthood or religious life." Funny, isn't it? We spend great amounts of time, energy, and prayer discerning our religious or priestly vocation, but relatively little time and energy discerning celibacy!

In our treatment of this first major content area in our model for celibacy formation, the primary question is: What landed you in the celibacy box? Or in other words: Why did you choose to become a celibate? We will proceed in this chapter by looking carefully at a variety of motives for pursuing celibacy before setting some concrete goals for formation in the chapter that follows.

The rest of this chapter leans fairly heavily on the work of Sr. Sandra Schneiders, who has written nicely on motives for celibacy in her book *Selling All: Commitment, Consecrated Celibacy, and Community in Catholic Religious Life.*[1] In her treatment, Sr. Schneiders points out the potential plurality of our motives for celibacy (i.e., that we may be motivated by more than one thing) and emphasizes the importance of examining the "validity" of a person's motives for celibacy. Below, we will spend more time examining the health and validity of our potential motives for celibacy and underscore the importance of developing healthy, sustaining motives for celibacy as part of the initial or ongoing formation process.

Motives as Multiple and as Multivalent

When exploring our motives for celibacy, we begin by acknowledging that for many, if not most, people, the primary reason for becoming celibate is that a vow or promise of celibacy simply came with the territory of priesthood or religious life. But it's probably not that simple. In truth, our motives are rarely pure, and we are most often motivated by several factors when making significant life decisions. Our motives are usually multiple or "plural," to use Sr. Schneider's terminology. True, you may have chosen celibacy primarily because it was part of religious life or priesthood, but it may also be possible that you didn't feel called to marriage. Or you may not have thought that marriage was possible for you for one reason or another.

In addition to having multiple reasons for choosing celibacy, it is also likely that those reasons will change or evolve over time. This is true for any vocation. You may have heard one of your parents say, "You know, the reasons I married your father are very different from the reasons we stayed married." People change, relationships change, and our understanding of our relationships change over time. Doesn't it follow that our motives for staying in those relationships would also evolve?

And if an individual's motives for celibacy are multiple, then we also have to acknowledge that our motives or reasons for choosing celibacy might also be multivalent—meaning that some of them might be con-

---

1. Sandra M. Schneiders, *Selling All: Commitment, Consecrated Celibacy, and Community in Catholic Religious Life* (Mahwah, NY: Paulist Press, 2001).

sciously known to us, while others may be subconscious or hidden from our awareness, at least for some time. Let's illustrate some of these ideas with an example.

> *Kim grows up in an emotionally chaotic family. Her parents divorce when she is eight years old, following several years of intense fighting and argument. Even after their separation, Kim continues to feel caught in the middle, especially when her parents express their dissatisfaction with one another either in front of her or to her directly.*
>
> *A year after the divorce, Kim's father remarries and starts a new family with a woman who is not very affectionate toward Kim and seems to compete with Kim for her father's attention. The result is more fighting—this time between Kim's father and his new wife.*
>
> *Following the divorce, Kim's mother becomes involved in a series of relationships, none of which last very long, and Kim moves in and out of various homes and schools each time her mother moves in with a new boyfriend. Kim grows up too fast and acts more like an adult than her mother, who leans on Kim for company and emotional support each time a relationship fails. By the time she reaches adolescence, Kim has a pretty low estimation of men, not to mention romance.*
>
> *After Kim graduates from eighth grade, she asks if she can live with her grandparents so she can go to one school and live in one place. While living with her grandparents, Kim goes to church with them and attends high school at a local Catholic girls academy. Kim looks up to a couple of the sisters who teach in the school and who show a particular interest in her. Kim admires what she sees of their life in the convent, which seems ordered, predictable, grounded in charity, and free from drama. She expresses an interest in religious life to one of the sisters and agrees to stay in touch once she graduates.*
>
> *After high school, Kim attends a local community college, earns an associate's degree, and decides to enter the community of sisters that taught her in high school. In her interview with the vocation director, she is asked what she thinks about celibacy. Kim replies: "Well, I've never been really interested in dating, so I think celibacy will not be all that hard for me. Sometimes I think about whether or not I would want to have children, but I think I'd be okay not having a family of my own."*

What are Kim's motives for choosing celibacy? It's safe to assume that Kim has not given much thought to celibacy and why she wants to be celibate. We might also assume that one of her primary motives is simply that she wants to be a sister and celibacy comes with the territory of religious life. But are there other possible reasons? It is possible that Kim's unpleasant childhood experiences of love and marriage have left her with little interest in romance and maybe even a desire to avoid the messiness of romantic relationships in her own life. It may also be that Kim fears getting close to men, particularly if she has grown up hearing her mother complain that "men will always disappoint you" or that "men just aren't worth it!" At some point, Kim may have sworn to herself that she would grow up to be independent and never as emotionally needy as her mother had been.

Are these experiences influencing Kim's decision to pursue celibacy? If they are, it may be at a subconscious level. Kim is probably not consciously saying to herself, "I think I will be celibate to avoid the messiness of marriage and risk becoming too dependent on men." When she is asked why celibacy might be a good choice for her, she is more likely to say that she wants to be a sister and celibacy is part of religious life than to say that she wishes to avoid the possibility of being hurt all over again by relationships and marriages that never seem to work out.

Kim's story highlights the potential for multiple motives and the possibility of subconscious versus conscious reasons for choosing celibacy. It also stirs in us some concern about the quality or appropriateness of Kim's motives for wanting to be a celibate. In her treatment of motives for celibacy, Sr. Schneiders raises the question of the "validity" of a person's motives and goes on to describe the possibility that a person may have reasons for celibacy that are not only not valid, but also may be rooted in poor psychosexual health. Let's proceed in the sections ahead to explore these two ideas—validity of motives and health of motives—separately in order to facilitate an honest examination of motives as part of our initial or ongoing formation for the celibate life. While there will be some overlap between these two ways of categorizing motives (health and validity), we will also see that just because some motives are not rooted in psychosocial or psychosexual (i.e., unhealthy) concerns doesn't mean they are going to be helpful in sustaining and directing a life of celibate chastity toward the theological and spiritual ends for which it is intended.

Evaluating Motives: Healthy versus Unhealthy

If there are a variety of possible motives for choosing the celibate life, then we would be wise to begin sorting them out in terms of whether they are healthy or unhealthy reasons. We have all known, either in real life or in films or novels, people who have gotten married for "all the wrong" (i.e., unhealthy) reasons: in order to get away from or to please their parents; because they are overly dependent and need to be with someone to feel valuable; or because they need someone to control.

There are just as many unhealthy reasons for choosing celibacy. Here is a list, though not necessarily an exhaustive one:

- sexual or emotional naiveté or underdevelopment

- fear of marriage or sex

- fear of relating to people of the opposite sex

- fear of intimacy and getting hurt

- a desire to avoid dealing with one's sexual orientation

- a desire to avoid dealing with a history of being sexually abused or assaulted

- an attempt by someone with same-sex attraction to find a potential partner or mate

- an attempt to control sexually compulsive or harmful behaviors

- a belief that sexuality is unholy or disgusting

If you were a vocation director and a candidate gave you any of these reasons for choosing a life of celibacy, you would probably put on the brakes.

We already have one illustration of unhealthy motives in the case of Kim, but let's add another.

> *Kyle lives with his mother, who is a single parent. His mother married very young, at seventeen, after getting pregnant with Kyle. The marriage lasted only three years—long enough for Kyle and his sister, Amy, to be born. Kyle has no memory of his father, who has been out of the picture since his parents divorced. Kyle's mother dropped out of high school upon getting pregnant with Kyle, and although she*

was able to get her GED, she did not go to college as she had always planned. Instead, she found a job in a furniture factory and worked hard to support herself and her children. She never remarried or even dated, believing that her sole responsibility was to care for her children.

Kyle's mother has always been very determined that her children "will not make the same mistakes I made," and she lectures them often about the importance of abstinence and the dangers of sex. She tells Kyle and Amy that they should finish their education and get their lives settled before they start dating. "There will be plenty of time for romance and sex," she reminds them. "Sex can ruin everything!"

Growing up, Kyle was a very devout and compliant child who was eager to please his mother. Each Sunday at church, his mother would introduce Kyle to her friends and to the parish priest as "Kyle, our little priest." She would often say in front of her son, "I really think he's going to be a priest one day!"

In high school, Kyle does not date and takes seriously the suggestion from his mother and others that he would make an excellent priest. In his senior year of high school, Kyle makes contact with the vocation director of his diocese and applies to college seminary. When interviewed by the psychologist about why he thinks celibacy will be a good fit for him, Kyle responds: "I've known I was going to be a priest since I was ten. I've never really seen any point in dating, since dating can easily lead to sex and that could be dangerous to my vocation. I've seen lots of kids already mess up their lives by having sex. That's the problem with our society—everything is about sex—and I want to show that there is something more to life than sex."

Kyle's motives for celibacy are complex. They do not scream psychopathology and they may not be entirely unhealthy. However, Kyle's choice to be celibate may be influenced, whether he recognizes it or not, by fairly negative views of sexuality, by a possible fear of sexuality, and by a certain naiveté about himself as a sexual person. Kyle is young, just barely eighteen when he enters college seminary, and he risks prematurely deciding on his identity as a sexual person based on limited knowledge and a negatively skewed notion of romance and sexuality. These are not the healthiest motivations for choosing celibacy.

Sometimes the choice for celibacy is motivated by the impression that it will help an individual escape or control dangerous, compulsive, or even illegal sexual behaviors (e.g., child pornography, serial anonymous encounters, attraction to minors). Vocation directors sometimes receive inquiries from individuals, for example, who wish to enter a religious community or seminary because they believe that the requirement of celibacy will help deliver them from temptations and provide the support and external controls needed to live more sexually virtuous lives. As a vocation director myself, I have often had to explain to candidates that people's sexual histories, temptations, limitations, and proclivities follow them into the convent, seminary, or monastery. Consequently, candidates must have already achieved a certain degree of internal discipline and proven ability to resist temptation and curb sexual impulses prior to entering religious life or seminary. While it is true that in some traditions, celibacy has been conceived of as an ascetical practice aimed at doing penance for past sins, its adoption in the context of religious life or priesthood is never intended to be a treatment for sexual compulsions or a means of controlling deviant sexual behaviors.

A young man or woman who hopes to avoid dealing with difficult sexual issues (e.g., same-sex attraction) or a painful sexual history (e.g., sexual abuse or assault) might also be choosing celibacy for unhealthy reasons. We must always remember that in the context of the priesthood or religious life, celibacy represents a movement toward a theological and spiritual good, not a movement away from a perceived threat or danger.

Evaluating Motives: Valid versus Invalid

When discussing the validity of a person's motives for celibacy, it is probably safe to say that unhealthy motives for celibacy (as discussed above) are almost always invalid motives. But it is also possible to have motives that, while not pathological or unhealthy, are still not "valid" in the sense that they are not consistent with the purpose for which celibacy as a religious and spiritual discipline is intended. The obvious example, of course, is one we have mentioned a number of times: "I chose celibacy because it came along with priesthood/religious life." There is nothing pathological or dysfunctional here. But if this is the only motive underpinning a lifelong pursuit of celibacy, perseverance could be a real struggle. And even if individuals should manage to persevere in a life of celibacy with this limited motive alone, they are likely to find little meaning, joy, or spiritual growth in the sacrifice they have made.

In her discussion of motives for a freely chosen life of celibacy, Sr. Schneiders reminds us that our vows or promises (including celibacy) are characterized by three dimensions: unitive, communitarian, and ministerial dimensions. This notion moves us into a discussion of the theological motives for celibacy, which will be the focus of the next section of this volume. Let it suffice to say here, though, that when assessing the validity of a person's motives for celibacy, the primary concern is spiritual and theological in nature. In other words, does the individual have motives that are capable of sustaining, inspiring, and informing a life of celibate chastity, ultimately aimed at increasing his or her capacity for love—love of God and love of neighbor?

I have spoken with many older priests and religious whose formation for celibacy was very limited and who, to this point, have engaged in minimal examination of their motives for choosing celibacy. It would be wrong to say that their gift of self as celibate men and women has been meaningless, ill-founded, or invalid simply because their primary motive for choosing celibacy had been or maybe even continues to be the view that it was "part of the deal" of their chosen vocation. Still, it is possible that an opportunity lies before them—that is, the opportunity to delve more deeply into the richness of the church's tradition and teaching in order to inspire (perhaps for the first time) a deeper call to intimacy with God and the rest of his creation.

Initial versus Ultimate Motives

A final distinction in sorting out motives is the difference between a person's initial motives and ultimate motives for choosing to be a celibate. We will use the term "initial motives" to refer to those reasons that moved a person initially—in other words: What has landed you in the celibacy box to begin with? These we will distinguish from the motives a person has at the time of ordination or final vows, when he or she is expected to make a permanent or lifelong commitment to celibate chastity.

This distinction between initial and ultimate motives is important because it allows for the possibility that a person may initially choose to pursue the celibate life for invalid or even unhealthy reasons, but in the course of formation may adopt or grow into healthier, stronger, and more promising motives. As we will point out again in the next chapter, formation should help candidates identify and evaluate the health and validity of their initial motives for celibacy, then assist them in exploring healthy and valid reasons that may eventually form the basis for their ultimate or final profession of celibacy.

Older generations of priests and religious, many of whom received minimal initial formation for celibacy, may recognize that even after several decades of priesthood or religious life there is still lot of work to do with respect to clarifying their initial and current motives for celibacy. That work may result in a little uneasiness, especially if it leads to the recognition that their lifelong choice of celibacy was and perhaps continues to be motivated by mostly unexamined or undeveloped reasons. Although we would certainly advocate for the bulk of this work to be done in initial formation, it is never too late to develop insight into the motives behind one of our most important life decisions and hopefully to discover the potential for greater inspiration and deeper meaning in the life we are already living.

Summary and Conclusions

In this chapter we have established a framework and some vocabulary for formation in the area of motives for the celibate life. The key questions are: What initially landed you in the celibacy box? and What will your reasons for a lifelong commitment to celibacy ultimately be?

We have pointed out that the initial motive for many celibates has been that celibacy simply came along with the territory of priesthood or religious life; and while this motive does not indicate any level of psychosocial or psychosexual dysfunction, it is probably not the most "valid" motive for celibacy, in that it does not hold much promise for perseverance in a life of celibate chastity, a life intended and designed in the church's wisdom to increase the candidate's capacity for love for God and his people.

Having now explored the ideas of multiple and possibly multivalent (conscious versus subconscious) motives, having also practiced classifying motives according to their health and their validity, and having finally distinguished between initial and ultimate motives for celibacy, we will proceed in the next chapter to establish four concrete goals for formation in the area of motives for celibacy.

CHAPTER 4

MOTIVES FOR CELIBACY:
GOALS FOR FORMATION

Initial formation has two primary purposes: preparation and discernment. Whether it is formation for religious life or for priesthood, initial formation aims first to prepare candidates for their vocation. To this end, a formation program imparts information, skills, attitudes, and the vision required for individuals to inhabit the vocation to which they are aspiring. The theology, spirituality, customs, history, human predisposition, and mind-set are all made explicit and available so that they may be internalized and eventually personified by the aspirant. Pope John Paul II beautifully organized the primary aspects of formation as they relate to priesthood according to four "pillars": human, intellectual, spiritual, and pastoral formation.[1] These have also been applied to formation for religious life, and Pope Francis has suggested "communitarian" formation as an important dimension to consider as well.[2]

But initial formation is also every bit as much about discernment as it is about preparation. In fact, we cannot think about discernment and formation as two separate tasks or discrete, sequential steps in a progression toward ordination or religious profession. The overlap between the

---

1. John Paul II, *Pastores Dabo Vobis: On the Formation of Priests in the Circumstances of the Present Day* (Washington, DC: United States Catholic Conference, 1999), 117.

2. Antonio Spadaro, "'Wake Up the World!': Conversation with Pope Francis about the Religious Life," trans. Donald Maldari, *La Civilta Cattolica*, I (2014): 3–17. English translation available at http://jpicformation.wikispaces.com/file/view/Wake_up_the _world-2.pdf/495026180/Wake_up_the_world-2.pdf, last accessed May 8, 2017.

two is considerable. Once we decide to enter a seminary or formation program, discernment has just begun. For a young religious in formation, the opportunity to move in and begin living a communal life, working and praying alongside one's sisters or brothers, participating in the community's mission and apostolates while still temporarily professed, affords the luxury of "trying on" the vocation for a while, assessing along the way whether this new expansion of his or her Christian identity fits. Similarly, the seminarian's training in theological knowledge, the gradual accumulation of ministries, his closer association with the administration of the church, and the practice of supervised ministry all help him to inhabit the vocation of priesthood in increasing increments and to generate more information for discerning a permanent call to priesthood. The availability of and emphasis on spiritual direction, yearly evaluation procedures, and periodic community votes (in the case of religious life) all underscore the reality that discernment is an ongoing endeavor throughout the course of initial formation and that discernment is both the work of the candidate and the work of the diocese or the religious community sponsoring and supporting the young man or woman in formation.

This notion that formation is equally about discernment is probably no truer anywhere in our model of celibacy formation than in the area of motives for celibacy. In the previous chapter, we acknowledged that many make an initial choice of celibacy based on reasons that are less than ideal or not always in total alignment with the church's intent and vision for celibacy. Some motives may be still unknown to individuals when they enter formation. To the degree that candidates are unaware of what is motivating their choice of celibacy, they lack freedom. Church formation documents talk frequently about freedom of choice with respect to celibacy and vocation. As we turn to articulating some concrete goals for formation in the area of motives for celibacy, let us keep in mind the overarching goal of growing in self-knowledge and self-acceptance—both of which are aimed at facilitating freedom in discernment.

Four Concrete Goals to Guide Formation

In the last chapter, we took a number of approaches to thinking about motives for celibacy and established several criteria for sorting our motives: healthy versus unhealthy; valid versus invalid; conscious versus unconscious; and initial versus ultimate. In this chapter, we will use these concepts and vocabulary to articulate four concrete goals for celibacy formation in the area of motives for the celibate life:

1. To identify and clarify one's initial motives for choosing celibacy

2. To evaluate the health and validity of one's initial motives for choosing celibacy

3. To learn and begin to adopt strong and valid reasons for choosing the celibate life

4. In the last six to twelve months leading up to ordination or final profession, to revisit the question: Do I presently have motives that are capable of sustaining a fruitful life of celibate chastity, consistent with the church's intention and vision for celibacy?

As we look at each of these goals, we will discuss who is responsible for the work to be done and in what settings the work is accomplished in the course of initial formation. Toward the end of the chapter, we will also draw some implications for ongoing formation.

Goal 1: To identify and clarify one's initial motives for choosing celibacy

The work of identifying and clarifying our initial motives for celibacy begins the first time we are asked the question: Why did you decide to be a celibate? Ideally, this question is asked early in our discernment by the vocation director, who expresses interest not only in our motives for priesthood or religious life in general, but in our reasons for choosing celibacy more specifically. If not asked in the first stages of discernment, then the question should be raised early in initial formation. Judging by conversations I've had with many older men and women in religious life and priesthood, many celibates waited years before someone asked them this critical question. Many are still waiting.

The question itself places the ball squarely in the candidate's court, but seminarians and religious do not need to be left alone to struggle with this most basic of questions. The work of identifying and clarifying initial motives for celibacy can and often does happen in a number of important relationships within the context of formation, including interviews with vocation and formation personnel, conversations with friends, spiritual direction, and counseling.

Given that our motives are rarely simple or "pure," we should not be satisfied with an answer as limited as: "I guess I chose celibacy because it came along with the territory of priesthood/religious life." This may be one of the motives; however, others should be considered. Sometimes candidates need a trusted other to help them entertain additional motives by suggesting a range of possibilities. For example: "Some men and women who have grown up in divorced families choose celibacy as a way of avoiding intimacy and the messiness of marriage. Do you think this could be true of you to some degree?" A formation director should be careful not to pin specific motives on a candidate, but the director can certainly help the person articulate other motives by providing a list of those identified by others. Readings and conversations with a spiritual director or formation director can also elicit and generate a range of possible reasons why others have chosen celibacy (both healthy and unhealthy) and prompt candidates to think more deeply about their own reasons and motives.

Novels, poems, and movies can also help us explore motives by examining first the motives of fictional characters. Why has Philippa in Rumer Godden's novel *In This House of Breed*, for example, chosen celibacy? Or Antoine, the young Trappist, in the more recent book *All We Know of Heaven* by Remy Rougeau? What has motivated the priest in Georges Beranos's *Diary of a Country Priest*, or Sister John in Mark Salzman's novel *Lying Awake* to choose celibacy? One of the great gifts offered by art and literature is the invitation to project ourselves onto characters, to see ourselves reflected in them, and then sometimes to have an aspect of our personalities revealed to us—perhaps one we have not yet considered or have not yet been brave enough to acknowledge.

Although we ideally begin this work of identifying and clarifying our motives for celibacy early in the discernment and formation process, it is good to revisit the question of initial motives periodically throughout initial formation and even after ordination or final profession. The perspective that comes with age, life experience, and maturity often provides deeper insight into the choices we made long ago. "I see now that I was choosing celibacy in part because I thought being sexually abused meant I would never be able to fall in love," one might say. Another may eventually realize, "I am beginning to see how my sexual orientation really played a role in my decision to enter religious life."

Formation staff may know or suspect that certain candidates are struggling with an aspect of their sexuality or think others seem inappropriately naive about themselves as sexual beings. In such cases, these candidates or seminarians may need some external encouragement or compassionately applied pressure to look more closely at motives. Because unhealthy motives are often protected by defense mechanisms such as denial, repression, or intellectualization, formation staff may need to take caution in how they direct their charges toward a greater self-honesty, careful not to "break the bruised reed," as St. Benedict cautions. Formation staff will first need to foster an atmosphere of acceptance, trust, and reassurance before challenging the validity or health of the candidate's reasons for pursuing celibacy. Sometimes—especially if the motives are rooted in psychosocial or psychosexual concerns—counseling or psychotherapy is warranted, allowing qualified mental health professionals to assist in the needed work while leaving the formation and spiritual direction relationships free to address the religious and spiritual dimensions of formation.

Goal 2: To evaluate the health and validity of one's initial motives for choosing celibacy

Once initial motives have been identified and clarified, we move quickly to assessing their health and validity. Remember, when considering the "validity" of a person's motives for the celibate life, the primary consideration is whether these motives can sustain a life of fruitful celibate chastity consistent with the church's intentions and vision for the celibate life in the church.

Again, this work is done by the candidate, but often in the context of relationships with formation personnel, spiritual directors, close friends, and in some cases, counselors or psychotherapists. And although the work of evaluating the health and validity of motives for celibacy is the work of the candidate, it is ultimately the formation director's responsibility, acting in the best interests of both the individual and the community or diocese, to make sure that work is being done and the right questions are being asked. Accountability for clarifying and evaluating motives for celibacy can be achieved by conducting yearly evaluations in the course of initial formation. The inclusion of questions such as "What have you learned so far about your initial motives for choosing celibacy?" or "How would you evaluate your current motives for choosing to be celibate?" can help hold candidates responsible for addressing these issues and help formation staff monitor their charges' progress along these lines.

If in the course of formation, candidates recognize that that they have chosen celibacy based on unhealthy, incomplete, or invalid motives, some important decisions must be made. First, they must discern whether priesthood or religious life (with its expectation of a properly motivated celibacy) is truly what they are called to. If candidates were attracted to the celibate vocation based primarily on an errant hope that they would not have to deal with their sexuality, they will hopefully recognize the insufficiency of this motive to support a vocation and leave formation. On the other hand, if candidates were studying for priesthood or joining a religious community for reasons not *solely* tied up with unhealthy or invalid motives for celibacy—if they also had a strong attraction to priestly ministry or to the charism of religious life—then there may be some benefit from continuing formation, working toward the goal of adopting more appropriate and promising reasons for pursuing a life of celibate chastity.

We will say more about this in following chapters, but it is worth noting here while addressing motives that candidates should have a clear understanding of the distinction between celibacy and chastity. Sometimes in the course of initial formation, candidates find themselves struggling with loneliness, temptation, and sexual attraction and begin to question their decision to be celibate. In reality, these are struggles that all Christians, celibate or not, deal with and primarily relate to efforts to be chaste, not celibate. In such cases it will be helpful for formation staff and spiritual directors to help clarify whether these are challenges to celibacy or to chastity.

An illustration may help clarify some of what we have talked about so far:

> *Jordan is a twenty-three-year-old seminarian who has struggled most of his adolescence and young adulthood with masturbation. He is not compulsive in his masturbation but experiences occasional, if not regular, lapses despite his honest and sincere efforts not to masturbate. Jordan was especially disillusioned and disappointed in himself when, after only a couple of months in the seminary, he gave in to the temptation to masturbate. The experience caused him to question whether he is truly called to be a priest. In discussing this with his spiritual director, Jordan came to recognize that part of what had motivated*

him to celibacy in the first place was the thought that "celibacy would
be good for me"—that the promise and expectation of celibacy itself
would make him less vulnerable to the temptation to masturbate.

Here is an example of where life experience has led to a clarification of
an individual's initial motives for celibacy. If Jordan could have articulated
this initial motive at the very beginning, before he entered seminary, by
saying, "I want to be celibate because it will help me not to masturbate,"
his vocation director would have certainly challenged Jordan's motives
and helped him to recognize that a history of struggling to rein in sexual
impulses is not a good (valid) reason to pursue clerical celibacy. Still, if
Jordan is a pious individual with other sincere reasons for wanting to be a
priest (e.g., he loves the liturgy and the sacraments and desires to minister
to others who are suffering), then his formation director or spiritual director might invite Jordan to remain a while longer and see if he can grow in
his understanding of celibacy and what it might offer him and the church.
They might begin by pointing out that his struggles with masturbation
represent a more fundamental struggle with chastity (not celibacy) and
that he would likely be struggling with this temptation whether married,
single, or celibate. They might tell Jordan that his struggles do not necessarily mean that he is not called to celibacy any more than a husband
occasionally feeling attracted to another woman means he is no longer
called to be married to his wife. With some assistance and support in
continuing to work on chastity, and with some help in seeing that there
have already been some fruits to his commitment to celibacy—perhaps an
experience of deeper intimacy with God in prayer—Jordan may come to
realize that he is indeed called to celibacy, the point of which is a greater
capacity for love, not a means of achieving sexual continence.

This example leads us to the third goal for formation in the area of
motives for celibacy.

Goal 3: To learn and begin to adopt strong and valid reasons for choosing the celibate life

Of course, the strongest motives for celibacy are theological and spiritual, and before these can be adopted by the candidate, they must be
presented and made explicit by the formation program. Once candidates
have begun the work of identifying, clarifying, and evaluating their initial

motives for celibacy, they must be introduced to the church's goals for the celibate life and encouraged to consider whether these can inspire, support, inform, and sustain them in a life of self-gift that does not include marriage or genital sexual expression.

We will talk extensively in the chapters ahead about the theology of celibacy and the importance of applying theological knowledge to our lived experience in order to derive meaning from the celibate life; however, let us emphasize here that it is the role and responsibility of the initial formation program to provide a strong theological education from which seminarians and candidates for religious life can draw motivation, inspiration, meaning, and support. This work of educating candidates about the church's theology of celibacy may include academic coursework, spiritual conferences, workshops, and assigned readings. A variety of personnel may be involved. A seminarian's or candidate's progress toward this goal can likewise be assessed in a number of ways, including written assignments (in academic courses), self-evaluations, and conversations with formation staff, all aimed at better understanding how well the candidate grasps the church's intention and theological vision for celibacy. In the yearly evaluation procedures in my religious community, our men in formation are asked to reflect on the following questions: What is your understanding of the church's vision for celibacy? How have you seen this vision play out in your own life so far as a celibate monk? Personally owning and living out the church's full vision and hope for celibacy is surely the work of an entire lifetime; however, by the end of initial formation, candidates should have had some experiences of that vision coming to fruition if they are going to be able to say with any confidence that they are called to a permanent commitment to celibate chastity.

Goal 4: In the last six to twelve months leading up to ordination or final profession, to revisit the question: Do I now have motives that are capable of sustaining a fruitful life of celibate chastity, consistent with the church's intention and vision for celibacy?

The fourth goal for formation in the area of motives for celibacy once again has to do with discernment, but this time not the discernment of *initial* motives, but of *ultimate* motives for choosing the celibate life. In other words, after several years of careful formation, can candidates now say that they have healthy and valid motives for choosing a lifetime of celibate chastity?

We should acknowledge that it is impossible to know ourselves completely at any given point in our lives. Consequently, it may be similarly impossible to completely understand the depth and complexity of our motives for choosing celibacy—even after several years of the best formation. There are certain dimensions of ourselves that we come to know only with time and experience. That being said, people can and should aim to increase their freedom and improve the quality of their decision by embarking on a careful and honest exploration of motives while working to inhabit or "try on" the church's vision for celibate chastity.

In the final six or twelve months of initial formation, then, the fourth goal should be to evaluate whether the individual has motives that are truly capable of sustaining a fruitful and meaningful life of celibate chastity consistent with the church's intention and vision for celibacy. A series of questions asked in the contexts of individual reflection and conversations with formation directors, spiritual directors, and superiors can guide this process of discerning one's ultimate motives. These include the following:

1. What is my theological understanding of the celibate life as I approach final profession or ordination?

2. Is this theological understanding consistent with the church's intention for celibacy and with the charism of the vocation I am embarking upon (i.e., diocesan life, contemplative religious life, apostolic life, etc.)?

3. Has this theological understanding helped to motivate, direct, and make meaning of my experience of living the celibate life so far?

4. What have been the discernable fruits of my commitment to celibacy so far? In other words:
   a. Has celibacy resulted in a greater capacity for love of God? What are the indications?
   b. Has celibacy resulted in a greater capacity for love of other people? What are some concrete examples or indications?

Note that the primary questions of discernment do not have to do with personal happiness—in other words, "Am I *happy* living a celibate life?" It is not that happiness is not an important consideration—after all, we are not looking for miserable and joyless witnesses to the celibate life! The more immediate question, however, is whether the practice of celibacy has resulted in and holds promise for future conversion in the individual's life.

We can safely assume that if in the candidate's years of formation the practice of celibacy has resulted in a greater capacity for love—a pouring out of oneself for God and others, as well as greater openness to receiving the love of God and neighbor—then we can be confident that the individual will continue to find meaning and fulfillment in life as a celibate, even amid the inevitable challenges, sorrows, and doubts that the vocation may bring. Ultimately, it is this meaning and fulfillment that bring a deep and enduring sense of happiness, peace, and joy in any life we have chosen.

In the two chapters that follow, we will explore the strongest motives for celibacy—the theological and spiritual motives—and discover how the discipline of theological reflection assists us in deriving meaning and fulfillment from the celibate life.

SECTION III

THEOLOGICAL DIMENSIONS

CHAPTER 5

THEOLOGICAL DIMENSIONS
OF CELIBATE CHASTITY

Having completed an exploration of motives for leading the celibate life, we move to the second major content area within our model for celibacy formation: theological dimensions. As you will recall, we concluded the previous chapter with four goals relative to motives, the third of which was to learn and begin to adopt strong, valid motives for choosing celibacy, with theological motives being the strongest and most valid. Therefore, in this second content area we focus on two primary goals: first, to explore the theology (or theologies) of celibacy; and second, to learn and practice the discipline of theological reflection on the experience of living the celibate life. These will be the topics of this and the next chapter, respectively.

It is perhaps difficult to speak of the *theology* of celibacy because, in actuality, there are several *theologies* of celibacy, or at least several dimensions or facets of the theology of celibate chastity. It will be our task in this chapter to survey these various theological dimensions with the understanding that a sound theological basis for celibacy is necessary not only to make sense of and to derive meaning from the experience of living the celibate life, but also to derive the inspiration needed to persevere when challenges, struggles, and temptations inevitably arise.

I always remind the men and women with whom I work that celibacy is difficult. That is not to say that marriage and parenting are not also difficult; but there are real and particular challenges that come with not marrying and with refraining from genital sexual expression, especially when we are surrounded by many beautiful and attractive examples of married friends and family members, and because our secular and highly sexualized culture often fails to understand and support the celibate witness. Like their married peers, if celibates do not have a strong spiritual and theological foundation for their commitment, the risk of abandoning their vocation is great, especially once boredom, temptation, or other unanticipated difficulties set in. And even if celibates do manage to stay committed in the face of challenges and struggles, without a deeper rationale or motive than "I agreed to this because I wanted to be a priest/religious," they are at great risk for disillusionment or regret in the long run. Theological understanding and reflection are the tools we use to make sense of the difficulties and to transform challenges into opportunities for greater depth and expressions of self-gift.

Answering My Aunt Joyce

One way I ask men and women in formation to begin articulating a theology of celibacy for themselves is to imagine how they would explain it to another. I give them the following scenario:

> You have been assigned to a parish/school/ministry in the small rural town where my aunt Joyce lives. Joyce is in her early seventies and has been Catholic her entire life. Like most Catholics, she does not have a degree in theology and has never taken a college-level theology course; however, she is a very devout and generous Catholic. She grew up attending Catholic school and attends Mass faithfully. She has worked every parish picnic for the last fifty-five years and has worked several years as the secretary in the local Catholic school. Joyce has never really understood the reason for celibacy, but she has never asked a priest or sister about it for fear of seeming disrespectful or questioning church teaching. But Joyce has grown to feel very comfortable with you, and one day she says: "You know, there is one thing that I have never fully understood, and I think you could probably help me: I don't really understand celibacy. Why are priests, sisters, and brothers not allowed to get married?"

What are you going to tell her? The challenge here is to provide a rationale—a theological rationale—that is compelling, that doesn't diminish the witness of married and single Christians, and that is accessible to most Catholics (after all, you shouldn't have to have a master's degree or doctorate in theology to make sense of celibacy). For the exercise, I usually forbid my students to use prepared phrases such as "for the sake of the kingdom" or "an undivided love of Christ," and I push them to use their own words and experience to articulate the intention of the celibate witness. How would you answer?

As important as it is to be able to explain this to people like my aunt Joyce, it is more immediately important that celibates are able to articulate *for themselves* a clear rationale for why they have chosen celibacy. Throughout this volume, we will repeatedly return to the theme that the bottom line of celibacy is love. Every theology of celibacy we explore in this chapter has love as its ultimate aim—love of God and love of others. In preparing my own response to Aunt Joyce, I would begin by saying, "It's how we love, Joyce." And go from there.

We should always remember, and therefore aim to communicate to others in words and actions, that celibacy is a charism—not merely an obligation. It is *charismatic*, not only in that it characterizes or distinguishes a particular vocation, but also in that it is meant to be attractive, maybe even compelling. It is not an obstacle to overcome. When people are charismatic, we say they have a certain something that draws us to them and reflects some kind of virtue. If lived properly, celibacy should make us more attractive and generous and our witness more compelling. It should result in an outpouring of grace, not a hoarding of gifts, talents, and energies. If lived correctly, celibacy has the capacity to draw others to us and to make us irresistible to God.

Sexuality, Marriage, and the Call to Chastity

We begin a discussion of the theology of celibacy by briefly reviewing the theology of sexuality and marriage. Unless we have a firm grasp on the essential purpose and goodness of these from the Christian perspective, we cannot understand more fully the purpose and value of celibacy. Recall that the parameters of celibacy are that we choose to refrain from marriage and from genital sexual expression; however, we do so not out of a conviction that either of these are evil or to be generally avoided. Rather, sexuality and marriage have great value in their capacity to draw us closer to God and to one another. We must remember that celibacy draws both its value and its meaning from the goodness and holiness of marriage and sexuality.

The *Catechism of the Catholic Church* reminds us that sexuality is a deeply human experience that has as its essence both a unitive and a procreative end. This means human sexuality is designed by God both to draw humans into relationship to himself and to one another (the unitive dimension) and to generate new life (the procreative dimension): "Sexuality affects all aspects of the human person in the unity of his body and soul. It especially concerns affectivity, the capacity to love and to procreate, and in a more general way the aptitude for forming bonds of communion with others."[1]

Like any of God's gifts—e.g., the earth, human ingenuity, freedom—sexuality can be used for good or evil purposes; and any harm, negativity, injustice, abuse, or fear associated with sexuality is of our own human making. Sexuality in itself is not ugly or fearsome; it is a manifestation of God's love for us. When used correctly and toward the proper ends, sexuality presents opportunities to better understand God's loving nature. In his *Theology of the Body*, Pope John Paul II reminds us that in his perfection, God is not fractured into male and female, but encompasses all.[2] Consequently, in a marriage, and in particular in the "conjugal act" (or sexual intercourse) when two become one flesh, humans realize in a special way the reality that we are made in God's image and likeness.

Further, there are countless examples in the Catholic tradition of human sexuality as a vehicle for communicating important truths of faith. Recall, for example, the many medieval depictions of the Jesse tree used to illustrate the human genealogy of Christ. In this iconography found throughout the church in stained glass windows and manuscript illuminations and alluded to in liturgical texts, Jesse the patriarch is typically portrayed lying down on a bed with a tree trunk (the "rod" or "root" of Jesse) springing from between his legs. In each of its branches are his descendants, with Christ at the very top.

There is also sexual imagery in the liturgy. For example, at the Easter Vigil the paschal candle—a phallic form and symbol of fertility—is

---

1. *Catechism of the Catholic Church,* 2nd ed. (Washington, DC: United States Conference of Catholic Bishops, 1997), Article 2332.

2. John Paul II, *The Theology of the Body: Human Love in the Divine Plan* (Boston: Pauline Books and Media, 1997), 25.

brought into the darkened church and used to light the myriad candles held by the believers, filling the church with light. Later in the liturgy, the paschal candle is thrust into the baptismal font (a feminine form) several times before its waters are used to baptized the catechumens who will continue to help populate the church and testify to the ongoing fertility of Christ's loving presence in the world. And we need only to read from the Song of Songs in Scripture or from the mystical poetry of St. John of the Cross to further appreciate how our erotic and sexual sensibilities are not only acceptable, but powerful windows into the all-consuming love that God calls us to with himself.

In the church's wisdom, marriage is a vocation with its own charism and particular witness for the world. As with every vocation in the church, the purpose of marriage is to challenge and support Christians in their journey of conversion, of becoming the most Christlike (in other words, the most loving) individuals they can be. Therefore, the goal of marriage is not one's own personal happiness, but the creation of a bond and the formation of a community (whether it includes just the spouse or expands to include children) within which the members love, serve, and lay down their lives for one another, and in so doing, love and serve God who is present in the spouse and in each member of the family.

Marriage and parenthood are thus blessed and holy vocations in which Christians experience the love of God through one another. When this is understood, the celibate vocation becomes a complement to marriage. Marriage is not a mediocre institution to be rejected by celibates, but another valuable witness in reference to which celibates more clearly see and understand the end to which their sexuality and impulse to love is directed. Fr. Raniero Cantalamessa summarizes this point convincingly: "Indeed, what merit would there be in not marrying, if marriage were something bad or simply dangerous and inadvisable? To abstain from it would be a duty and nothing more, like abstaining from any occasion of sin. But precisely because marriage is good and beautiful, the renunciation of it for a higher motive is even more beautiful. . . . When you think of it, it is only the existence of marriage that makes virginity a choice, and only the existence of virginity that makes marriage a choice."[3]

---

3. Raniero Cantalamessa, *Virginity: A Positive Approach to Celibacy for the Sake of the Kingdom of Heaven* (New York: St. Paul's Press, 1995), 61–62.

Chastity is a final concept considered foundational to a proper theological understanding of celibacy. Chastity is a virtue to which all Christians are called and can be defined in brief as a properly ordered living out of one's sexuality according to the person's state in life. The *Catechism of the Catholic Church* talks about the proper "integration" of one's sexuality into the moral and relational life of the individual whereby he or she is able to "imitate the purity of Christ."[4]

Celibacy, by distinction, is one state according to which a Christian man or woman is called to live chastely, as the following selection from the *Catechism* suggests: "People should cultivate [chastity] in the way that is suited to their state of life. Some profess virginity or consecrated celibacy which enables them to give themselves to God alone with an undivided heart in a remarkable manner. Others live in the way prescribed for all by the moral law, whether they are married or single. Married people are called to live conjugal chastity; others practice chastity in continence."[5]

Let us now survey the various theologies or theological dimensions of celibate chastity.

Celibacy for the Sake of the Kingdom: The Eschatological Dimension

When I ask my students to articulate a theology of celibacy, most respond by saying that celibacy is pursued "for the sake of the kingdom." Even if they are not exactly sure how further to articulate this, they have a clear understanding that celibacy is pursued with a goal in mind, and that goal is the realization of the kingdom of God. This basic theology of celibacy derives its scriptural support from the Gospel of Matthew where, in reference to those who do not marry, Christ teaches: "Some are incapable of marriage because they were born so; some, because they were made so by others; some, because they have renounced marriage for the sake of the kingdom of heaven" (Matt 19:12; NABRE).

In his highly recommended treatment on the theology of celibacy entitled *Virginity*, Cantalamessa suggests that there are two facets to this notion of celibacy "for the sake of the kingdom"—an eschatological

4. *Catechism*, Article 2345.
5. *Catechism*, Article 2349.

dimension and an apostolic or missionary dimension.[6] We begin with the eschatological dimension.

The word "eschatological" refers to the end of the world (or the "eschaton"). When we say something is eschatological, we mean that it somehow reflects the end times, or how it will be when the world as we know it passes away and everything is brought to its ultimate fulfillment in God. With this in mind, recall the story in the gospels wherein the Sadducees challenge Jesus with a riddle about a woman who marries seven brothers one after the other, after each previous one dies. After explaining the predicament, the Sadducees then ask Jesus: "In the resurrection, then, whose wife of the seven will she be?" Jesus replies: "For in the resurrection they neither marry nor are given in marriage, but are like angels in heaven" (Matt 22:28, 30). In his response, Christ teaches that at the end times, all people will be gathered back into God in Christ. There will be no marriages—no husbands or wives—because God's all-consuming love will eclipse any need for our human arrangements. We all will belong to one another because all will belong completely and eternally to God.

When we say, then, that celibacy is pursued "for the sake of the kingdom" in the eschatological sense, we mean that the celibate makes real in our present reality the kingdom of God. By not marrying and by devoting their life to the worship and praise of God, celibates live now as we will all live at the end of time. In this way, a celibate life is a sign of confidence in both the kingdom to come and in God's eternal love to which we are all called and into which we are all drawn if we hold fast to our faith. Celibate men and women remind the world that the kingdom of God is not only a future possibility, but a present reality. The kingdom is already underway. It is already in our midst!

This eschatological or prophetic theology of celibacy aligns well with contemplative traditions and particularly informs celibacy lived out in the context of the consecrated, communal life. We like to say, for example, that the role of the monastery in the church and in the world is to provide a foretaste of heaven—a community of men or women gathered into one, attempting to live as we will all live in eternity: in perfect charity, in constant praise of God, preferring nothing to the love of Christ, rejoicing that the bridegroom is here. With this as their goal, monasteries and religious

---

6. Cantalamessa, *Virginity.*

communities become places of pilgrimage, bastions of hospitality, and centers of worship where Christians and even non-Christians are welcomed, offered a vision of paradise, and given strength and inspiration for their own journey toward the new Jerusalem.

Celibacy for the Sake of the Kingdom: The Apostolic Dimension

The *apostolic* notion of celibacy comes closest to what most people have in mind when they consider why priests and religious are required to be celibate. We most often hear that priests, sisters, and brothers refrain from marrying and having a family of their own in order to love more broadly or to love a larger group of people; for example, parishioners, students, the homeless, or another group served by a priest or religious community's charism. The choice not to marry and parent in order to serve the spiritual, educational, and even basic needs of others is driven by an apostolic zeal and aims to build the kingdom of God in a way that is different but complementary to how the contemplative gives witness. Cantalamessa refers to this as the missionary dimension of celibacy:

> Now here is the motive that flows from this: since God's Kingdom has not yet come but is on the way, we need men and women who will devote themselves full-time and wholeheartedly to the coming of that Kingdom. . . . It is difficult to imagine what the Church would be like today had there not been, through the centuries, this host of men and women who have left "house, wife or children" for the sake of the Kingdom of Heaven (cf. Lk18:29). The proclamation of the Gospel and mission work have rested to a large extent on their shoulders. Within Christianity, they have promoted knowledge and the Word of God through study; they have opened up new ways of Christian thought and spirituality; abroad, they have carried the message of the Kingdom to the most remote peoples. They are the ones who brought into being nearly all the charitable institutions that have so enriched the Church and the world.[7]

When considering this apostolic or missionary dimension of celibacy, the primary focus is usually on the time and attention that is freed to devote to meeting the needs of God's people. Priests are free to leave

---

7. Cantalamessa, *Virginity*, 12–13.

the rectory in the middle of the night to anoint someone in the hospital without having to worry about who will stay with their children. Religious brothers and sisters are free to cook at a soup kitchen or tutor children late into the evening without having to worry about who will cook for their own family or help their own children with homework. The notion of spiritual fatherhood or motherhood fits nicely within this larger concept.

But there is something more than just the availability of time and energy that is "freed up"; there is also a potential increase in the expendability of one's life that comes with not having a spouse and children who depend on you. Let me explain.

Ever wonder why all the superheroes—Batman, Superman, Wonder Woman, Spiderman—are never married? There is a dimension to this apostolic notion of celibacy for the sake of the kingdom that I like to call the "superhero theology of celibacy." Consider what might happen if superheroes married. If Spiderman had a wife and children at home, he would have to think twice before placing himself in such danger for the sake of others. The last thing Wonder Woman needs running through her mind before she puts her life on the line to save the world against a heinous villain is: "If this doesn't go so well, who is going to care for my children? Is my husband's income going to be enough to support them?"

One of the fruits of celibacy is that it gives individuals more freedom to lay down their life in radical, heroic, and what the world might even call "foolish" ways. This notion of celibacy for the sake of the kingdom is not just about an economy of time and energy, but it is literally about the freedom to die for others. Maximilian Kolbe is an excellent model: a celibate who takes the place of a husband and father sentenced to die in a concentration camp. We could also hold up the Trappist monks of Tibhirine Abbey in Algiers (documented in the movie *Of Gods and Men*), or the El Salvadoran martyrs Sisters Ita Ford, Maura Clarke, and Dorothy Kazel, as well as Archbishop Oscar Romero—all of whom died for the rights of the poor and oppressed. These martyrs and countless others serve as compelling reminders of the gift of celibacy by their willingness to lay down their lives in the most radical ways to serve justice, defend the rights of the oppressed, and meet the basic human needs of others—in other words, to bring about the kingdom of God here on earth.

Whether it is the smaller death-to-self that comes with going out in the middle of the night to anoint the dying, or the great risk of standing up in the face of grave danger to represent and meet the needs of the hungry, the poor, and the powerless, all are acts of love facilitated by celibacy. All are opportunities for conversion to Christ who serves as our ultimate model of what it means to lay down one's life for the sake of others, for the sake of the kingdom.

Spousal Theology of Celibacy: An Unmediated Love of God

The notion of a spousal theology of celibacy can be confusing and perhaps even uncomfortable, especially for those who may be reluctant to think of themselves as "married to God" or Christ. Many find it difficult to identify with a theology of celibacy that, on the surface, may seem overly pious or sentimental. Yet the spousal theology of celibacy is one of the most ancient and bears a profound depth of meaning with significant implications for both men and women, particularly those in contemplative orders.

To better understand this spousal theology of celibacy, begin by recalling that the *entire church* is considered to be the bride of Christ. Scripture—Old and New Testaments alike—frequently employs spousal imagery to communicate the depth of God's loving relationship with his people. In the book of the prophet Isaiah, we read:

> For your maker is your husband,
>   the Lord of hosts is his name;
> the Holy One of Israel is your Redeemer,
>   the God of the whole earth he is called. (Isa 54:5)

And again:

> I will greatly rejoice in the Lord,
>   my whole being shall exult in my God;
> for he has clothed me with the garments of salvation,
>   he has covered me with the robe of righteousness,
> as a bridegroom decks himself with a garland,
>   and as a bride adorns herself with her jewels. (Isa 61:10)

And of course the Song of Solomon employs this spousal motif throughout:

Come with me from Lebanon, my bride;
  come with me from Lebanon.
Depart from the peak of Amana,
  from the peak of Senir and Hermon,
from the dens of lions,
  from the mountains of leopards.
You have ravished my heart, my sister, my bride,
  you have ravished my heart with a glance of your eyes,
  with one jewel of your necklace.
How sweet is your love, my sister, my bride! (Song 4:8-10)

In the Gospel of John, John the Baptist introduces Christ as the bridegroom (John 3:29) and Christ himself makes the spousal relationship abundantly clear by referring to himself as the bridegroom in the ninth chapter of Matthew's gospel: "And Jesus said to them, 'The wedding guests cannot mourn as long as the bridegroom is with them, can they? The days will come when the bridegroom is taken away from them, and then they will fast'" (Matt 9:15). St. Paul in his letter to the Ephesians (5:22-23) uses the image of Christ as bridegroom to the church to describe how husbands and wives ought to relate to one another.

If we consider the entire church as being the bride of Christ, then we can think of the celibate as one who inhabits this facet of the church's identity and relationship with God in a particular way and with expanded intention. For the celibate, it means the pursuit of a relationship with God that is deeply personal and intimate, one that is not mediated through husband or wife and children, as Sr. Sandra Schneiders points out: "The religious chooses to engage in the God-quest in an immediate way, exclusive of all mediating life commitments. The renunciation of the paradigmatic primary commitment, to spouse and family, is the symbolic expression of that exclusive commitment to the unmediated God-quest."[8]

In his treatment of the charism of celibacy, Thomas Dubay similarly champions the notion of the contemplative vocation as "a vocation of being in love with God," asserting that "the individual consecrated virgin [or celibate] embraces a way of life in which she so exclusively focuses on her one Beloved that she declines a marital relationship with any other

---

8. Sandra M. Schneiders, *Selling All: Commitment, Consecrated Celibacy, and Community in Catholic Religious Life* (New York: Paulist Press, 2001), 128.

man."[9] Dubay likewise reminds us that this spousal way of relating to God in Christ is not unrelated to the charism of the entire church: "What the whole Church is to be, the individual virgin does by vocation" and, "the celibate woman or man after the example of the Master, is to be a model of the Church at prayer."[10]

Although the spousal theology of celibacy is often associated with cloistered women—Carmelites, Poor Clares, cloistered Benedictines—celibate men have also drawn inspiration and meaning from a spousal theology. St. John of the Cross, whose mystical poetry is emblematic of this theological orientation, is probably the most famous example:

> O guiding night!
> O night more lovely than the dawn!
> O night that has united
> The Lover with His beloved,
> Transforming the beloved in her Lover.
>
> Upon my flowering breast
> Which I kept wholly for Him alone,
> There He lay sleeping,
> And I caressing Him
> There in a breeze from the fanning cedars.[11]

Proving that this type of relationship is not only for cloistered contemplatives, St. Augustine employs similarly intimate language in one of the most famous passages of his *Confessions*: "I have learnt to love you late, Beauty at once so ancient and so new! I have learnt to love you late! You were within me, and I was in the world outside myself . . . You called me; you cried aloud to me; you broke my barrier of deafness. You shone upon me; your radiance enveloped me; you put my blindness to flight. You shed your fragrance about me; I drew breath and now I gasp

---

9. Thomas Dubay, ". . . *And You Are Christ's*": *The Charism of Virginity and the Celibate Life* (San Francisco: Ignatius Press, 1987), 41.

10. Dubay, ". . . *And You Are Christ's*," 42–43.

11. Kieran Kavanaugh and Otilio Rodriguez, eds., "Stanzas," in *The Collected Works of St. John of the Cross* (Washington, DC: Institute of Carmelite Studies, 1979), 69.

for your sweet odour. I tasted you, and now I hunger and thirst for you. You touched me, and I am inflamed with love of your peace."[12]

Informed by a spousal theology, the celibate's relationship with God is an unmediated one, and in order for it to be pursued, the celibate is afforded the time and space to pray, meditate, adore, and develop a relationship with the word of God in our *lectio divina* and our praying of the Liturgy of the Hours—all activities that our married, parenting, and even diocesan counterparts are not likely to find possible with all of their holy obligations. In turn, the entirety of the church relies on the celibate having this special relationship with God. Proof is on the bulletin boards found in every religious community in the world. They are universally littered with small scraps of paper with prayer requests printed on them: *Please pray for my husband who has just been diagnosed with cancer. Please pray for my daughter who is suffering from depression. Please pray for me because I have lost my job and I have three small children.*

It may embarrass celibates when people ask for their prayers because they have "a special relationship with God," but they do, and the structures of their life allow for it. It is a gift celibates receive from the church and one they give back to the church. It is the celibate's charism and responsibility. The rest of the church knows and expects that if celibate men and women have been living the charism of consecrated celibacy zealously and as intended, then—on behalf of the entire church—they have been afforded the privilege of pursuing the kind of relationship with God in which petitions become personal favors asked by those who endear themselves in a particular way to the heart of God.

At its very core, the spousal dimension of celibacy is relational. It does not aim to deny or diminish the often heroic ways in which the husbands, wives, parents, diocesan priests, apostolic religious, or missionaries love and therefore love God. Still, it represents another facet of how we as the church are called to love and be in love with God. Sr. Schneiders's simple but profound insight follows: when the celibate is inspired by the spousal theology, "Fidelity . . . [is] not to a vow but to a Person."[13]

12. Saint Augustine, *Confessions*, trans. R. S. Pine-Coffin (London: Penguin, 1961), 231–32.

13. Schneiders, *Selling All*, 142.

An Ascetic Theology of Celibacy

Asceticism is the practice of sacrificing something of value in the interest of achieving or gaining some higher good. Although we tend to associate asceticism with men and women living in the desert centuries ago, or with emaciated monks and nuns sequestered in austere monasteries, the fact is that people all around us (including ourselves) engage in ascetic practices all the time. Dieting, for example, is an ascetic practice by which people deprive themselves of food for the sake of losing weight, feeling better, looking more attractive, or fitting into last summer's wardrobe. Competitive athletes also practice asceticism when they give up time, comfort, food, and sometimes even sleep for long hours of training. In fact, the word "asceticism" comes from the Greek word *asketikos* and originally refers to rigorous exercise or training for athletic competitions. Ascetic monks and nuns were often thought of as "spiritual athletes," and St. Paul likens himself to an athlete for the sake of the gospel when he writes: "I have fought the good fight, I have finished the race, I have kept the faith. From now on there is reserved for me the crown of righteousness, which the Lord, the righteous judge, will give me on that day" (2 Tim 4:7-8).

Christian asceticism involves making sacrifices for the sake of a spiritual good: a more intimate association with Christ; the coming of the kingdom of God; or the evangelization of others. The *Program of Priestly Formation* includes asceticism as a discipline to be cultivated among those preparing for priesthood: "Spiritual formation initiates seminarians to a path of voluntary renunciation and self-denial that makes them more available to the will of God and more available to their people. Asceticism and the practice of penance is a path of learning to embrace the cross and, in an apostolic context, a way of rendering priests unafraid to bear their 'share of hardship for the gospel with strength that comes from God (2 Tim 1:8).'"[14] Hermits and anchorites practiced deprivations of sex, food, and sleep as means of disciplining their bodies and minds and removing any obstacle that might interfere with their contemplation and relationship with God. The essential point is that Christian ascetic practices are always adopted for the sake of the love of God or for the love of God's people.

---

14. *Program of Priestly Formation,* 5th ed. (Washington, DC: United States Conference of Catholic Bishops, 2006), 45.

Once again, the bottom line of celibacy is always love. Individual sisters, brothers, or priests might be perfectly continent, but they might still be lousy celibates if their discipline has not resulted in a greater capacity for love. In his Rule for monks, St. Benedict beautifully links discipline and the ascetic life to the love of God when he writes: "The good of all concerned, however, may prompt us to a little strictness in order to amend faults and to safeguard love. Do not be daunted immediately by fear and run away from the road that leads to salvation. It is bound to be narrow at the outset. But as we progress in this way of life and in faith, we shall run on the path of God's commandments, our hearts overflowing with the inexpressible delight of love" (RB Prol. 47–49).[15]

In other words, the ascetic practice of celibacy should not leave one miserable, irritable, distant, and emotionally chilly. If the point is to deprive ourselves of thoughts or obsessions that might interfere with our ability to relate to the indwelling God, then the result of our efforts ought to be joy and gratitude, not fatigue and resentment.

Be warned, also, that taken too far, an ascetic approach to celibacy can lead to theological problems and can be used to justify unhealthy notions of sexuality. Evagrius and Cassian, champions of ascetic practices in the desert, were criticized by their contemporaries as leaning in the direction of semi-Pelagianism—the idea that one could achieve purity of heart by his or her own efforts, therefore minimizing the need for God's grace. Most of us are acutely aware of our own limits and failures when it comes to ascetic practices such as celibacy, and we need reminders that the work is not ours alone. The same God who initiates these good works in our lives also provides the grace and mercy to bring them to perfection. Writing on the spiritual disciplines, the Quaker author Richard Foster nicely describes the relationship between our efforts and God's grace: "The needed change within us is God's work, not ours. . . . God has given us the Disciplines of the spiritual life as a means of receiving his grace. The Disciplines allow us to place ourselves before God so that he can transform us."[16]

15. Timothy Fry, Imogene Baker, Timothy Horner, Augusta Raabe, Mark Sheridan, eds., *The Rule of St. Benedict in English* (Collegeville, MN: Liturgical Press, 1981), 18–19.

16. Richard J. Foster, *Celebration of Discipline: The Path to Spiritual Growth,* rev. ed. (San Francisco: Harper & Row, 1988), 6–7.

We call again upon St. Benedict, who concludes chapter 4 of his Rule, the "Tools for Good Works" (a long list of over seventy-five works, attitudes, and disciplines for the monk to cultivate) with the ultimate admonition: "And finally, never lose hope in God's mercy" (RB 4.74).[17] If nothing else, adopting ascetic practices can result in a new appreciation of our human weaknesses and a greater realization of our dependence on God.

Another potential danger associated with an ascetic notion of celibacy is the risk of going too far and denouncing sexuality altogether as sinful and evil. We should always be mindful that even if it has been used for harm or evil by some, God created sexuality in his goodness to humankind, to bring people together, to bring life into the world, and to draw us to himself. Rather than being possessed by a spirit of fear or distrust of sexuality, the healthy celibate recognizes that, even if the world has made an "idol" of sexuality, the sacrifice of living joyfully and meaningfully without genital sexual expression can help redeem sexuality and restore its true value as something created by God as good, not something to be worshipped. This is Fr. Cantalamessa's point when he reminds us that by adopting the ascetic practice of celibacy (as well as the other evangelical counsels of poverty and obedience), the priest or consecrated religious participates in the sufferings of Christ and in the saving mission of the paschal mystery: "Poverty, chastity and obedience are not a renunciation—or worse, a condemnation—of a created *good*, but a rejection of the *evil* that has come to overlay that good. Therefore they are, by definition, a proclamation of the original goodness of created things."[18] Of course, to do this, the celibate must sacrifice freely and joyfully—not grudgingly, unwittingly, coldly, or fearfully.

In Persona Christi Capitis: Celibacy in Imitation of Christ

A final theological dimension relates specifically to priestly or clerical celibacy. In *Pastores Dabo Vobis,* Pope John Paul II writes: "And so priestly celibacy should not be considered just as a legal norm, or as a totally external condition for admission to ordination, but rather as a value that is

---

17. Fry and others, eds., *The Rule of St. Benedict*, 29.
18. Cantalamessa, *Virginity*, 45–46.

profoundly connected with ordination, whereby a man takes on the likeness of Jesus Christ, the good Shepherd and Spouse of the Church, and therefore as a choice of a greater and undivided love for Christ and his Church, as a full and joyful availability in his heart for the pastoral ministry."[19]

Here again, a spousal metaphor is invoked; however, in this context the celibate priest, assuming the place of Christ, head of the church, is regarded as bridegroom to the church (and not bride). In modeling himself after Christ, therefore, the priest adopts celibacy and devotes himself entirely to the love of Christ and the church in his priestly ministry and prayer.

As we have seen, these various theological dimensions begin to overlap, and so it is useful to think about all of these dimensions (for the sake of the kingdom, spousal, ascetic, *in persona Christi*) as facets of a single theological reality—that our celibacy is motivated by a love of God that spills over into a love of God's people and a desire for his kingdom in our midst.

It is also worth pointing out that while the various facets of the theology of celibate chastity may have grown out of or are more closely identified with different charisms in the church (i.e., contemplative, apostolic, missionary, priestly), all celibates—regardless of type of religious life—benefit from being acquainted with all of these dimensions, understanding that in the course of a single lifetime, the celibate is likely draw upon each of them in order to inform, inspire, and help make meaning of the experience of living a celibate life.

Drawing Up a Curriculum

It is impossible to exhaustively explore the theology of celibate chastity in one chapter. Here, I have attempted to survey the major theological dimensions of celibate chastity as they relate to various forms of priestly and consecrated life. One could add additional readings to this summary in order to arrive at a more tailored curriculum for learning the theology of celibacy.

As I have mentioned previously, an effective curriculum should begin with an adequate review of the Catholic theology of sexuality in general with an appropriate understanding of chastity. Although I will leave it to

---

19. John Paul II, *Pastores Dabo Vobis: On the Formation of Priests in the Circumstances of the Present Day* (Washington, DC: United States Catholic Conference, 1999), 137.

the theological experts to make a more exhaustive list of recommendations in this area, one could certainly not go wrong including a reading of
the *Catechism*, Pope John Paul II's *Theology of the Body* (or more popular-
ized treatments of this body of teaching), and some of the official Vatican
documents offered on the subject of human sexuality. Among these, the
1995 document *The Truth and Meaning of Human Sexuality: Guidelines
for Education within the Family* offers a clear and straightforward review
of basic Catholic teaching on sexuality. Pope Benedict XVI's Encyclical
Letter *Deus Caritas Est* is highly recommended to candidates for its inspiring and beautifully written exploration of love, including erotic love
(eros) and its place in God's generous providence and plan for humankind. From these readings, candidates should also come to appreciate the
meaning of marriage and the larger concept of chastity so they can more
easily discern in their experiences whether something is a specific challenge of the celibate life or the chaste life. This will be critically helpful as
men and women discern whether they are called to celibacy.

Beyond a survey of the theological facets of celibate chastity, candidates
ought to draw on sources that explore a theological understanding of
celibacy more closely linked to their particular charism. Monastic men
and women, for example, will surely want to familiarize themselves with
the works of the Desert Fathers and Mothers, including Cassian and
Evagrius, as well as explore Bernard of Clairvaux's sermons on the Song
of Songs. Carmelites in particular will benefit from reading more deeply
in the writings of the Spanish mystics or Therese of Lisieux to better appreciate how their celibacy was informed and inspired by a more strictly
contemplative and spousal theology. Formation directors of apostolic
and missionary orders will want to direct their charges to the appropriate
writings of their founders and members who articulate the theology and
spirituality of celibacy within their own tradition. Diocesan seminarians,
priests, and deacons will surely be inspired by writings on the distinctive
charism of priestly celibacy found in the church's formation documents
and by the many priests, bishops, popes, and saints who have championed
and encouraged celibate chastity over the centuries.

At the conclusion of initial formation, candidates should be able to answer the question: What is a *Benedictine* (*Dominican, Franciscan, priestly,*
etc.) theology of celibacy? They should be able to articulate—not only for
people like my aunt Joyce, but especially for themselves—why the church

has asked them to be celibate and why they have chosen celibacy as the context in which they will endeavor to lead a chaste life. A bottom line, regardless of the context in which they are endeavoring to live the celibate life, is that candidates should be able summarize their explanation with the simple, but definitive statement: "It's how we love."

CHAPTER 6

THEOLOGICAL REFLECTION

Theological reflection is probably the most important skill we can teach young candidates who hope to persevere for a lifetime of celibate chastity. It is probably universally accepted that celibates must have a solid grounding in the theology of celibacy; however, theological knowledge makes little difference unless candidates also have the ability to apply that knowledge to their lived experience and use it to derive meaning and inspiration. Consequently, our second formation goal relative to the major content area of theological dimensions of celibacy is to acquire and practice the skill of theological reflection.

I begin this chapter by describing what theological reflection is and making a case for its inclusion in formation programs. Following this introduction, we will explore a concrete model for practicing theological reflection and conclude with two case studies to help us develop a concrete sense of how theological reflection works and its potential benefits in the life of the celibate.

What Is Theological Reflection?

Theological reflection is a discipline that helps us to explore the relationship between our theological knowledge and our experience. When used in the context of ministry training, the process of theological reflection involves examining (or *reflecting* upon) an experience of ministry through a theological lens. There are two goals: (1) to better understand the incident as an experience of applied theology; and (2), to allow the experience to deepen theological knowledge or understanding. Patricia O'Connell Killen and John de Beer define *theological reflection* in the following way: "Theological reflection puts our experience into a genuine conversation with our religious heritage. . . . It helps us access the Christian tradition as a reliable source of guidance as we search to discover the meaning of what God is doing now in our individual and corporate lives."[1] In the context of celibacy, the practice of theological reflection invites us to examine specific experiences related to living the celibate life through the lens of the theology of celibacy in order to derive meaning, deeper theological knowledge, and greater inspiration for our commitment to celibate chastity.

Knowledge and Experience

Let's first explore the relationship between the two key components of the process of theological reflection: knowledge and experience. These can be thought of as relating to one another in a circular fashion, a dynamic often described as the "hermeneutic circle." The word "hermeneutic" refers to the act of interpreting or finding the meaning in something (a text, an experience, etc.). This relationship between knowledge and experience is circular in the sense that it is ongoing, it is evolving over time, and it is almost impossible to determine where it begins and where it ends. What we know (knowledge) helps us to interpret the experiences we have. And our experiences provide us with the practical, sensory information that helps to deepen our ever-expanding knowledge base.

Knowledge   Experience

1. Patricia O'Connell Killen and John de Beer, *The Art of Theological Reflection* (New York: Crossroad, 1994), viii.

Let's illustrate with a simple example. A young child learns what a thorn is from his mother while reading the fairy tale "Sleeping Beauty" (Sleeping Beauty's tower is surrounded by a thicket of thorns). While reading this part of the story, the mother points to the thorns in the picture and says: "Ouch, thorns! Those are very sharp and they can cut you. The prince will have to be careful not to get hurt!" The child now has knowledge—*intellectual* knowledge—of thorns and what it means for something to be sharp. But this knowledge is limited by the fact that thus far the boy has no real experience of thorns. One day a few months later, the boy is playing soccer with his sister in his grandmother's backyard and follows the ball into his grandmother's rose garden. He gets tangled in the bushes and is scratched up by the thorns. Experience! Now he understands thorns on a whole new level. He says to himself: "Oh, *these* are the thorns I learned about when we were reading "Sleeping Beauty." Man, those are sharp! I'm going stay far away from thorns from now on!" The boy's previous knowledge helps him to understand what is happening to him (application of knowledge to experience), and his firsthand experience serves to expand his knowledge and understanding of what a thorn really is (experience deepens knowledge). With any reflection at all, the boy's experience will lead him to make decisions about how close he will allow himself to get to those rose bushes in the future.

Now let's apply this to celibacy. As we grow into the celibate life, there should be an ongoing relationship between our intellectual knowledge of the theology of celibacy and our lived experience. In the previous chapter, we explored the various facets of the theology of celibate chastity. This could represent just the beginning of an intellectual understanding of these theologies. But just as in the illustration above, in which the boy's knowledge was limited without a firsthand experience of thorns, our theological and spiritual understanding of celibacy is limited until we have some experience living it.

As we live the celibate life, we encounter certain experiences—some challenging (e.g., loneliness, temptations, falling in love) and some joyful (e.g., an experience of prayer in solitude or the experience of being available to someone in a way enabled by not having a spouse or family of one's own)—that make our commitment more real. When these occur, we use our theological knowledge not only to recognize them as experiences of celibacy, but also to interpret them, make sense of them, and derive meaning from them. The meaning and sense we make contribute to our ever-expanding theological knowledge.

But why is this so critically important?

First of all, because celibacy is difficult. It's not impossible, but it is difficult, and recent research shows that religious men (and likely women) tend to underestimate the challenge of celibacy at the time of their final profession.[2] Research also indicates that issues related to celibacy (falling in love, discovering new aspects of one's sexuality) are among the most frequent precipitating events leading priests and religious to leave the priesthood or religious life within the first five or ten years.[3]

An interesting and related finding, however, is that if priests and religious are feeling adequately supported and manage to maintain a balance between their spiritual life and ministerial demands, then they will usually weather the challenge of falling in love or some other celibacy-related crisis without leaving their vocation. This should not surprise us. Another recent study of young men and women entering religious life in the last ten years clearly shows that one of the primary motivators for joining religious life is the opportunity to live a life that is prayerful and explicitly spiritual in nature.[4]

It's not rocket science. Theological and spiritual meaning is what draws us to priestly and religious life—the celibate life—in the first place. If opportunities for theological and spiritual meaning are absent, squeezed out, or neglected, a priest or religious is at much greater risk of abandoning the vocation. And what are these "opportunities for theological and spiritual meaning"? Time designated for theological reflection on this life. Let's recall the second half of Killen and de Beer's definition: "[theological reflection] helps us access the Christian tradition as a reliable source of

2. John Mark Falkenhain and Jane Becker, "The First Ten Years of Solemn Vows: Benedictine Monks on Reasons for Leaving and Remaining in Monastic Life," *The American Benedictine Review* 59, no. 2 (June 2008): 184–97.

3. Falkenhain and Becker, "The First Ten Years of Solemn Vows"; Dean R. Hoge, *The First Five Years of the Priesthood: A Study of Newly Ordained Catholic Priests* (Collegeville, MN: Liturgical Press, 2002), 5–8.

4. Mary E. Bendyna and Mary L. Gautier, "2009 Vocations Study—Executive Summary," last accessed June 9, 2017, https://nrvc.net/247/publication/913/article/1022-executive-summary-english.

guidance as we search to discover the meaning of what God is doing now in our individual and corporate lives" (emphasis added).

At some point, every celibate will hit a patch of unhappiness in his or her vocation as a priest or religious. They may feel overworked or perhaps disappointed in their community or diocesan leadership. On top of that, they may encounter a period of loneliness compounded by seeing peers marry and begin families. Envy may set in, as well as the feeling that they are missing out on something important. As the demands of ministry pile up and their prayer life grows a little flat, celibates are likely to begin to wonder what it's all about. And then, when all these stressors pile up, if someone walks into their life—someone who understands them, someone they can talk to, someone with whom they can really talk about their faith, who makes them feel more spiritually alive than they have for months if not years, someone who is very attractive—what will keep them committed to celibacy? The research suggests that celibates are most likely to stay committed to celibacy if the life has proven meaningful and a path to conversion and transformation. Of course, meaning and depth don't happen on their own; they are the result of a commitment to prayer and thoughtful theological reflection.

An Adapted Model for Theological Reflection

Theological reflection as a formal practice and discipline has developed primarily in the arena of field education or supervised ministry training. To my knowledge, no one has yet proposed a model of theological reflection on the celibate life for the purposes of celibacy formation. Fortunately, several models have been proposed for supervised ministry, and one that is particularly appealing for its simplicity and generalizability to our purposes is by Kathleen McAlpin. This model can be found in *Ministry That Transforms: Contemplative Process of Theological Reflection.*[5]

McAlpin was influenced by Bernard Lonergan's "dynamics of human knowing," which involve four activities: experiencing, understanding,

---

5. Kathleen McAlpin, *Ministry That Transforms: A Contemplative Process of Theological Reflection* (Collegeville, MN: Liturgical Press, 2009).

reasoning, and deciding. Based on these, McAlpine suggests a four-stage model for engaging theological reflection on ministry:[6]

1. Recalling the "thoughts and feelings from a historical incident"

2. Analyzing "the cultural context of the situation"

3. Using theological knowledge to reflect on the experience

4. Deriving the spiritual meaning of the experience in order to arrive at a "conscious decision for transformed action"

We can adapt McAlpin's model to celibate life. Although a few modifications are needed, the general process and goals remain the same: bringing our experience into dialogue with our theological knowledge in order to extract meaning and direction for our ongoing transformation.

1. Identify and explore a key experience of celibate living

Theological reflection begins with identifying and describing a specific event—in this case, an experience of celibacy. The phrase may sound a little odd at first, but by "an experience of celibacy" we mean a specific life experience related to one's lifestyle as a celibate man or woman. Loneliness, feeling attracted to or falling in love with someone, and grieving over the loss of the chance to marry or raise children are all examples of experiences tied to the celibate life. Some of these experiences of celibacy may be ongoing, always humming in the background, and may become particularly salient when provoked by a specific incident such as visiting with several of your married friends and feeling like the odd one out, or watching your brothers and sisters interact with their children. I recall reading somewhere that one of the most challenging parts of a diocesan priest's week is watching all the families leave church after the last Mass on Sunday, then returning to the rectory and having lunch alone. This would be an experience of celibacy.

Some experiences of celibacy come in the form of more acute crises: falling in love, giving in to temptation of some kind, becoming ensnared in internet pornography. While some of these are also challenges related to chastity (even married people are vulnerable to these experiences),

6. McAlpin, *Ministry That Transforms*, 24–25.

they occur in the context of our celibate life and are influenced to some extent by our commitment not to marry and to refrain from genital sexual expression.

Still, most experiences of celibacy are not crises and they are certainly not limited to negative or unpleasant experiences. Solitude, friendship, and mentoring are positive experiences of celibacy. Certain aspects of ministry—for example, being free to show up at the hospital in the middle of the night to comfort a grieving family—represent experiences of celibacy, as do extended opportunities for private prayer or time spent praying for people who have asked for your prayers.

And don't forget that some experiences of celibacy can be vicarious. Watching a movie or engaging with art and literature can evoke certain emotions or insights that turn these experiences into experiences of celibacy. Watching a romantic comedy and identifying with the romantic lead can become an experience of celibacy, as can having our sadness, loneliness, fears, and possible regret provoked by a song or reflected in the story line of a play or a novel.

Once we have identified a specific experience of celibacy, then we spend some time describing it. We can ask ourselves: What feelings does it generate in me? Where do these emotions come from? How would this experience be different had I not made the choice to be celibate? And how does this experience make me feel about my choice of celibacy? The aim is to raise our awareness of what is happening to us as a result of our commitment to celibate chastity and in the end to increase the intentionality with which we live this life. If the unexamined life is not worth living, then it is probably because the unexamined life is devoid of meaning and closed to the possibility of transformation and conversion.

2. Analyze the intrapersonal and interpersonal contexts

In her model for theological reflection on ministry, McAlpine describes the primary task of this second stage as analyzing the "cultural context of the situation." Here McAlpine invites the student to consider the larger culture in which the event took place. This might include the ethnic culture, but also the historical and socioeconomic variables that influence the event.

For the purpose of theological reflection on the celibate life, we proceed the same way: once candidates have identified an experience of celibacy, they are asked to consider both the interpersonal and the intrapersonal context in which the event takes place. In other words, what are the external and internal variables that might be affecting the situation? In examining the *interpersonal* context, we take into account what other people (if any) are involved, what role they play, and how they might have influenced the situation or might still influence the outcome. For example, did the situation occur

- While you were away at graduate studies and therefore isolated from your community?

- In a group setting in which you were the only celibate?

- In the context of a joyful community celebration—e.g., a profession or shared holiday?

- In the context of an intimate ministry experience—e.g., comforting the sick or hearing a confession?

- When you were entirely alone or surrounded by people who had no concept of what a commitment to celibacy means?

- When your entire family was gathered?

- After you had just come from a heated argument with a community member, coworker, or family member?

- With another person who was vulnerable due to a significant loss, divorce, or illness?

Beyond the interpersonal context, we consider what variables *within* the individual (*intrapersonal* factors) may have influenced the experience. For example, at the time of the experience

- What was your primary affective state: lonely, angry, or self-pitying; happy or satisfied?

- Were you doubting your vocation or, more specifically, your decision to be celibate?

- Were you feeling well-supported by your community, diocese, or fellow priests?

- Were you grieving the loss of a parent?

- Were you drinking?

- What was the state of your prayer life?

- Were you feeling satisfied in your ministry?

- Had you experienced a recent loss, a recent promotion, or recent profession?

- What was the general state of your relationship with your parish or community?

When examining these intrapersonal variables, we can categorize them as "trait" or "state" variables. Traits have to do with personality characteristics or conditions that are stable over time. For example, sexual orientation; the personality types you tend to be attracted to; a history of impulse-control problems; a long-standing pattern of isolating yourself when stressed; or a natural inclination to seek out other people to distract yourself from personal problems are all examples of traits a person brings to various experiences of celibacy. By states, in contrast, we are referring to variables that are tied specifically to that time period. For example, being drunk at the time; grieving the recent loss of a parent; feeling stressed due a major crisis in your work; or feeling excited because of a promotion or elevation to a leadership position.

It may seem as though this part of theological reflection could take a long time. The idea, however, is not to get too bogged down in the details, but rather to give a fair consideration to the most important internal and external factors that might be at play in the moment upon which we are prayerfully reflecting. Being especially aware of the interpersonal and intrapersonal factors can lead to a better understanding of whom our commitment to celibate chastity affects; which factors cause us to feel closer to God and which interfere with our relationship with God; patterns in our vulnerability to temptation; and patterns in our ability to remain dependent on God.

3. Use theological knowledge to reflect on the incident

This third stage is the heart of theological reflection. It involves applying our theological knowledge of celibacy to the actual lived experience of being celibate in order to better understand the experience and to derive meaning from it. This presumes, of course, that celibates have had a sufficient education in the theology of celibacy since we are asking them to apply perhaps a number of different theological ideas in their efforts to arrive at the meaning of the event. A useful metaphor is to think about examining an experience through a series of theologically tinted lenses—lenses that will help the meaning of the experience become clearer. The result is further insight, new meaning, a deeper understanding of the theology, and perhaps some decisions about how to continue living as celibates in the future.

To get started, I suggest the following questions to guide this reflection:

- Is the primary issue one of celibacy or chastity?

- Among the various theological dimensions of celibacy (i.e., apostolic, eschatological, spousal, ascetical, *in persona Christe*), which one (or ones) help to inform this experience in particular?

- How does my understanding of the theology of celibacy help me understand the situation? For example:

  How could this loneliness deepen my relationship with God?

  How does saying "no" to this relationship make me more available to others when it seems to give me new energy?

  What are the implications of my being a spouse to the church in this situation?

  How does saying "no" to my desire to be married right now point to the kingdom of God?

- What were the invitations to a greater love of God in this situation?

- What were the invitations to a greater love of others in this situation? Who are the others?

- What factors enabled me to seize on this opportunity to grow in my capacity to love?

- What factors prevented me from seizing the opportunity to grow in my capacity to love?

- Overall, what has this experience taught me about the celibate life?

- How might this experience change how I live or think about celibacy?

It is important to note here that candidates must bring a disposition of faith to the practice of theological reflection. They must have faith in the value of celibacy and a basic belief in the theological meaning of celibacy that the church in her wisdom has proposed. Consequently, the mind-set must not be one of, "Let's see *if* this spousal theology of celibacy is true," but rather one of, "*How* is it true? And how might it be playing out in my life at present?" Consequently, theological reflection is an act of faith, accompanied by prayer and done in relationship with God to whom celibates hope to draw nearer by their very act of theological reflection.

In supervised ministry settings, theological reflection is often conducted in groups; however, given the nature of experiences being reflected upon, theological reflection on the celibate life is more likely to be an individual activity (that is not to say it cannot be attempted in a group setting). Candidates may find it advantageous to approach theological reflection similar to the way they approach *lectio divina* or meditation: sitting quietly with an experience, paying attention to their posture and breathing, and making efforts to draw their attention back to the task at hand. Others may find writing or journaling a helpful way of exploring the meaning of the situation, using questions like those proposed above.

At its core, theological reflection involves simply setting aside the time to observe and explore the relationship between our theological knowledge and what we have experienced in order to derive meaning from those experiences. This might involve asking questions of oneself such as the following: How could this loneliness possibly be drawing me closer to God? How can my experience of attending my friend's wedding help me to see more clearly what my celibacy is offering the church? What theology of celibacy is going to help me stay committed to celibacy when it feels inadequate and I find myself feeling attracted to one of my coworkers?

Remember that practitioners of theological reflection should not expect jewels of insight and meaning the first time or each time they engage in theological reflection. Like prayer, it is a discipline, and practice should be regular and consistent. The celibate should be mindful that, aside from the possibility of gaining deeper meaning and insight, the simple act of setting time aside expresses a desire to be closer to God and lays the foundation for deeper meaning and insight into the celibate life when it finally does develop. Again, great moments of insight may not occur each time we sit down for theological reflection, but we can be fairly certain that they will likely never (or at least rarely) happen if we never set the time aside and engage in the practice.

4. Allowing meaning to deepen one's theological understanding and shape future experience

In this fourth and final stage of theological reflection, candidates are asked to briefly summarize what they have learned about the celibate life, both from an experiential point of view and with respect to their theological understanding of celibacy. The experience may lead to resolutions as they continue to live as celibates. A young sister may resolve to welcome feelings of loneliness in the future and see them as windows into an unmediated relationship with God, rather than experience them as simply one of the "harsh" parts of celibacy to which she will have to resign herself. A young priest may come to better understand the burden of late-hours ministry as the spiritual counterpart to what his married peers are doing as they care for their children at all hours of the day and night. Practicing theological reflection on an experience of celibacy, once the experience has passed, can yield insights that allow celibates to approach future experiences with the awareness and intentionality necessary to see more of God's grace as the moment unfolds.

Before we provide some illustrations of theological reflection at work, let us expand our model of the hermeneutic circle to more accurately describe what happens as a result of theological reflection. Recall that initially we depicted the relationship between our knowledge and experience as follows:

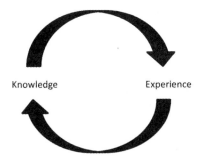

Knowledge   Experience

This illustration is limited, however, in its failure to demonstrate that once we have completed the circle of applying our knowledge to our experience, the depth of our knowledge is no longer the same. Our knowledge has advanced and will further affect future decisions and experiences, which in turn will teach us yet something new again. Consequently, there is not only a circular, but a linear movement that occurs with the ongoing practice of theological reflection. We can designate this linear dimension as transformation or conversion:

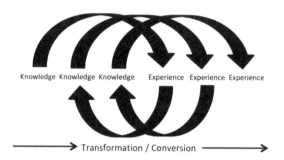

Case Studies

Case study 1: Sr. Elizabeth

Sr. Elizabeth is twenty-seven years old, in her third year of temporary vows as a Dominican sister. Elizabeth lives in a convent with six other sisters, all of whom work as either teachers or administrators in a grade school run by their community. Elizabeth has satisfactory relationships with the other sisters in the convent, though none of the women with whom she was in the novitiate are assigned in the same community, nor are either of the younger sisters to whom she feels closest. Her prayer life is consistent, with set times for common Eucharist, morning prayer, and evening prayer, and, as is the custom in her community, a forty-five-minute period of meditation between Vespers and supper.

With final vows approaching next year, one area of uncertainty for Sr. Elizabeth is celibacy. She understands the incompatibility of marriage with community life and knows that by not having a family her own, she is free to love more widely and consider the students her children, in a way. Still, she wonders how true this is when she observes some of the lay teachers who have children of their own and are *still very generous and effective teachers. Even after five years in the community, Elizabeth still feels a great desire at times to be a mother and feels especially resentful when she sees some of her students being neglected by their parents. Elizabeth often thinks to herself, "I could do a better job of giving these children the love and attention they need if they were mine." Elizabeth is confused by these feelings and wonders if they mean she is not called to celibacy.*

One day, Alison, one of the lay teachers who is close in age to Elizabeth and whom Elizabeth greatly admires as a teacher and mother, catches up to Elizabeth after a faculty meeting and asks if she can speak with her for a few minutes. Alison breaks down unexpectedly and asks Elizabeth's prayers for her three-year-old, who is being tested for leukemia. "I know you are especially close to God and I think you are such a wonderful person. Could you please pray for Luke? And for me? If he has cancer, I don't know what I am going to do. I don't think I could handle it."

Let's put ourselves in Sr. Elizabeth's shoes and walk through the steps of theological reflection.

Stage 1: This experience of celibacy is a combination of the ongoing questioning by Sr. Elizabeth about the value of her own celibacy and her desire to be a parent, and the more acute situation of her colleague's request for her prayers.

Stage 2: Several groups of people comprise the interpersonal context of this situation. There is Sr. Elizabeth's religious community, in which she feels generally satisfied, though maybe isolated at times. There are her students, whom Elizabeth truly appears to love and who meet some of her needs to nurture and provide care. At the same time, some of her more neglected students remind her of her desire and her potential to give more if she were free to be a parent herself. Finally, there is her relationship with Alison, who is requesting her prayers. This is an especially rich relationship considering that Alison's life represents in many ways the type of life Elizabeth imagines she might want. In some ways, Elizabeth is in the midst of grieving not being a parent, and her relationship with Alison underscores some of the struggles she experiences in her celibate life.

When considering the intrapersonal context (the variables at play within the person), Elizabeth will have to acknowledge that, in general, she is a caring person with a great desire and capacity to love in all kinds of ways, including as a romantic person and as a caregiver. Elizabeth recognizes that these desires were present at the time she entered the community, though she imagined that her desire for romance and parenting would eventually fade as her love for God continued to grow along with her religious vocation. Internally, Elizabeth is probably feeling some pressure to make a decision about her vocation and celibacy as final profession looms ahead, and her uncertainty about celibacy is apparent as she continues to find herself attracted to romance and parenting despite being reasonably happy and satisfied in her religious life.

Stage 3: What are the theological dimensions that might help Sr. Elizabeth make sense of this experience? We begin by acknowledging that up to this point, Sr. Elizabeth's celibacy has been informed and motivated by an apostolic notion of celibacy for the sake of the kingdom. She has understood her celibacy as means of loving more broadly, and her students are the objects of that love, especially those who need extra attention (the same ones who have led her at times to wish that she could have children of her own). But more recently, Elizabeth has struggled with this theological understanding, wondering if she is loving any more broadly as a celibate than her married peers are able to do. As she reflects on her very moving encounter with Alison, however, Elizabeth finds the phrase "I know you are especially close to God" particularly provocative. She has heard this comment before, and it makes her feel uncomfortable. If she were to reflect on why it seems to have a different meaning when spoken by Alison, she might recognize that it is because it is coming not only from a peer whom she admires (whose life Elizabeth admires and even envies), but also from someone who actually knows something about her life from working closely with her.

In trying to make sense of this experience of celibacy and Alison's claim that she is somehow "especially close to God," Elizabeth recalls a spousal theology of celibacy in which she recognizes that, as a result of her choice not to marry and have children, she has been allowed the time and the space, and subsequently the luxury and responsibility, of cultivating an unmediated relationship with God. For the first time, Elizabeth understands that her celibacy has allowed not a necessarily *closer* relationship with God, but an "especially close"—meaning, *close in a special way*—relationship with God. This special relationship with God is what Alison is invoking as she asks for Sr. Elizabeth's prayers. It is as if she were petitioning the best friend, the daughter, the son, the wife, or the spouse of a powerful person for some favor. And in fact, she is.

Stage 4: Sr. Elizabeth has a newfound appreciation for a number of aspects of her life as a religious sister: the time allowed for praying the Liturgy of the Hours; the time allowed for personal prayer and contemplation; the myriad notes on the community bulletin board asking the sisters for prayers; her religious name and its reference to Mary's visitation to invoke the assistance of her cousin during her own time of wonder and excitement; the expectations others have of her "special" relationship with God; and the responsibility that all of these bear. As a result of her reflection, Elizabeth gains a new perspective on the value of her celibacy, which she sees does not come at the cost of the value of marriage and parenthood. As a result of this new insight and the new meaning she has found in her commitment to celibacy, she resolves to have greater gratitude for the gift of time allotted for communal and private prayer; to be more assiduous in reading and taking to heart the prayer requests from others; and to pray more earnestly for the parents of her students and the "special" way that they, too, love God as married people.

Case study 2: Fr. Robert

> Fr. Robert has been ordained for ten years and has spent the last five years as pastor of St. Pius X, a large and active suburban parish. Fr. Robert found the assignment challenging, but it was also an exciting environment in which to grow his skills as a pastor, with responsibility for parish schools and a variety of ministries. Fr. Robert is from an upper-middle-class background and related well to the parishioners while challenging them to think outside their comfortable existence, initiating several food and clothing drives throughout the year and an annual mission trip for the youth.
>
> Last year, Fr. Robert was asked by his bishop to leave St. Pius and assume pastorship of St. Francis of Assisi, an old and dwindling parish in a dangerous part of the city known for drug trafficking and high

crime rates. *The bishop hoped he might help rejuvenate the area by creating a vibrant parish life at St. Francis. Fr. Robert's predecessor at St. Francis generally kept to himself and initiated little else other than providing Mass for a few elderly churchgoers.*

Robert feels out of his element in his new assignment. He has little knowledge or experience of serving in the inner city and had previously drawn much meaning and direction for his priesthood, including celibacy, from a notion of himself as leading the church as a "spiritual father" who "pours himself out" for the needs of the people. At St. Francis, however, Robert finds he has an abundance of time on his hands with so few parishioners and no established programs. Consequently, he isn't entirely certain where to begin pouring himself out for those he serves.

Upon the recommendation of the diocesan social outreach coordinator, Fr. Robert decides to assess the needs of the local community by talking to his new neighbors face-to-face. Overcoming his own fear of what he might encounter, he begins visiting the local housing projects in his parish boundaries, simply listening to how people answer the questions "What do families in this neighborhood need?" and "What do you need from the church?" Fr. Robert is overwhelmed by most of what he hears—people want an end to gang activity, a way to stop gun violence, to keep their young people from getting involved in drugs, jobs for the unemployed—however, he listens with some hope as several mothers and fathers wished for a safe place for their children to play.

Fr. Robert goes to work, with the help of some grant money, converting an old boarded-up gym next to the church into an indoor playground and gathering place for neighborhood parents. Unfortunately, he soon runs into resistance from gangs and drug traffickers who used the abandoned building and the area around it for meeting and making drug deals. Shortly after Fr. Robert posts a sign announcing the renovation project, his garage is broken into and his car is vandalized. With some reassurance from the police that will they more carefully watch the church property, Fr. Robert proceeds with his plans.

One evening Fr. Robert is beaten and left unconscious on the front steps of the rectory. When he regains consciousness, he is able to drag himself inside the house and call 911. His main thought as he waits for help to arrive is that he has never felt so alone in his life.

Stage 1: Let's put ourselves in Fr. Robert's shoes and walk through the process of theological reflection on the specific experience of feeling lonely while waiting for assistance. While his loneliness may initially seem like an odd detail to focus on—after all, we would imagine issues of trauma and safety to be foremost in Robert's thoughts—he nonetheless keeps returning to that feeling of loneliness, which dominates his memory of the event and which he returns to over and over again during his recovery.

Stage 2: When taking stock of the *interpersonal* context of the incident, Fr. Robert acknowledges that there really is no interpersonal context—that it is actually the absence of people that is most remarkable. In his new parish assignment, Robert is separated from his former parishioners and the roles he felt most comfortable and successful functioning in, along with the social reinforcement of an engaged and active parish. Fr. Robert has tried to develop relationships with his neighbors in the local housing projects; however, these are men, women, and families with a life experience very different from his own. Some are even hostile toward him and clearly wish he were not there. In many ways, he is truly alone.

One other interpersonal dimension that seems especially remarkable to Robert is that when he was assaulted, there was no one at home who could help. He has no spouse to comfort him, no children to buoy him up and distract him from his worries, not even a roommate or fellow priest to find him or assist him after the assault.

At the *intrapersonal* level (what is going on inside him), Fr. Robert acknowledges both the uncertainty and the excitement of his new parish assignment. He admits that he has felt disconnected and perhaps even unsupported, "out there on his own" on an unfamiliar frontier few of his fellow priests would be likely to envy. Still, he has been happy, somewhat flattered by the bishop's confidence in him to take on the challenge, and inspired by the thought of ministering to people very much in need.

Stage 3: What theology of celibacy can help Fr. Robert make new sense of his loneliness and his traumatic experience? Before now, Fr. Robert's celibacy has been supported by a theology of mission, of a building up of the kingdom. At St. Pius, he could more easily see how his not having a wife and children left him free to dedicate long hours, especially in the evening, to serving the needs of his parishioners. All of the parishioners were his "children" in a way and he was reminded of this each time he was called "Father." As he reflects on it, Robert admits this source of inspiration felt a little inadequate in his current environment with little social interaction and so much more time on his hands.

But it is the loneliness, and in particular the experience of being assaulted and left alone, that leads him to doubt celibacy. As he thinks through the various theological dimensions of celibacy, Robert recalls the notion of the celibate priest as imitating Christ—as being *in persona Christi*. He is struck by the parallel to his situation—being beaten, abandoned, and left for dead by the people whose lives he hoped to improve. And he recalls that Christ was, in one way, freer to literally lay down his life because he endangered no one else's life—no wife or dependent children—by endangering his own. True, Christ was alone in the Garden of Gethsemane and alone on the cross; but he was also free in his aloneness to spend his life carelessly, radically for the sake of the kingdom. Fr. Robert's aloneness has been a source of suffering for him, but for the first time he sees it as a condition that allows him to lay down his life in a unique way and more freely than his married siblings and friends. He also recalls the heroic acts of love of Maximilian Kolbe, Oscar Romero, Mother Teresa, and the sisters martyred in El Salvador.

Stage 4: As Fr. Robert recovers, he is faced with the decision of returning to St. Francis, and if he does return, whether to pursue the playground project and the likelihood of continued dangerous resistance. Several of Robert's friends and family members tell him he would be foolish to return: "They clearly don't want your help! You could do much more good somewhere you're wanted." But Fr. Robert's reflection leaves him with nagging questions: If I am not called and *free* to lay down my life, then who is? Whose life is more expendable than mine?

Fr. Robert decides to return to St. Francis after he is promised increased security. The news of his attack brings new attention to the plight of the neighborhood and attracts more assistance from people inside and outside the neighborhood. He continues to live with some fear, but also with gratitude for the opportunity to be biologically childless, so that like Christ, he might also be free to take on the cares and needs of some of God's most imperiled children.

Conclusion

I began this chapter stating that theological reflection on the celibate life is probably the most important skill we can teach men and women embarking on a life of celibate chastity. We will never be without "experiences of celibacy": the myriad ups and downs, the sudden joys, the unexpected challenges, the predictable woes, the minor and the major life crises that come with the territory of the celibate vocation. These are the experiences that reveal the meaning of our vocation. But it is more likely revealed to those whose eyes are prepared and trained to see it.

Theological reflection is best taught across a number of settings. As we have already said, it assumes a strong grounding in the theology of celibacy in all its various dimensions. Beyond this, candidates must be trained to begin identifying experiences of celibacy and then be assisted in applying their theological knowledge to these experiences in order to arrive at meaning, insight, and future direction. In classroom settings or in formation conferences and workshops, formators can work to establish the rationale, goals, and process for theological reflection. Group settings may also be appropriate to work through case studies, giving students practice at applying various theological dimensions to scenarios like the ones outlined above. Formation directors might also be encouraged to speak of their own past experiences and share how their theological knowledge of celibacy helped them derive meaning and direction from particular incidents in their own lives. Eventually, and while exercising appropriate boundaries, men and women in formation may be able to share with one another their own experience of practicing theological reflection, including what they have learned about the celibate life from the experience.

Spiritual direction is probably the forum in which individuals are most likely to receive assistance in learning how to reflect theologically on their experience of living the celibate life. This may happen naturally, without a systematic approach; however, having a method or system in place helps not only to facilitate the process, but also assists directees in internalizing the discipline so they are able to continue the practice independently, outside of spiritual direction meetings. Practicing theological reflection within the context of spiritual direction can be initiated either by the spiritual director or the directee. The spiritual director might say, for example, "Next time we meet, I would like you to come in with a particular experience related to living the celibate life so that together we can explore it through our theological lens." In a trusted spiritual direction setting, candidates are likely to appreciate the insights of a more experienced celibate, who can help shed light upon and draw meaning from his or her experiences. Candidates, too, can initiate the process by letting their spiritual director know that they would like to spend the next session exploring a particular experience of celibacy.

Regardless of where the skills are taught and practiced, the formation director is ultimately responsible for ensuring that the skill of theological reflection is taught and practiced in initial formation. Since this is likely to occur over the course of several years, it is recommended to set formation goals or benchmarks for each year of formation so that formation staff and candidates alike can monitor and assess their progress. An example of such a schema arranged over four years of initial formation (either seminary or house of formation for consecrated religious) follows:

- **Year I:** Is able to articulate three different theological dimensions supporting the celibate life.

- **Year II:** Has learned and practiced a model of theological reflection on the celibate life.

- **Year III:** Is able to articulate an experience of practicing theological reflection to derive meaning from an experience of celibate life.

- **Year IV:** Regularly practices theological reflection on the celibate life and can articulate how his or her theological understanding of celibacy has developed in formation.

The title of Sr. Sandra Schneiders's book on celibacy and community life is *Selling All.*[7] The reference is the gospel in which Jesus compares the kingdom of God to a treasure buried in a field. If accepting celibacy—giving up opportunity for marriage and a rightly ordered sexual and romantic life—is one of the primary ways in which priests and religious "sell all" they have in order to gain the treasure of God's kingdom, then wouldn't it be a shame to live only on the surface of that field, never digging, never

7. Sandra M. Schneiders, *Selling All: Commitment, Consecrated Celibacy, and Community in Catholic Religious Life* (Mahwah, NY: Paulist Press, 2001).

uncovering and discovering the richness? Theological reflection is the best tool we possess to unearth the meaning, joy, and inspiration of our celibate commitment. Without it, we run the risk walking around on a very expensive field, leaving treasure buried everywhere under our feet.

SECTION IV

SEXUAL IDENTITY AND INTEGRATION

CHAPTER 7

SEXUAL IDENTITY:
WHO ARE YOU AS A SEXUAL PERSON?

Having explored in the previous sections the first two major content areas in our model of celibacy formation—motives for the celibate life and theological dimensions—we turn now to the dimension of sexual identity. One of St. Thomas Aquinas's foundational statements to which we refer often in considering the development of our Christian identity is his assertion that "Grace builds on nature." We accept as truth the notion that God's will and providence works with and through our humanity, not despite it. Pope John Paul II applies this fundamental precept to formation when he describes human formation as "the basis of all priestly formation,"[1] and this assertion also applies to formation for religious life.

Extended to celibacy formation, the notion that grace builds on human nature leads us to the recognition that the graces of the celibate life build on our specific nature as sexual people. We bring our entire human experience, including and perhaps *especially* our sexuality, to the enterprise of celibacy. If the commitment to celibacy is to be built on a firm foundation, then celibates must begin with an honest and sincere understanding of themselves as sexual people. In other words, celibates must have a clear, accurate, and healthy sense of their sexual identity.

1. John Paul II, *Pastores Dabo Vobis: On the Formation of Priests in the Circumstances of the Present Day* (Washington, DC: United States Catholic Conference, 1999), 116.

For several years I conducted psychological evaluations of men and women for seminary formation and religious life, and as vocation director, I continue to conduct extensive interviews of candidates for our community. In the course of interviewing candidates, once adequate rapport has been established, I ask the following question: "How would you describe yourself as a sexual person?" Most candidates come expecting that we will eventually talk about sexuality, but the question can still seem a little shocking.

When faced with this question, most candidates look for a little more detail before answering and ask, "What do you mean?" But I usually offer little additional direction and allow them to struggle a bit with the vagueness of the question. It's not that I particularly enjoy watching people squirm, but I have yet to find a better and more efficient way to evaluate the amount of time and energy young men or women have spent developing knowledge and insight about themselves in the area of sexuality and romantic intimacy.

When we ask candidates to describe themselves as sexual beings, we are asking them to begin articulating a sexual identity. Perhaps nowhere under the larger umbrella of human formation is the value of self-knowledge and self-acceptance more important than around sexual identity. Research shows that experiencing a sexual crisis is one of the most frequent precipitating events leading priests and religious to leave their vocation within the first five or ten years following ordination or final profession.[2] Sexual and emotional underdevelopment is one of the primary contributing factors to child sexual abuse among priests and religious.[3] It is a critical question, and one that must be asked not only at the beginning, but throughout our formation for the celibate life: Who are you as a sexual person?

The goal of this chapter is to provide a helpful conceptual framework for answering this question. In addition to establishing a helpful and common vocabulary for articulating who we are as sexual people, we

2. Dean R. Hoge, *The First Five Years of the Priesthood: A Study of Newly Ordained Catholic Priests* (Collegeville, MN: Liturgical Press, 2002), 63; John Mark Falkenhain and Jane Becker, "The First Ten Years of Solemn Vows: Benedictine Monks on Reasons for Leaving and Remaining in Monastic Life," *The American Benedictine Review* 59, no. 2 (June 2008): 184–97.

3. Marc A. Falkenhain and others, "Cluster Analysis of Child Sexual Offenders: A Validation with Roman Catholic Priests and Brothers," *Sexual Addiction and Compulsivity* 6 (1999): 317–36.

will also conduct a careful review of church documents and the scientific literature on the way to facilitating a better understanding of our basic human and sexual nature.

A Multifactored Model for Sexual Identity

If we step back from sexuality for a moment and consider the notion of identity in general, we quickly conclude that identity is a complex phenomenon. If someone asks, "Who are you?" or "What kind of person are you?" you would more than likely launch into a lengthy response that includes information about where you grew up, what kind of family you grew up in, defining experiences in your childhood and adulthood, the values instilled in you by your parents, your core beliefs, your work, your hobbies, your important relationships, and maybe even something about your physical appearance and attributes.

Similarly, the construct of sexual identity cannot be reduced to one particular aspect of sexuality—for example, sexual orientation or whether you have been sexually active. This chapter offers a five-factored model of sexual identity, which we will use in the next chapter to better understand what integrity and integration look like in the context of the chaste and celibate life. While this model may not be exhaustive, it has significant value in its ability to advance our understanding of some important concepts related to sexuality and sexual identity. Our freedom to discern celibacy and enter into the process of formation is enhanced by having a vocabulary and accurate information with which to better understand ourselves and communicate who we are to others.

Let's begin by thinking of sexual identity as comprised of five primary dimensions—sex, gender, sexual orientation, history of sexual experiences, and attitudes and values regarding sexuality.

Sexual Identity = Sex +
           Gender +
           Sexual Orientation +
           History of Sexual Experiences +
           Attitudes and Values regarding Sexuality

We will look at each of these five dimensions separately before exploring how they interact and sometimes come into conflict with one another.

A. Sex

Technically speaking, our sex is our biologically determined status as male or female. Sex is primarily a dimorphic construct, meaning we are one sex or the other—male or female. Understanding one's sex is not a source of confusion for the vast majority of people.

Biologically speaking, there are two critical periods when a person's sex is determined. They are the early fetal period and puberty. This may get a little technical, but it's worth knowing.

During the first several weeks of pregnancy, a chromosomal male (XY) fetus and chromosomal female (XX) fetus are for the most part indistinguishable. The ultrasound scan of a fetus to identify the sex is not conducted until the second trimester of pregnancy. This is because, around the fifth and sixth weeks of pregnancy, the chromosomal male fetus begins to secrete androgens, which we can think of as masculinizing hormones. In response to these androgens, the genetic material that would otherwise have developed into the ovaries of the female (XX) fetus instead develops into the testicles of the male fetus. Similarly, the same genetic material that would have developed into the clitoris of the female becomes the penis, and the material that would have otherwise become the labia of the vagina, instead develops into the scrotum of the male fetus. This "androgen signaling," as it is sometimes referred to, is responsible for the development of "primary sex characteristics": the penis, scrotum, and testicles in the male. Without this secretion of androgens, the female *phenotype* (or the observable characteristics) develops with its primary sex characteristics: the labia, clitoris, and ovaries.

Typically, this prenatal process of sex differentiation occurs without complication; however, there are some rare anomalies that can result in discrepancies between the chromosomal sex of the child and the phenotype of the developing individual. In the case of androgen insensitivity disorder, the androgen receptors in the male fetus fail to respond to the androgens, thus resulting in a chromosomal male child who develops the primary sex characteristics or the outward appearance of a female. In the case of congenital adrenal hyperplasia—meaning "too much" (*hyper*) "androgens" (*adrenal*) "in the blood" (*plasia*)—a chromosomal female fetus is exposed and responds to heightened levels of androgens, thus resulting in the development of male primary sex characteristics in a chromosomal female. Again, these conditions are rare, but may have something to do with the phenomenon of sexual identity disorder or transsexualism in a small segment of the population—men and women whose internal experience of themselves as male or female is at odds with their actual sex.

The second critical period for sex differentiation is puberty, when, again, heightened levels of hormone production—estrogen and testosterone—result in the development of *secondary* sex characteristics, including enlargement of the breasts and commencement of menstruation in females; enlargement of the penis and testes as well as the commencement of sperm production in males; and muscular and skeletal growth and the development of pubic and axillary (e.g., armpit) hair in both sexes.

B. Gender

Although the words "sex" and "gender" are often used interchangeably, they are not the same in technical terms. Whereas our sex refers to our biologically determined status as male and female, gender refers to the more subjective internal and psychological experience of ourselves as male and female.

Gender is both a cultural and a personal phenomenon. The American Psychological Association (APA), for example, defines gender as "the attitudes, feelings, and behaviors that a given culture associates with a person's biological sex."[4] The term "gender identity" is often used to describe how men or women experience and communicate themselves at the individual level. In speaking about gender or gender identity, we use the words "masculine" and "feminine" to communicate an idea or experience that is more continuous in nature than the dimorphic (either-or) construct of sex.

As suggested by the APA definition above, gender is manifest in our affect (emotions), behaviors (how we act), and in our cognition (thoughts) and is influenced by many factors, including our biology, the culture in which we live, and the more immediate environment of our families and close relationships. The development of one's personal "gender identity," therefore, is the result of both nature (biological factors) and nurture (environmental factors).

---

4. American Psychological Association, "Guidelines for Psychological Practice with Lesbian, Gay, and Bisexual Clients," *American Psychologist* 67 (2012): 10–42.

Within every culture there are gender stereotypes that help to establish and reinforce gender expectations within that culture, and these are learned very early in life. Within our Western culture, masculinity is stereotypically associated with physical strength, rationality, problem-solving, action, assertiveness, and even aggression. Western stereotypes of femininity, on the other hand, are associated with caring, nurturing, emotionality, beauty, receptivity, passivity, and spirituality. Of course, very few (if any) individuals adhere completely to these gender stereotypes, and so we begin to see the more continuous nature of an individual's gender identity.

To further demonstrate the difference between sex and gender and to reinforce the continuous nature of gender identity, we can observe how all the following people have the same sex but have different gender identities or levels of adherence to gender stereotypes: Abraham Lincoln; Arnold Schwarzenegger in *The Terminator* movies; the children's television personality Mr. Rogers; and St. Joseph. We could do the same with women: Mother Teresa; the supermodel Gisele Bundchen; Hillary Clinton; Martha Stewart; and the cartoon character Betty Boop (for the older folks reading this!). All of these individuals are female (sex), but are different in how they adhere to the gender stereotype of femininity (gender identity).

At this point, it might be helpful to introduce another term that can help us to better understand and develop a vocabulary for the more continuous phenomenon of gender. "Psychological androgyny" is a term that is often misunderstood to mean "sexless" or "gender neutral"; however, as defined by prominent sex-role researcher Sandra Bem, psychological androgyny more accurately refers to one's capacity to incorporate personality characteristics typically associated with the opposite sex into one's primary gender identity.

Bem challenges the understanding of gender as falling on a single continuum with masculinity at one pole and femininity at the opposite pole, as illustrated below.

```
I------------------------------------------------------------------I
Masculine                                                  Feminine
```

She instead suggests thinking of masculinity and femininity as falling on separate continua.

```
I---------------------------------------------------------X-----I
Less Masculine                                     More Masculine

I-----X---------------------------------------------------------I
Less Feminine                                        More Feminine
```

Bem's paradigm enables us to consider that a woman might be able to incorporate characteristics typically associated with the opposite sex (e.g., assertiveness or problem-solving) into her personality without suggesting that this somehow makes her less feminine, as would be the case when considering gender along a single continuum. To pose another example, a father might share some of the more "nurturing" roles in the family, such as helping to feed the children or change diapers, without the supposition that this makes him less masculine.

Bem developed the Bem Sex Role Inventory (BSRI) to measure levels of psychological androgyny, and subsequent research using instruments like the BSRI has helped to establish that certain levels of androgyny among men and women are associated with positive social, relational, and personal outcomes such as marital happiness, success in establishing intimate relationships, the capacity for shared leadership, and overall psychological adjustment.[5]

What is of particular interest for us within the context of priesthood and religious life is that a certain amount of androgyny or gender transcendence, as it has also been called, is simply assumed. We expect priests, who are male, to be caring, good listeners, and sensitive to the emotional and spiritual needs of their parishioners. Women religious have similarly transcended traditional female roles. An older Dominican sister once shared with me that when she was a young religious in the sixties and seventies, there were few places in society outside of religious life where women had the opportunity and even were expected to lead large institutions such as high schools, universities, and hospitals.

5. Spencer A. Rathus, Jeffrey S. Nevid, and Lois Fichner-Rathus, *Essentials of Human Sexuality* (Needham Heights, MA: Allyn and Bacon, 1998), 126–28.

C. Sexual Orientation

Sexual orientation, the third dimension in our model of sexual identity, is a much-debated and often controversial topic, especially when discussed in the context of religion and morality. This tension is heightened in today's culture, where attitudes and values regarding sexual orientation appear to be shifting much more rapidly than in our churches and religious institutions. While some tension is understandable, conflict and contention (or negative tension) can be harmful, especially when they result from poor communication or limited and inaccurate information. Strong feelings coupled with limited or inaccurate knowledge tend to result in defensiveness and a breakdown in healthy discourse, and can further hinder self-knowledge and self-acceptance within individuals. It is helpful in this context to discuss sexual orientation in light of Catholic Church teaching as well as information from the scientific community. It is worth noting that just as attitudes and values regarding sexual orientation have shifted and continue to shift within the context of our larger culture, so does the language we use. While there are many terms used to describe the phenomenon of same-sex attraction and those who identify as having same-sex attraction, we have elected to use the terms "same-sex attraction," "homosexual," and "bisexual" since these have recently been the most commonly used words in the writings of the Church and in the field of professional psychology (although this is rapidly changing).

In its 1986 *Letter to the Bishops of the Catholic Church on the Pastoral Care of Homosexual Persons*, the Congregation for the Doctrine of the Faith under the leadership of Cardinal Joseph Ratzinger (later Pope Benedict XVI) asserted, "The Church is thus in a position to learn from scientific discovery but also to transcend the horizons of science and to be confident that her more global vision does greater justice to the rich reality of the human person in his spiritual and physical dimensions, created by God and heir, by grace, to eternal life."[6] We will follow this lead by first reviewing Catholic Church teaching on homosexuality before learning what we can from science regarding prevalence rates of homosexuality, determining factors, and whether sexual orientation appears to be changeable.

6. Congregation for the Doctrine of the Faith, *Letter to the Bishops of the Catholic Church on the Pastoral Care of Homosexual Persons* (1986), 2.

For our purposes, we define sexual orientation as a person's *primary* and *persistent* pattern of sexual arousal—*primary* in the sense that it refers to the pattern of arousal the person experiences most if not all of the time; and *persistent*, indicating a pattern that endures over time and is not based on temporary experimentation, curiosity, or other situational factors.

Church teaching

In the *Catechism* the Catholic Church carefully distinguishes between a homosexual orientation and homosexual acts, and asserts that while the orientation itself is not sinful (that is, one does not commit a sin by having a homosexual orientation or experiencing same-sex attractions), homosexual acts are considered sinful and "disordered" because they are inconsistent with the natural ends to which sexuality is ordered, namely procreation: "[T]radition has always declared that 'homosexual acts are intrinsically disordered.' They are contrary to the natural law. They close the sexual act to the gift of life. They do not proceed from a genuine affective and sexual complementarity."[7]

In church teaching, the word "disordered" is used in a Thomistic, philosophical sense. Because the church understands all sexual activity, according to natural law, as "ordered" toward procreation or the creation of new life, homosexual acts are considered "disordered" in that they go against this natural order. It is important to recognize that the church is speaking from a philosophical, theological, and moral authority but not from a medical or psychiatric authority. Consequently, the church is not suggesting that homosexuality is a medical or psychiatric disorder.

At the same time that the church teaches that homosexual acts are sinful and therefore to be discouraged, it also deplores the maltreatment of homosexual or same-sex-attracted persons, strongly reaffirming the dignity of all people in the eyes of God: "It is deplorable that homosexual persons have been and are the object of violent malice in speech or in action. Such treatment deserves condemnation from the Church's pastors wherever it occurs. It reveals a kind of disregard for others which endangers the most fundamental principles of a healthy society. The

---

7. *Catechism of the Catholic Church*, 2nd ed. (Washington, DC: United States Conference of Catholic Bishops, 1997), Article 2357.

intrinsic dignity of each person must always be respected in word, in action and in law."[8]

It is also notable that the church recognizes that an individual's sexual orientation is not chosen. While all of us make choices about how we act in response to our sexual attractions, sexual orientation is not perceived as something people choose for themselves. Again from the *Catechism*: "The number of women and men who have deep-seated homosexual tendencies is not negligible. They do not choose their homosexual condition; for most of them it is a trial. They must be accepted with respect, compassion, and sensitivity. Every sign of unjust discrimination in their regard should be avoided. These persons are called to fulfill God's will in their lives and, if they are Christians, to unite to the sacrifice of the Lord's cross the difficulties they may encounter from their condition."[9] The *Catechism* goes on to say that homosexual persons are called to chastity, which, given the church's teaching, entails refraining from any kind of genital sexual expression outside the context of marriage and which is not open to the creation of new life.

While many appreciate the church's careful distinction between orientation and acts, and its condemnation of discrimination and maltreatment of homosexual persons, some homosexual individuals express feeling misunderstood and occasionally hurt by some of the language in church teaching. Some same-sex-attracted individuals have, for example, found the description of their sexual orientation as a "more or less strong tendency ordered toward an intrinsic moral evil"[10] a bitter pill to swallow.

With respect to admitting homosexual individuals into the priesthood and religious life, more direction has been provided regarding priesthood, though some have found the church's teaching in this area a little unclear. In its 2005 document *Instruction Concerning the Criteria for the Discernment of Vocations with Regard to Persons with Homosexual Tendencies in View of Their Admission to the Seminary and to Holy Orders*, the Vatican Congregation for Catholic Education offers three criteria to indicate that an individual is unsuitable for priestly formation. After a review of the

---

8. Congregation for Doctrine of the Faith, *Letter to Bishops*, 10.
9. *Catechism*, Article 2358.
10. Congregation for Doctrine of the Faith, *Letter to Bishops*, 3.

church's general teaching on homosexuality, the *Instruction* states: "In light of such teaching, this Dicastery, in accord with the Congregation for Divine Worship and Discipline of the Sacraments, believes it necessary to state clearly that the Church, while profoundly respecting the persons in question, cannot admit to the seminary or to holy orders those who practice homosexuality, present deep-seated homosexual tendencies or support the so-called 'gay subculture.'"[11]

While the first and third of these conditions (i.e., practice homosexuality and support the "gay subculture") are fairly clear, the second (i.e., "present deep-seated homosexual tendencies") has been a subject of some debate. Some take it to mean that anyone who identifies himself as having a homosexual orientation should not be admitted to seminary. Others have offered more nuanced interpretations—suggesting, for example, that an individual might be unsuitable for admission if his homosexual orientation is the sole or primary filter through which every other aspect of his life is processed.

The intent here is not to offer a specific interpretation of the document. It is recommended for consideration, however, that dioceses, seminaries, and even religious communities—both men's and women's—be clear for themselves, and for the sake of those who might be interested in joining their ranks, what their policy is regarding the admission of individuals who identify as having a homosexual orientation or same-sex attraction. Individuals with same-sex attraction have both a right and a need to know whether they belong in a particular place or community. If policies are unclear, or if there is lack of agreement within the institution, it increases the likelihood that candidates will hide their sexuality, receive mixed messages, or be caught in the crossfire of disagreements. All of these situations can pose significant obstacles to open and healthy formation. In short, dioceses, seminaries, and religious communities should have a clear policy regarding admission of same-sex attracted individuals so that freedom of discernment is optimized on the part of both the candidate and the community or diocese.

11. Congregation for Catholic Education, *Instruction Concerning the Criteria for the Discernment of Vocations with regard to Persons with Homosexual Tendencies in view of their Admission to the Seminary and Holy Orders* (2005), 2.

Now we will examine what scientific research says about sexual orientation in terms of prevalence, sex differences, and causation or determination of sexual orientation.

What is the prevalence of homosexuality?

Establishing a prevalence rate for homosexuality in the general population is challenged by definitional and measurement issues. Early studies by Alfred Kinsey famously asserted a prevalence rate for homosexuality of 10% based on research with college students in the 1940s and 1950s. The current validity of his finding is compromised by a number of concerns, including the dated nature of the research (social desirability factors would likely be greater in the 1950s than in our current times) and the population surveyed (college students are generally accepted to be in a more experimental time of their life and represent a subpopulation that tends to be more liberal in attitude and behavior when compared to the general population). In the decades following Kinsey's famous research, subsequent studies have produced a wide range of prevalence rates, with literature reviews estimating the prevalence of homosexuality in the United States to be around 5% of the general population.[12]

Among clergy and religious there is no definitive or recent research. Donald Cozzens and A. W. Richard Sipe, both counselors working with clerical populations, have suggested the prevalence of homosexuality among priests to be much higher than in the general population, with estimates ranging from 20 to 50%.[13] Again, the validity of these estimates is compromised by their age and by the possibly skewed nature of the sample (men and women in treatment). Still, if we give their conclusions some credence, taking the lower end of their estimated ranges as a conservative possibility, we could assume that there has been and might continue to be a disproportionally higher prevalence of homosexual individuals among clergy and religious compared to the general population.

12. John C. Gonsiorek and James D. Weinrich, "The Definition and Scope of Sexual Orientation," in *Homosexuality: Research Implications for Public Policy*, ed. John C. Gonsiorek and James D. Weinrich (Newbury Park, CA: Sage Publications, 1991), 1–12.

13. Donald B. Cozzens, *The Changing Face of the Priesthood: A Reflection on the Priest's Crisis of Soul* (Collegeville, MN: Liturgical Press, 2000); A. W. Richard Sipe, *A Secret World: Sexuality and the Search for Celibacy* (New York: Brunner/Mazel, 1990).

Discussion of the reasons for this prevalence will likely lead again to an exploration of motives for celibacy, thereby underscoring the importance of carefully and honestly evaluating the health and validity of one's reasons for pursuing the celibate life.

What determines a person's sexual orientation?

Theories about what causes homosexuality have evolved over time and have included Freudian (or psychodynamic) theories, social learning theories, and, most recently, research into possible biological contributions. We will spend some time reviewing each.

Sigmund Freud's theories about homosexuality stemmed from his conviction that all mature sexuality is heterosexual in nature. Freud understood homosexuality, therefore, as the result of being fixated or arrested at an earlier stage of development. He theorized, for example, that a flawed resolution of the oedipal stage (during which the sexual drive of young males was believed to be focused on the mother) could lead to an overvaluation of the penis (the believed result of extreme castration anxiety derived from the assumption that females had been castrated) or to the redirection of all sexual energies away from women as a consequence of avoiding competition with his father or siblings for the mother's attentions. Freud accounted for homosexuality among women by suggesting that some girls, perceiving themselves as socially inferior for not having a penis, cultivated a strong masculine identity (including sexual attraction to women) as a means of compensating or even hoping to achieve male genitalia. Freud's theories sound far-fetched to our modern sensibilities and have little empirical support. They are worth acknowledging, however, insofar as they have shaped our historical understanding of homosexuality and continue to influence how we think and talk about homosexuality and its origins. For example, notions of same-sex attraction as the result of growing up with an absent or disapproving father or being raised by a dominant mother grew out of Freudian theory.

Social learning theories are built on the hypotheses that a homosexual or bisexual orientation has been learned or conditioned, or that it results from inadequate skills in relating romantically or sexually to persons of the opposite sex. The idea that homosexuality might have been modeled for the developing individual or that it has been reinforced by certain experiences in childhood or adolescence is consistent with social learning theories. A corollary of this approach to understanding sexual orientation is to suggest that if a particular pattern of sexual arousal can be learned or conditioned, it might be able to be unlearned or reconditioned. This hypothesis, along with the skills-deficit theory, forms many of the underlying principles upon which conversion therapies are built.

Conversion therapies (also sometimes referred to as reparative therapies) are treatments that attempt to change an individual's sexual orientation. The effectiveness of conversion therapies has been investigated in numerous studies, with a wide range of results reported. When there is disagreement among studies, literature reviews that examine an entire body of published research taking quality of research design and sources of potential bias into consideration are helpful in reaching general conclusions. Literature reviews published by Ellis and Mitchell,[14] Haldeman,[15] and Bieschke, Paul, and Blasko[16] have concluded that while treatments may be somewhat effective in helping highly motivated individuals refrain from acting out on homosexual impulses, there is little empirical evidence to suggest that conversion therapies are effective in changing sexual orientation and therefore lack adequate support to justify their use. Because of their apparent ineffectiveness and some evidence of harm associated with conversion therapies, several states have outlawed the use of these with minors.

In one carefully conducted review published in *Professional Psychology: Research and Practice,* a well-regarded refereed journal, Shidlo and Schroeder identified 202 individuals who had participated in conversion

14. Alan L. Ellis and Robert W. Mitchell, "Sexual Orientation," in *Psychological Perspectives on Human Sexuality*, ed. Lenore T. Szuchman and Frank Muscarella (New York: John Wiley & Sons, 2000), 196–231.

15. Douglas C. Haldeman, "Sexual Orientation Conversion Therapy for Gay Men and Lesbians: A Scientific Examination," in *Homosexuality: Research Implications for Public Policy*, ed. John C. Gonsiorek and James D. Weinrich (Newbury Park, CA: Sage Publications, 1991), 149–60.

16. Kathleen J. Bieschke, Parrish L. Paul, and Kelly A. Blasko, "Review of Empirical Research Focused on the Experience of Lesbian, Gay, and Bisexual Clients in Counseling and Psychotherapy," in *Handbook of Counseling and Psychotherapy with Lesbian, Gay, Bisexual and Transgender Clients,* 2nd ed., ed. Kathleen J. Bieschke, Ruperto M. Perez, and Kurt A. DeBord (Washington, DC: American Psychological Association, 2007), 293–315.

therapies and were willing to share their experience of treatment.[17] The researchers carefully screened participants to include only those who identified themselves as predominantly homosexual (with a subjective rating of 5 or 6 on the 6-point Kinsey Scale) and who had persevered in conversion therapy for a lengthy period of time. Participants' average time spent in treatment was twenty-six months (over two years) with an average number of sessions of 118. Of Shidlo and Schroeder's 202 participants, 176 (87%) reported failing in their efforts to change their sexual orientation. Of the 26 participants reporting some success, nearly half (12) reported repeated "slips" of homosexual behavior. Six participants reported greater success in refraining from homosexual activity, but declined to classify their current orientation. Only 8 of the original 202 subjects (4%) denied any homosexual behavior and reported being involved in heterosexual relationships post-treatment.

While these results do not rule out the possibility of environmental and social factors contributing to the determination of sexual orientation, they do clearly suggest that sexual orientation does not appear to be a malleable or changeable trait. They further indicate that while psychotherapy or counseling may help individuals clarify their sexual orientation and integrate it into the larger context of their personality in ways consistent with values and perceived moral obligations, treatments aimed specifically at changing orientation are not likely to be successful and could possibly lead to further internal distress. It is also important to keep in mind, especially within the context of celibacy formation, that while the church asks men and women with a homosexual orientation to refrain from homosexual activity and to lead celibate lives, nowhere in its official documents does the Catholic Church ask or encourage individuals to try to change their sexual orientation.

The research on the biological foundations of sexual orientation is complex and ongoing. Although it is not entirely conclusive at this time, it does point to the likelihood of some type or types of biological contribution to the determination of sexual orientation. In our survey of the research in this area, we will look at twin studies, the role of androgen-signaling, and the fraternal birth order effect as some of the

---

17. Ariel Shidlo and Michael Schroeder, "Changing Sexual Orientation: A Consumers' Report," *Professional Psychology: Research and Practice* 33, no. 3 (2002): 249–59.

accumulating evidence supporting the likelihood of at least a partial biological foundation.

Twin studies compare concordance rates (i.e., the percentage of times that two related individuals share a particular trait) of siblings with increasing levels of shared genetic material. Of particular interest is the comparison of concordance rates between monozygotic twins (from a single fertilized egg or zygote) and dizygotic twins (resulting from the simultaneous fertilization of two separate ova or zygotes). While both types of twins share the same intrauterine environment, they differ in amount of shared genetic material, with monozygotic twins having 100% genetic relatedness. Twin studies have repeatedly shown concordance rates for homosexuality to be significantly higher (typically around twice as high) in monozygotic twins compared to dizygotic twins.[18] These findings suggest that while there appears to be some genetic contribution or predisposition to same-sex attraction, sexual orientation does not appear to be solely determined by genetic factors since the concordance rate of homosexuality among monozygotic twins does not appear in any of the studies reviewed to be 100% despite sharing 100% of the same genetic material.

Androgen-signaling has also been implicated as a possible biological factor in the determination of sexual orientation. Recall from our earlier discussion that the secretion of androgens (masculinizing hormones) in the early fetal period leads to the development of the primary sex characteristics in the chromosomal (XY) male fetus, but can also errantly lead to the development of male genitalia in a chromosomal female in the case of overexposure to androgens (congenital adrenal hyperplasia, or CAH). Several studies have shown that women with CAH are more likely than unaffected women to be lesbian or bisexual.[19] A complementary finding is reported in chromosomal males affected with androgen insensitivity

18. Alexander K. Hill, Khytam Dawood, and David A. Puts, "Biological Foundations of Sexual Orientation," in *Handbook of Psychology and Sexual Orientation*, ed. Charlotte J. Patterson and Anthony R. D'Augelli (New York: Oxford University Press, 2013), 55–68; Margaret Rosario and Eric W. Schrimshaw, "Theories and Etiologies of Sexual Orientation," in *APA Handbook of Sexuality and Psychology, Volume 1: Person-Based Approaches*, ed. Deborah L. Tolman and others (Washington, DC: American Psychological Association, 2014), 555–96.

19. Hill, Dawood, and Puts, "Biological Foundations of Sexual Orientation."

syndrome, who show higher levels of same-sex attraction compared to their unaffected male counterparts.

Finally, a repeatedly documented phenomenon referred to as the "fraternal birth order effect" points again to the likelihood of at least a partial biological involvement in the occurrence of same-sex attraction. The fraternal birth order effect refers to the fairly robust finding (noted only among males) that the chance of having a homosexual orientation increases with each older male sibling a man has. Although the exact mechanism is still uncertain, it is hypothesized that each time a mother carries a male child, her endocrine system may react to the introduction of androgens into her own bloodstream by producing anti-male antibodies. It is proposed that the accumulation of these antibodies passing back across the placental barrier could have increasing canceling effects on the androgen signaling in subsequent male fetuses.[20] Although the fraternal birth order effect has been well-established, it still accounts for only a relatively small percent of the variance with respect to sexual orientation. In other words, boys with a number of older male siblings should not jump automatically to the conclusion that they will have a homosexual orientation!

What can we conclude? The simple answer is that we still do not know entirely what determines sexual orientation or what causes someone to have a homosexual or bisexual orientation. We can say with a fair amount of confidence that same-sex attraction is probably a multifactorial phenomenon, meaning there are likely many factors that combine in different people and in different ways to result in someone having a homosexual or bisexual orientation. Like most complex personality characteristics, there are probably many "paths" that result in this particular trait, and research is beginning to show that these paths likely involve a biological contribution or genetic predisposition upon which other social and environmental influences may build.

It is important here to make one final and important note regarding the phenomenology (or experience) of sexual orientation and how it appears to differ between men and women. It is becoming increasingly clear that for women, emotional attraction and relationship context plays a more significant role in the determination of sexual arousal and attraction

20. Hill, Dawood, and Puts.

(compared to men, for whom physical attraction and the gender of the partner is more prominent). Consequently, sexual orientation is increasingly regarded as a more fluid construct in women, with women more likely than men to report histories of feeling sexually attracted to both men and women and reporting greater variability in the age at which they first experienced same-sex attraction and behaviors (as late as middle and late adulthood).[21] Because sexual orientation appears to be a more fluid construct for women, we are more likely to encounter women in our formation programs who, when asked to articulate themselves as sexual people, may describe themselves as bisexual, struggle to define their sexual orientation, or even resist categorizing their sexual orientation in the traditional terms of homosexual versus heterosexual. Simply acknowledging the fluidity and complex nature of sexual attraction among many women may help allay concerns, address confusion, and assist candidates in arriving at a better understanding and acceptance of themselves as sexual people. What is most important is that men and women have a clear understanding and acceptance of their capacity for romantic and sexual attraction and are able to recognize who they find attractive and what they find attractive in others.

D. History of Sexual Experiences

An individual's history of sexual experiences is the fourth factor in our model of sexual identity. It goes without saying that our identities in general are shaped by the things that happen to us and by the experiences we seek out. When it comes to our sexual identity, our experiences also play a defining role and ultimately affect our experience of celibacy. Those who have never been sexually active or who have never dated, for example, are likely to have a different experience of living the celibate life compared to people who have been involved in several romantic relationships and maybe even some sexual relationships. Their self-knowledge will include what they have learned about themselves from relating closely to another. Their understanding of what it means to have been in love and perhaps

21. Lisa M. Diamond, "Gender and Same-Sex Sexuality," in *APA Handbook of Sexuality and Psychology, Volume 1: Person-Based Approaches*, ed. Deborah L. Tolman and others (Washington, DC: American Psychological Association, 2014), 629–52.

to have been disappointed in love will become part of their consideration and future understanding of the celibate life. The experience of having been sexually active can pose particular challenges to the celibate, or may result in a greater appreciation of the power of sexuality and the complexities that a physical relationship brings to intimacy. Regardless, the experience becomes part of who people are as sexual beings and how they will experience the celibate life.

Candidates' history of sexual experiences may include a wide range behaviors and events, some of which are obvious in their sexual nature: dating, kissing, masturbation, and sexual intercourse. Others are more subtle, ambiguous, and even subject to being misinterpreted or overlooked. Hugging, for example, may or may not be a sexual behavior, depending on the type of hug, the intent of those involved, and the type of relationship in the context of which it occurs. These same conditions—type, intent, and context—can define the sexual or romantic nature of other types of behaviors or interactions, including talk, humor, how a person dresses, and the proximity to which we sit or stand next to another person. Because sexual experiences can sometimes be very subtle, people may not be aware of the degree to which something they have said or done has a sexual valence.

A person's history of sexual experiences might also include unpleasant, harmful, or violent sexual experiences. Sexual abuse in childhood, sexual assault (rape), or bullying because of one's sexuality are examples of experiences that deeply affect people and may motivate future decisions about how to live out their sexuality, including the choice of celibacy. When individuals present with a history of unpleasant or traumatic sexual experiences, it is important to carefully explore the possible impact of these on their decision to pursue celibacy.

In addition to sexual behaviors and interactions, our history of sexual experiences also includes the manner in which sexuality and physical affection were handled in our families of origin. Growing up in a family in which physical affection was never on display is a very different experience than growing up in a family environment in which the children regularly saw their parents hold hands, kiss, or even flirt with one another. Some children grow up in families in which the physical and sexual boundaries are inappropriate, irresponsible, and even abusive. What is modeled for us in our families helps to form our later perceptions of what is normal and acceptable behavior.

Sexual practices and society's norms for what practices are considered acceptable change over time and have differed for men and women. Use of internet pornography has become an increasingly common phenomenon over the last ten or fifteen years, and although it is more commonly associated with men, research indicates that internet pornography use among women is also on the rise. Types of preferred cyber sexual experiences appear to differ from men to women, with males tending to access more visually stimulating sexual content while women appear to prefer types of pornography and sexual experiences that depend more on narrative, emotional content, and relational contexts.[22]

The meanings and motivation associated with our sexual experiences are also important to consider. Some men and women, for example, walk away from romantic and physical relationships feeling hurt and untrusting of future relationships, while others gain new appreciation and respect for the power of love and the sacredness of sexuality. For a man or woman who has been sexually active in the past, it will be important to examine what these experiences might have to say about personality, capacity for intimacy, and what aspects of the celibate life might be most challenging and rewarding. It will be fruitful to consider what role the physical dimension played in the larger relationship: whether physical intimacy developed early in the relationship as a means of trying to meet emotional needs, or whether it was the result of a well-formed, loving relationship. Anonymous sexual encounters point to a very different understanding of love and sexuality altogether and may indicate an impoverished sense of self-worth or signal an inability or disinterest in pursuing affection and emotional intimacy in more genuine and healthy ways.

When a person has had no sexual or romantic experience, it is equally important to explore the meaning and motives associated with this kind of history. Young adults who have never dated or had any kind of sexual experience (including hand-holding, kissing, or flirting) might be considered atypical compared to their peers. Although this history is not necessarily problematic, it is important to be sure that the choice not to date or relate romantically or sexually to others has not been the result of

22. Gert Martin Hald, Christopher Seaman, and Daniel Linz, "Sexuality and Pornography," in *APA Handbook of Sexuality and Psychology, Volume 2: Contextual Approaches,* ed. Deborah L. Tolman and others (Washington, DC: American Psychological Association, 2014), 3–35.

fear, naiveté, confusion, or denial of one's sexuality. Here again we see the implications for exploring motives for celibacy, and it is worth repeating that the choice to lead a celibate life should not ultimately be rooted in emotional or psychological dysfunction.

A person's history of sexual behavior can also include compulsive sexual behaviors such as compulsive masturbation, sexual acting out, or internet-based sexual activity. Behaviors are considered to be compulsive when, beyond being habitual, they increasingly demand more and more time and resources and begin to interfere with the ability to function professionally, socially, or academically. When online sexual behaviors interfere with or substitute for real-life relationships, or when they place an individual at risk of suffering major negative consequences (e.g., divorce, job loss, scandal, significant financial loss, legal problems), intervention is needed and the individual is not adequately free for proper vocational discernment or religious formation.

Msgr. Stephen Rossetti has listed extremes in developmental sexual experience as a red flag for identifying potential sexual offenders among clergy and religious.[23] Note that the word "extreme" can signify either an overabundance of sexual experience or a near absence of sexual interest and awareness. Emotional and sexual maturity is manifest at least in part by the discretion and moderation with which individuals conduct themselves as sexual people.

Just how much life experience is necessary or even desirable for one approaching the celibate life? There is no simple answer to this question. What we can be sure of is that men and women will enter priestly and religious formation with a range and variety of sexual and romantic experiences. A good formation program is a flexible one that takes each individual's history of experience into account as it fosters self-knowledge and self-acceptance as a means of discerning a life of celibacy as a free and generous self-gift to God and others.

E. Attitudes and Values regarding Sexuality

The final dimension in our five-factored model of sexual identity is one's attitudes and values regarding sexuality. This includes the attitudes

---

23. Stephen J. Rossetti, *A Tragic Grace: The Catholic Church and Child Sexual Abuse* (Collegeville, MN: Liturgical Press, 1996), 72.

and values one holds about sexuality in general; for example: Is sexuality seen as something beautiful, engaging, and life-giving; or is one fearful, threatened, or even disgusted by sexuality? We should also consider one's attitudes and values related to specific topics within the realm of sexuality, including premarital sex; homosexuality; use of artificial contraception; and attitudes toward the opposite sex, including the roles of women in society or in the church.

Attitudes and values have a variety of influences and these influences may change in relative importance over the course of our development. In early and middle childhood, our parents, family, and the institutions in which our parents place authority (e.g., schools, church) exercise the greatest influence. In adolescence and young adulthood, the influence of peers, media, and the larger culture increases. The attitudes and values we come to hold as adults are a complex hybrid of our earlier and later influences, further shaped and defined over time by our own personal experiences.

It is important to consider how our attitudes and values have been shaped by the things that have happened to us and by the experiences we have sought out for ourselves. An individual's strong, negative attitudes toward people who are homosexual, for example, may become more nuanced or even change dramatically in response to discovering that a close friend is attracted to people of the same sex. A young woman with very liberal or recreational attitudes regarding premarital sex may find her attitudes changing in response to a pregnancy scare or having to console a friend who became the victim of a coercive sexual experience.

Influences and Interactions among These Five Dimensions of Sexual Identity

We have mentioned a number of times so far how each of these individual dimensions (i.e., sex, gender, sexual orientation, history of sexual experiences, and attitudes and values regarding sexuality) can influence and relate to one another. We have just explored, for example, how our history of sexual experiences can have a significant impact on the development of our attitudes and values regarding sexuality.

With respect to history of sexual behaviors, society has traditionally perceived men as being more sexually adventurous than women, and there is some historical evidence to support this. Research on generational cohorts shows, however, that in more recent generations the prevalence of various sexual practices among women (e.g., premarital sex, extramarital affairs) has gradually increased and come close to equaling that of males. These findings obviously parallel the significant shifts in the perceptions and roles of women in western society.[24]

Thus, while there are many and clear interactions and influences to be considered among the dimensions within our model of sexual identity, we must also caution ourselves not to go the extra step to conflate these dimensions. We create potentially harmful overgeneralizations when we fail to recognize the distinction between these separate dimensions or constructs, assuming, for example that women (sex) are not really all that interested in sex (attitudes and values), or that all homosexual men (sexual orientation) are effeminate (gender identity) or promiscuous (history of experiences). Keeping these constructs separate, even while acknowledging their potential relatedness, can save us from harmful prejudices and even provide us in our own self-reflection with expanded room to better explore and understand who we are as sexual people.

In the next chapter, we will examine some possible conflicts within our sexual identity and continue to use the model to arrive at some useful definitions of sexual maturity and integration.

24. Edward O. Laumann and others, *The Social Organization of Sexuality: Sexual Practices in the United States* (Chicago: University of Chicago Press, 1994).

CHAPTER 8

SEXUAL INTEGRATION

Now that we have established a vocabulary and framework for understanding ourselves as sexual people, let's proceed to describe what it means to have integrated our sexuality into the larger picture of our personality and our identity as celibate men and women. Formation directors talk frequently about the importance of "sexual integration." But what exactly does it mean to be sexually integrated? This chapter offers three definitions of sexual integration that serve as formation goals in the area of sexual identity:

1. Possessing appropriate self-knowledge and self-acceptance in the area of sexual identity

2. Achieving a sexual identity that has integrity

3. Arriving at a proper placement of one's sexuality in the context of his or her personality

These three definitions of integrity or maturity will build on the model of sexual identity offered in the last chapter:

Sexual Identity = Sex +
                  Gender +
                  Sexual Orientation +
                  History of Sexual Experience +
                  Values and Attitudes regarding Sexuality

1. Self-Knowledge and Self-Acceptance

The first and perhaps simplest definition of sexual maturity is borrowed once more from the US bishops. Recall the line from the *Program of Priestly Formation*: "Human formation happens in a three-fold process of self-knowledge, self-acceptance, and self-gift."[1] We begin here when establishing formation goals for sexual identity. Our first goal is for candidates to develop adequate knowledge and acceptance of themselves as sexual beings. This means that candidates must have an honest understanding of each of the various dimensions of sexual identity (sex, gender, sexual orientation, history of sexual behaviors, and attitudes and values regarding sexuality) as they apply to themselves. And beyond understanding, they must be able to accept and to live within the truth of who they are as sexual people.

As we have discussed several times, knowledge and acceptance are key to developing the necessary freedom of choice when it comes to making a permanent and continuous gift of oneself as a celibate man or woman. Not only can ignorance or denial limit our freedom and possibly lead to later regret or an inability to persevere in the commitment to celibate chastity; but long-term denial, confusion, and inappropriate naiveté can also lead to more harmful consequences for others. This is particularly evident in the case of the sexual abuse crisis in the church.

Research on clergy child sexual offenders indicates that one of the largest subtypes of child sex offenders among Catholic priests and religious brothers is men who could be best described as "sexually and emotionally underdeveloped."[2] These individuals were not deeply disturbed from a psychiatric point of view or even criminally minded. Rather, they were described as having inadequate knowledge and insight into their sexual identity and their needs for intimacy. In his book *A Tragic Grace*, Msgr. Stephen Rossetti similarly lists *confusion about sexual orientation* as the

1. *Program of Priestly Formation,* 5th ed. (Washington, DC: United States Conference of Catholic Bishops, 2006), 33.

2. Marc A. Falkenhain and others, "Cluster Analysis of Child Sexual Offenders: A Validation with Roman Catholic Priests and Brothers," *Sexual Addiction and Compulsivity* 6 (1999): 317–36.

first of six red flags for identifying potential clergy sex offenders.[3] Note that the sexual orientation itself—whether heterosexual or homosexual—is not the issue; what's more important is the degree to which one has been able to integrate (i.e., have knowledge and acceptance of) his sexual orientation.

When individuals are ignorant of their sexual desires or refuse (consciously or subconsciously) to accept the truth of who they are as sexual people, there is a greater risk of desires and impulses being expressed in unhealthy or inappropriate ways. We have a much greater chance of making healthy and moral choices about how our sexual and emotional needs are met when we are aware and accepting of them. Danger comes when we have little understanding about how our feelings are affecting us and how they are motivating our behavior.

We should also note that the consequences of ignoring or denying one's sexuality are not limited to immoral and illegal behaviors such as abuse. More often, a failure to grow in self-knowledge and self-acceptance of one's sexual identity can lead to defensiveness, emotional unavailability, or even hostility, further causing a person to be ineffective in ministry or less capable of relating meaningfully to others in community. A young woman, for example, who is unclear or even defensive about her sexual orientation may have a difficult time negotiating healthy boundaries in her religious community. She might be physically or emotionally overinvolved with other community members or remain emotionally distant, unable to connect with others out of a subconscious fear that they might perceive something she has yet to accept. A young priest who keeps a history of sexual activity or pornography use compartmentalized or cut off from his new, preferred image of himself—"That part of me is dead and I have no memory of it!"—may become overly judgmental and impatient with the flaws of others. This could obviously affect his ability to effectively show God's mercy in the sacrament of reconciliation or to be authentically pastoral toward struggling parishioners.

As we grow in self-knowledge and self-acceptance, we usually become more tolerant of those around us and freer to draw on our own experience when serving others. The ability to freely access one's own experiences and emotional life is the foundation of empathy. As Pope John Paul II wrote so beautifully in reference to the human formation for priests in

3. Stephen J. Rossetti, *A Tragic Grace: The Catholic Church and Child Sexual Abuse* (Collegeville, MN: Liturgical Press, 1996), 68.

Pastores Dabo Vobis: "[I]t is important that the priest should mould his human personality in such a way that it becomes a bridge and not an obstacle for others in their meeting with Jesus Christ the Redeemer of man."[4] Whether we are talking about priestly or religious formation, the goal is always to be a bridge for others to experience Christ.

Self-knowledge and self-acceptance develop in the context of warm and loving relationships. Close friends and family members point out and help us see our strengths and weaknesses, our gifts, and our areas for growth. The experience of being of loved and accepted by others who see and know our vulnerabilities and limitations helps us accept ourselves as we are and keep our personal strengths and limitations in the proper perspective.

2. Having Integrity within Our Sexual Identity

Achieving a sexual identity that has integrity is our second goal and definition of sexual integration. When something has integrity, we say that it is genuine, solid, and true. If we say, "That woman has integrity," we mean that she does what she says, she is the same on the inside as on the outside, she is consistent and not two-faced. Another word for integrity is "sincere"—a Latin word that comes from the phrase *sin cero*—"without wax." It originally referred to the condition of stone columns or statues. A column made of several pieces of stone would need wax to seal or cover the cracks and make it appear whole when it was not. A column made of one solid piece of stone with no need for wax (*sin cero*) had a soundness and solidity desirable for its ability to withstand external stress and strain.

When applied to people, and more specifically when applied to sexual identity, integrity has to do with soundness of identity and consistency within one's personality. People have integrity when what they do is consistent with what they say—their behaviors are consistent with their professed attitudes and values. Individuals' sexual identity has integrity when the various dimensions or facets of their sexual identity—sex, gender, sexual orientation, history of sexual behaviors, and attitudes and values—are in harmony, not in conflict or battling against one another. Let's discuss a few examples of what dis-integration might look like within a person's sexual identity.

---

4. John Paul II, *Pastores Dabo Vobis: On the Formation of Priests in the Circumstances of the Present Day* (Washington, DC: United States Catholic Conference, 1999), 117.

Sexual Identity = **Sex** +
                             Gender +
                             Sexual Orientation +
                             History of Sexual Experiences +
                             Values and Attitudes regarding Sexuality

An obvious but rare example would be a conflict between one's sex and one's gender identity. An individual who is physiologically a male (sex) but identifies internally as a woman (gender) experiences what is clinically described as a gender identity disorder. Currently, we are hearing more in the media and in public discourse about *transgendered* individuals—a less clinical way of describing those who feel conflict between their biological sex and their gender identity. This growing public awareness might lead us to the impression that transgender is becoming more and more prevalent. In actuality, gender identity disorder or being transgendered appears to be a relatively rare phenomenon. It is likely that increasing levels of social acceptance is enabling those who may have previously kept their experience hidden to be more open about their struggle and their desire to have their biological sex align with their internal experience of themselves as male or female.

An example of conflict within one's sexual identity that we are more likely to encounter involves individuals whose attitudes and values are at odds with their sexual orientation or with their history of sexual experiences. Let's consider a couple of case studies.

Case study 1: Sarah

Sexual Identity = Sex +
                             Gender +
                             Sexual Orientation +
                             History of Sexual Experiences +
                             Values and Attitudes regarding Sexuality

Sarah grew up in a fairly traditional family whose attitudes toward homosexual people were negative and frequently verbalized. She frequently heard the words "fag" and "queer" used to describe men and women with same-sex attraction. Sarah recalls her mother saying often, "I just can't support how they live." As Sarah grows into ado-

lescence and young adulthood, she comes to the slow realization that she is physically attracted to other women instead of men, and she panics when her friends and family ask her why she is not dating. She laughs it off publicly and tells them: "I'm too picky. There's no man good enough! Plus, I want to focus on my education and career before I tie myself down." Over time Sarah feels more and more worried, often trying to convince herself that she has simply not met the right man or that she is just slow to develop.

Case study 2: Richard

Sexual Identity = Sex +

Gender +

Sexual Orientation +

History of Sexual Experiences +

Values and Attitudes regarding Sexuality

Richard is in his second year of seminary. He came to the seminary with relatively little dating experience. "I always knew I was going to be a priest," he says. Richard speaks enthusiastically about celibacy and is not shy about telling others that his celibacy is "a much-needed countercultural statement in our oversexualized and promiscuous culture."

"But isn't it difficult?" some of his friends ask him.

"No," he tells them. "I find complete satisfaction and joy in how God is calling me and I believe he has given me this gift to help spread his message about what is right and true."

In his third year of seminary, Richard develops a close relationship with Rebecca, one of the lay graduate students at the seminary. One day, a couple months into their friendship, Richard impulsively kisses Rebecca, then immediately apologizes, saying, "I don't know why I did that!" Rebecca responds by sharing that she, too, has feelings for him. Soon, their relationship becomes physical, and Richard occasionally goes over to Rebecca's home where they have intercourse. Each time, Richard feels regret and swears it will not happen again, but neglects to disclose the relationship to any of his friends or anyone on the formation staff, including his spiritual director.

Both of these scenarios illustrate the types of conflict that can develop within an individual's sexual identity. In both cases, the subjects are divided within themselves—Sarah coming to the slow discovery that her sexual orientation is in conflict with the attitudes and values that have been instilled in her by her family of origin; Richard facing the reality that his vision of himself as a standard bearer of the value of celibacy is no longer consistent with his behavior. We would probably be more tempted to say that Richard lacks personal integrity because he preaches one thing and does another; however, Sarah and Richard both suffer from a lack of internal consistency within their sexual identity.

When one dimension of sexual identity is inconsistent with another dimension, the result is internalized conflict or dissonance. We all know what it feels like to be conflicted within ourselves: we say something uncharitable, knowing it is wrong; or we recognize a personality trait in ourselves that we despise in other people. When we become aware of the inconsistency, we are uncomfortable. We feel out of sorts because our behavior or some aspect of our personality doesn't align with our value system or our deeply held beliefs. Our human response is a desire to resolve the conflict. We need our behavior to match our values. In the cases of Richard and Sarah, the internalized dissonance is complex and difficult to resolve because the issues are of great importance and the stakes are high. Consequently, the desire for a solution may also be more urgently felt.

Psychologically speaking, we are not designed to live with high levels of dissonance or internal conflict for very long. Something has to give. In Sarah's case, we can imagine two obvious solutions: either she can change her attitudes and values regarding homosexual people (which now includes herself), or she can try change her sexual orientation (which the research shows is not a very malleable trait). Sarah's best solution may be to find ways to adopt attitudes about same-sex attraction that are not so negative or self-condemning. If she is Catholic, she might benefit from a careful reading of what the church teaches—that the orientation itself is not a sin and that she deserves respect and compassion. She might also find peers or trusted older adults with whom she can share this side of herself and hopefully receive the compassion, respect, and acceptance she needs. Self-acceptance often comes as the result of being accepted as we are by others whom we love and respect.

A third way to deal with Sarah's internal conflict exists, though it is not a very healthy or adaptive long-term solution. Sarah could continue to avoid or suppress her sexuality through rationalization or denial. She might continue trying to convince herself that she really is not attracted to other women and has simply "not met the right man" or has just been too busy with school or work to develop a romantic interest in men. These "defense mechanisms," as Freud originally called them, protect her from having to deal with a truth that at some level she knows, but does not consciously admit because it seems too overwhelming. Freud suggested that defense mechanisms can be helpful in the short term if they help the individual assimilate a threat more gradually or buy a little time in order to build up the needed internal resources or external support to deal with the concern. But if used too rigidly or for too long, defenses such as denial, repression, or rationalization can interfere with an individual's ability to grow. Additionally, defense mechanisms require psychic energy to keep in place, and over time they may rob the person of energy that would be better spent on healthier personal investments such as relationships, meaningful work, or even spiritual pursuits.

Even when important aspects of ourselves are kept out of sight and buried in the subconscious, they still can be powerful motivators of our behavior and life decisions. Sarah might choose a religious celibate life, for example, as a way of not having to deal with her orientation. "My sexuality will no longer matter and people will stop wondering" (or so she perceives). When left unchallenged, denial as a motive for celibacy can be very problematic. A young person in priestly or religious formation who is rigidly defensive about sexuality may be closed to the formation process and become irritable or antagonistic when the conversation turns to celibacy and sexuality.

Richard has the same three options as Sarah. He can change his behavior to be more consistent with his attitudes, values, and commitment to the celibate life; or he can arrive at a different or more nuanced attitude and reevaluate whether he is truly called to celibacy. On the unhealthier side, Richard might deal with the conflict between his behavior and his values by intellectualizing or rationalizing what he is doing (another defense). He might try to convince himself that his sexual relationship is actually helpful to his vocation: "This relationship is an important part of my formation for celibacy! How else will I be able to know what I am giving up as a priest unless I have some experience of romantic and sexual love before ordination?" He might further convince himself that other seminarians have had this experience before entering seminary and that he is simply having the experience now. "It is probably good that this is happening," he may tell himself, "and I'm sure my spiritual director and the formation staff would agree. No need to tell them right now. I will do that after the relationship has ended."

There are obviously many problems with Richard's attempt to rationalize the relationship and therefore deal with the inconsistency between his behavior and his values. Especially problematic is the fact that there are other people affected by his decisions. Apart from the impact that Richard's "formation experience" (as he calls it) might have on Rebecca and her relationship with the church, Richard also runs the risk of scandalizing others—in or outside the church—who may eventually learn about his behavior and generalize from Richard's lack of integrity that the church as an institution lacks credibility when it comes to celibacy and other issues related to sexual morality.

Again, the aim is integrity or internal consistency within our sexual identity. This is not to say that healthy and mature celibates don't occasionally find themselves internally conflicted about something they feel or have said or done. But growth in chastity—a responsible living out of one's sexual and romantic impulses—is characterized by a willingness to look honestly at ourselves, to recognize inconsistencies and challenges, and to move quickly to the appropriate decisions and adjustments that bring who we are and what we do as sexual people into alignment with our attitudes, our values, and God's vision for us as sexual people.

3. Having Our Sexuality in Its "Proper Place"

Let's preface the third definition of integration with a brief story. One day when I was a young monk my novice master, Fr. Harry, shared his thoughts about sexuality in his typical, folk-wisdom manner. He told me with a thoughtful expression on his face, "I think sexuality is both *more* important and *less* important than we think." I confess, I scratched my head at first. Then I slowly began to comprehend Fr. Harry's point. The truth is, sexuality is important; it is a defining part of who we are, but it is not the *only* aspect of our personality that defines us.

When it comes to integrating our sexuality, the goal is to give our sexuality the amount of time, attention, and energy it requires—not a whole lot more, but not a whole lot less. Sexual prudishness is not what we are after, nor is a disposition that looks for every occasion possible to make a sexual innuendo or share a bawdy joke. When we examine this from a developmental perspective, we will understand how the process of integration typically unfolds for most individuals.

In prepubescence—childhood before the onset of puberty—relatively little of our time, energy, and attention goes to processing sexuality. Although young children have a developing sense of their sex and gender, and sometimes imitate the flirtatious behavior of adults, they spend very little time talking about sexuality, noticing the physical attractiveness of their peers, or dreaming about romantic or sexual adventures. To visualize this graphically, we might draw a pie graph with just a small sliver shaded in to represent the proportion of our conscious energies being occupied by sexual and romantic concerns as young children.

Prepubescence

In adolescence, with the onset of puberty and the convergence of a variety of other physiological and environmental factors, we devote a much greater portion of our time, energy, and attention to romantic and sexual concerns. When drawing the graphs in class, my students like to suggest that a proportion the exact opposite of prepubescence best depicts the experience of adolescence!

Prepubescence   Adolescence

While this depiction may be an exaggeration, it does attempt to represent the significant behavioral shift in adolescents. This increased attention to romantic and sexual concerns is triggered by adolescent hormone production, but it is also cued by social pressures, such as eager questioning of adults and peers who want to know whom they have crushes on. The preoccupation with sexual concerns is further enabled by the development of the prefrontal cortex, the part of the brain that allows teens and adults to reflect on their experiences, to analyze their emotions, to think of themselves as sexual people, and to see themselves through the eyes of their peers. The result is an awakening of the relational self, and it requires a significant amount of time and energy to figure out how to negotiate these newly understood romantic and sexual impulses effectively. I distinctly remember how in a very short period of time, my younger cousin went from arguing with his mother about having to take a shower every day to taking over the bathroom for hours, experimenting with hairstyles, aftershaves, acne control, and the best postures to show off the biceps he was working on in the gym! Adolescents talk and text on their phones, talk in class, and talk in the locker room about who is cute, whom they like, who might like them, and what they've done (or would like to do) on dates. Thank God this phase doesn't last forever!

But if puberty and other physiological and environmental cues move us from childhood to an adolescent experience of our sexuality, how does our sexuality eventually assume its place within the context of our larger adult identity, where it continues in importance but ceases to be the sole thing defining us?

Prepubescence   Adolescence   Adulthood

Life experience, especially relationship experience, is probably what most often moves us to a more balanced, integrated sense of our sexual identity. Let me offer an illustration of how this can happen:

Joe, a high school sophomore, decides to begin dating. He works up his courage and asks out the most attractive girl in his class, Julie. To his great pleasure and the envy of his friends, Julie says yes. After three months of dating, Joe tells his friends that he has to break up with Julie. When they tell him he's crazy, he explains that she is very demanding and is never satisfied with anything he says or does.

After breaking up with Julie, Joe begins to date Samantha. He enjoys being with Samantha because she is also attractive and fun to be around. Joe is smitten with her, but about a year into the relationship, Joe's best friend reluctantly tells him that he has seen Samantha out with other guys, even after they had agreed to date exclusively.

In his heartache over this failed relationship, Joe leans heavily on Katie, a good friend to whom he has never been particularly attracted. As time goes on, Joe begins to recognize how grateful he is for Katie, and for the first time he notices how attractive she is and wonders why he had never noticed it before. Joe begins to develop romantic feelings for Katie and he asks her out on a date. Joe and Katie date for the rest of their senior year, but their relationship eventually ends amicably when they attend college in different parts of the country and mutually agree to date other people.

One factor that influences Joe's decision to end the relationship with Katie is that she is not a person of faith, and this has always bothered him. He never felt he could share this meaningful part of his life with her. In his sophomore year of college, Joe meets and feels a deep connection with a young woman in his Bible study at the Catholic student center. Joe somehow knows right away: "This is the one!"

This simple but not unrealistic scenario illustrates how relationship experience often helps us to see what is important to us and, in turn, allows us view ourselves in a more complex, mature light. At first, Joe chooses a young woman to date based on physical attraction. He quickly learns he wants to be in a relationship with someone not just because of how she looks or how desirable she is; she also must be kind and enjoyable to be around. Subsequent relationships and breakups help him to learn the value of truthfulness and fidelity, as well as the role of faith and a spiritual connection in a relationship. With each relationship, Joe learns more about himself by discovering what he finds attractive in others. Sexuality will always be important. He will probably never date someone to whom he is not physically attracted, but his experience has also taught him that sexual attraction is only one of many dimensions of his personality and how he relates to others.

Dating relationships are not the only type of relationships in which our identity is reflected back to us and clarified. Investing in close friendships, interacting with professional colleagues, and even exploring relationships through literature, film, and other art forms can help us to learn more about ourselves as romantic and sexual people. While vicarious experiences can never replace our own lived experience, I often suggest reading novels and short stories or watching films as additional ways of learning about relationships, intimacy, and our own attractions. It is one of my favorite experiences when watching a movie to find myself, along with the protagonist, gradually becoming aware of how appealing another character is as a result of learning more about the person's virtue or emotional or intellectual qualities.

Now let's return to our developmental schema to ask some crucial questions.

Prepubescence   Adolescence   Adulthood

Where do we expect someone to be upon entering a formation program for priesthood or religious life? Where do we anticipate someone should be at the time of ordination or final profession? Where do you see yourself at present?

Vocation directors and formation personnel should also ask: What are the indications that candidates are still in a prepubescent stage or an adolescent stage with respect to their sexual integration?

It is important to remember that progress is not guaranteed by chronological age, and as we've already suggested, it is possible for someone to be emotionally and sexually underdeveloped well into adulthood.

What are the signs of underdevelopment? Indicators include sexual naiveté, a history of few close personal relationships outside one's family of origin, and denial of ever having felt sexually or emotionally attracted to anyone. Candidates should be able to articulate the types of people they find attractive, how they know they are attracted to someone, and what they typically do when they are feeling romantically or physically drawn to another. Mature candidates can speak insightfully and comfortably about the intimate relationships they have had in the past (physical or emotional). If they have not been romantically involved, then we look to see if the individual has ever recognized a desire to be physically or emotionally close to another in the past. Above all, we want to avoid confusing sexual naiveté or avoidance with a call to celibacy. As highlighted earlier in our discussion of the theological dimensions of celibate chastity, celibacy is a discipline pursued in the service of increasing one's capacity for love, not a means by which a person attempts to live a life free of emotional challenges or sexual provocations.

When I was a novice about to take my temporary vows, my abbot asked me to memorize a poem by Gerard Manley Hopkins entitled "Heaven-Haven (a nun takes the veil)."

> I have desired to go
> Where springs not fail,
> To fields where flies no sharp and sided hail
> And a few lilies blow.
> And I have asked to be
> Where no storms come,
> Where the green swell is in the havens dumb,
> And out of the swing of the sea.[5]

Hopkins's poem challenges the reader to wonder about the nun's motives for moving into the cloister: Is she genuinely desiring an intimate relationship with God in solitude (note that God is never mentioned), or is she rather motivated by a need to escape the tumults of life? Does her willingness to settle for "a few lilies" instead of entire field suggest

5. Gerard Manley Hopkins, "Heaven-Haven (a nun takes the veil)," in *Mortal Beauty, God's Grace*, ed. John F. Thornton and Susan B. Varenne (New York: Random House, 2003).

compromise rather than a leap of faith? Our knowledge of Hopkins as a religious priest causes us further to wonder whether the poem is written from the viewpoint of the nun entering the cloister or from his own perspective as an older religious watching a young nun embark on a similar path of celibacy. After all, there is no escaping the occasional sharp and sided hail of our human experience, or the swing of life's emotional sea.

Challenges to Integration

Finally, let's consider the possible impact of certain life events or circumstances on a young person's progress through our developmental schema of integration. How, for example, might the process of integrating one's sexuality or sexual identity be different or more challenging for someone who has been sexually abused, has a homosexual orientation, or has grown up with very harsh or negative attitudes around sexuality?

Any of these circumstances could cause a young person to become hesitant, conflicted, or fearful during the more overtly sexualized period of adolescence. A young woman with a history of sexual abuse may find herself revisiting the trauma of her abuse and therefore desire to have as little as possible to do with her peers once they become more interested in sex. A young man who finds other young men, instead of women, attractive is more likely to struggle to find a peer group with whom to share his emerging identity. He may also be at a loss for appropriate models for integration. Both individuals may find it very difficult to engage in the experiences of dating and self-disclosure typical of adolescence and young adulthood and be reluctant to appear different from their peers at a time when, developmentally speaking, the need for social approval and peer acceptance is especially high.

Under such circumstances, negotiating some of the typical psychosocial and psychosexual tasks of adolescence and young adulthood may be delayed, and individuals may need some additional encouragement, support, or assistance in finding peers, identifying appropriate models of adjustment, and growing in their knowledge and acceptance of themselves as sexual people.

Individuals grappling with a challenging or long-avoided aspect of their sexuality may experience their sexuality as suddenly consuming greater amounts of their attention or taking on greater importance in their efforts to define who they are. Their experience may mimic a delayed adolescence in some ways and may help explain why some people make very public pronouncements about their sexuality. After years of painfully denying their sexuality to themselves, they may now want to be able claim it publicly and experience a general acceptance that most people feel without having to fight for it. While the impulse to finally share their identity or their story with others may be understandable, it may not always be appropriate depending on the context, the commitments they have made, and the people or community they represent.

On the way to finding how their sexuality fits in the larger context of their personality, people who have a history of abuse or who are questioning their sexual orientation may feel like that is the most important and defining thing about them—especially if they have not dealt with that piece of their identity or have exiled it from their consciousness for a long time. The desired perspective often comes when individuals have taken a chance to share what they are concerned about with trusted others who can hopefully provide the needed response: "This doesn't change the way I feel about you; I still love you." When people receive such responses from loved ones such as parents, a sibling, or friends, they come to more fully understand that their sexual identity is but a part (even if an important one) of the larger picture of who they are.

In short, there are times in our development when our sexuality needs more of our focus and attention, but in the long run, the goal is for it to be integrated into the larger context of our identity, so that it is receiving the amount of time, energy, and attention it truly requires.

Summary and Conclusions

Having explored five dimensions of sexual identity in the previous chapter, in this chapter we established three definitions of psychosexual maturity and integration:

1. Growing in appropriate self-knowledge and self-acceptance in each of the five dimensions of sexual identity: sex, gender, sexual orientation, history of sexual experiences, and values and attitudes regarding sexuality.

2. Achieving a sexual identity that has integrity—i.e., each of these five dimensions of sexual identity is in harmony with one another and not creating conflicts within the person.

3. Arriving at a proper placement of one's sexuality in the context of the individual's personality in which it receives an appropriate amount of time, attention, and energy. Let's consider where this work is done in the process of initial and ongoing formation.

As stated above, self-knowledge and self-acceptance often develop in the context of relationships, and there are many key relationships in religious and priestly formation settings where this work might be done. Meetings with formation directors, spiritual directors, and counselors (when available or appropriate) are obvious examples. Yet it is important to determine when it is more appropriate for an issue to be addressed in counseling or psychotherapy instead of (or in addition to) spiritual direction or formation meetings. A referral or self-referral for counseling or psychotherapy may be indicated for a number of concerns related to sexuality and celibacy, including confusion about sexual identity, dealing with the consequences of sexual abuse, addressing compulsive sexual behaviors, struggling to achieve appropriate intimacy in friendships, and resolving conflicts between the various parts of one's sexual identity, as discussed above. While some of these topics inevitably arise in spiritual direction and formation meetings, psychological concerns should be addressed by qualified professionals; formation staff should not make recommendations beyond their areas of expertise; and spiritual direction and formation meetings should address their intended issues—those related to prayer, vocational discernment, and communal life. A helpful question to ask is: Is this a spiritual issue, a psychological issue, or both?

Friendships and peer relationships are also important crucibles for human formation. On a daily basis, our peers and friends not only support and challenge us, but they tell us who we are by giving us feedback about how we relate, the appropriateness with which we reveal ourselves, our mood, our attractiveness, our gifts, our limitations, and even the attractions and interpersonal struggles we have yet to acknowledge to ourselves. If we listen carefully to how people tease us or even subtly express their frustrations with us, we can learn much about our own personalities. People who are frequently teased about sharing too much or being flirtatious are probably being told that their boundaries need some attention. For example, if a young man's peers continually express frustration about his habit of cracking jokes when discussions become personal, he might discern that he is emotionally limited.

The candidates themselves are the only ones who truly can do the work of growing in self-knowledge and self-acceptance. At the same time, in initial formation, it is ultimately the formation director's responsibility to ensure that seminarians, novices, or the temporary professed are engaging in this process. We cannot always count on self-initiative when it comes to personal growth, particularly if an individual is unaware or in denial about the need for personal development.

We can put some mechanisms in place to make dealing with issues of celibacy and sexuality easier to address. Since topics related to sexuality vis-à-vis celibacy can be awkward or difficult to bring up, setting general expectations can be helpful. For example, a formation director or spiritual director might explain at the beginning of formation that once a month or once a quarter, candidates will be asked about their experience of celibacy so far. Discussing difficult topics can also be facilitated by anticipating them: "At our next meeting, I would like to talk about celibacy and what you are learning about yourself as a sexual and emotional person."

Candidates or people pursuing ongoing formation can hold themselves accountable to discussing issues of celibacy and sexuality by similarly anticipating these issues at a future spiritual direction or counseling appointment: "Next meeting, I would like us to talk about celibacy and what I am learning about myself so far as a sexual and emotional person." Or, "Next time we meet, I would like you ask me about some of the challenges I am experiencing with celibacy."

Routine, yearly, or semiannual evaluations are recommended for keeping the work of formation and discernment in the area of sexual and emotional maturity moving forward. Developing a standard set of questions for reflection and discussion helps to normalize the process and dispel any notions that a formation director is being intrusive or that a particular candidate is being singled out and put under the microscope.

Finally, open and honest discussions about sexuality and celibacy are also facilitated by possessing good and accurate information and by having informed consent. When formation personnel and candidates have a common, accurate, and dignified vocabulary for talking about sexuality, the conversation is easier and less intimidating. I recommend that formation personnel and candidates attend workshops or read books together to build a common ground for discussion.

Similarly, men and women in formation are freer to talk about sensitive topics if they know in advance who will have access to their information and what the consequences will be if they share something they are struggling with. A formation director may wish to offer some guidelines for what to expect (what psychologists like to call "informed consent") at the very beginning of formation. An example:

> If you find yourself ensnared in pornography or falling in love or questioning your sexuality, we hope that you will bring these issues to your spiritual director and a member of the formation staff so that we can work on them together. Such activities do not necessarily mean you will be asked to leave, but we can't work on these issues and discern together if you keep them hidden from the people who are assigned to assist you in formation and discernment. Celibacy is a challenging discipline that inevitably brings temptations, questions, and sometimes even mistakes. Above all, we want to know that you can use the systems of support and accountability that our life affords all of us on the way to becoming more chaste and more loving individuals.

To conclude, let me finally acknowledge that formation directors themselves must have arrived at an adequate sense of sexual integrity and integration in order to assist others. A formation director with poor self-knowledge and self-acceptance or whose integration remains at a pre-adult level is likely to communicate defensiveness and avoidance around issues of sexuality. When the topic of sexuality is avoided in formation, formation directors risk implying that human sexuality is unimportant or incompatible with the religious or priestly life. I recall a story from one of my older colleagues about the kind of formation he received about sexuality as an aspiring priest and religious. When he was in high school seminary, before heading home at the end of the school year, he asked his rector if it would be all right if he dated over the summer. The response he received was, "Sure, you can date over the summer. Just don't come back to seminary in the fall!" Formation staff who adopt avoidant, antagonistic, or even overly permissive stances with respect to sexuality in formation are not only likely to miss important opportunities to help candidates integrate this most human experience into their larger identity as priests or religious, but they may even contribute to the perpetuation of harmful behaviors among young men and women hoping to create bridges for others to encounter Christ.

SECTION V

SKILLS FOR LIVING THE CELIBATE LIFE

CHAPTER 9

EMOTIONAL INTELLIGENCE
AS AFFECTIVE MATURITY

Skills and strengths needed for the celibate life represent the fourth major content area in our model of celibacy formation. These are the skills and personal characteristics we must assess for and cultivate among candidates for priesthood and religious life. Vocation directors should consider what skills and personal characteristics are needed for living as a celibate in the specific context of their diocese or religious community. Some of the skills necessary for celibacy as a diocesan priest living in a rural diocese where his nearest diocesan brother is miles away, for example, will differ significantly from those required for celibacy in a religious community of fifty men or women. Once necessary skills are identified and assessed upon application to the community or diocese, formation directors can help candidates set early formation goals for this very important aspect of their vocation.

Some of the personal characteristics and skills needed for celibacy should already be in place when an individual approaches the diocese or community requesting affiliation, while others we can expect to work on developing as part of formation. For example, adequate impulse control and the ability to express affection in non-physical ways are personality characteristics a candidate should already possess upon entering a formation program. Proficiency at practicing theological reflection, on the other hand, is a skill we can expect to teach and cultivate among new members. Vocation and formation directors should discuss together which personal characteristics and skills are nonnegotiable prerequisites for a candidate entering the diocese or community.

The celibate life requires many more skills than the five we will explore in greater detail in this volume. In addition to those explored in depth here because of their critical importance—emotional intelligence; identifying and utilizing systems of support and accountability; coping with romantic and sexual attraction; establishing and maintaining effective boundaries; and finding solitude in loneliness—the following should also be evaluated for and cultivated among candidates for the celibate life (many of these are named in the *Program of Priestly Formation,*[1] *Pastores Dabo Vobis,*[2] and the 1998 NCEA document on priestly formation[3]):

- modesty and prudence
- ability to trust oneself to behave appropriately in the face of temptation
- adequate mastery over one's sexual impulses
- capacity for introspection and self-reflection
- commitment to a life of prayer
- capacity for theological reflection on the celibate life
- appropriate self-disclosure
- practice of asceticism
- care for others
- capacity to give and receive love
- capacity for deep and appropriate friendship
- capacity to overcome selfishness and individualism

We now address one of the most foundational skills needed for the celibate life, affective maturity.

---

1. *Program of Priestly Formation,* 5th ed. (Washington, DC: United States Conference of Catholic Bishops, 2006).

2. John Paul II, *Pastores Dabo Vobis: On the Formation of Priests in the Circumstances of the Present Day* (Washington, DC: United States Catholic Conference, 1999).

3. Thomas W. Krenik, *Formation for Priestly Celibacy: A Resource Book* (Washington, DC: National Catholic Education Association, 1999).

Affective Maturity

Affective maturity, or proper development of one's emotional life, is cardinal among the personal characteristics important to the chaste celibate life. The church's formation documents are filled with references to affective maturity, and Pope John Paul goes so far as to refer to affective maturity in *Pastores Dabo Vobis* as "a significant and decisive factor in the formation of candidates for the priesthood."[4] We could easily extend this level of emphasis to candidates for religious life as well. To say that something is a "decisive factor" suggests that it is a singular criterion upon which a person's acceptance for ordination or profession can and should hinge. That is not to say it is the *only* criteria for ordination or profession; however, the Holy Father's emphasis suggests that if a candidate for priesthood lacks adequate affective maturity, he should not be ordained.

In *Vita Consecrata*, Pope John Paul's apostolic exhortation on the consecrated life, affective maturity is linked to other important qualities to be developed in religious men and women: "In present day circumstances, special importance must be given to the interior freedom of consecrated persons, their affective maturity, their ability to communicate with others, especially in their own community, their serenity of spirit, their compassion for those who are suffering, their love for the truth, and a correspondence between their actions and their words."[5] These characteristics nicely complement the qualities associated with affective maturity in the most recent edition of *Program of Priestly Formation*: "Signs of affective maturity in the candidate are prudence, vigilance over body and spirit, compassion and care for others, ability to express and acknowledge emotions, and a capacity to esteem and respect interpersonal relationships between men and women."[6]

There are two common insights in these formation documents that are worth highlighting as we explore the concept of "emotional intelligence" as a way of understanding affective maturity. First, both of these selections underscore the relationship between candidates' personal level of emotional maturity and their interpersonal relationships. This makes sense given the interpersonal nature of ministry and community life. More

---

4. John Paul II, *Pastores Dabo Vobis*, 119.

5. *Vita Consecrata*, no. 71.

6. *Program of Priestly Formation*, 61.

specifically, both documents establish a link between affective maturity and compassion or care for others. As we will see, higher-level emotional skills such as empathy and sympathy depend on the more basic *abilities to know and understand one's own affective or emotional experiences* (a basic definition of "emotional intelligence"). If, as we have already established, compassion and love are the strongest and most valid motives for choosing the celibate life in the first place, then proper development of one's emotional life is truly a "decisive factor" when evaluating and discerning the call to celibate chastity.

The research literature on clergy sexual offense also underscores the foundational importance of affective or emotional maturity. In my own research on child sexual offenders among Catholic priests and religious brothers, a cluster analysis of offenders' MMPIs (Minnesota Multiphasic Personality Inventory) indicated that nearly half (41%) of clergy and religious offenders were not men suffering from acute psychiatric illness or characterized by long-term personality flaws, but rather men who were best described as "emotionally and sexually underdeveloped."[7] In other words, these were individuals who had very little insight into their emotional lives, their sexual and romantic impulses, and how to relate effectively in interpersonal relationships. Simply stated, they lacked affective maturity.

While the effects of clergy sexual abuse have been devastating for the church at so many levels (especially for the victims and their families), there are other ways poor emotional maturity among priests and religious has affected the life of the church and thereby eroded the credibility of priests and religious in the eyes of the laity. Poor boundaries, failures to empathize, selfishness, emotional coldness, and poorly controlled tempers are just a few. At a time when the value of celibacy is already questioned among many sitting in our church pews, it is all the more important that celibate men and women are experienced as relatable, well-adjusted, and generous individuals, especially if we want others to follow us into the vocations of priestly and consecrated life.

---

7. Marc A. Falkenhain and others, "Cluster Analysis of Child Sexual Offenders: A Validation with Roman Catholic Priests and Brothers," *Sexual Addiction and Compulsivity* 6, no. 3 (1999): 317–36.

Emotional Competence as Affective Maturity

But how do we know exactly what it means to be affectively mature? Carolyn Saarni, a prominent researcher in the area of emotional intelligence, proposes eight skills associated with "emotional competence."[8] In the section that follows, Saarni's eight skills are explored as benchmarks for directing the formation and evaluation of affective maturity among candidates for priesthood and religious life. Although Saarni does not suggest that these are hierarchical in nature or developmentally sequential, in general, the arrangement progresses from very basic level skills (i.e., awareness of one's emotions and the emotions of others) to higher level skills associated with emotionally intelligent or competent people (i.e., capacity for empathy and sympathy).

Saarni's Eight Skills:[9]

1. Awareness of one's emotional state

2. Skill in discerning others' emotions

3. Skill in using the vocabulary of emotion

4. Capacity for empathic and sympathetic involvement in others' emotional experiences

5. Skill in understanding that inner emotional state need not correspond to outer expression

6. Skill in adaptive coping with aversive or distressing emotions

7. Awareness that the structure or nature of relationships is in part defined by both the degree of emotional immediacy or genuineness of expressive display and by the degree of reciprocity or symmetry within the relationship

8. Capacity for emotional self-efficacy

---

8. Carolyn Saarni, "Emotional Competence," in *The Handbook of Emotional Intelligence: Theory, Development, Assessment, and Application at Home, School, and in the Workplace,* ed. Reuven Bar-On and James D. A. Parker, (San Francisco: Jossey-Bass, 2000), 68–91.

9. Saarni, "Emotional Competence," 77.

Skill 1: Awareness of one's emotional state

The remainder of Saarni's identified skills for emotional competence builds on the foundation of this first one: having awareness of one's emotional state. The ability to identify what someone else is feeling, for example, depends on having experienced (and having been aware of experiencing) something similar yourself. It seems like such a basic—even universal—skill; however, there are state (situational) and trait (longer-term personality) variables at play that make this more complicated than it may seem. We all at some point use defenses such as denial or repression to keep threatening emotions out of our awareness. Grief, worry, and fear are normal emotions that we occasionally bury or deny in order to keep on functioning or to accomplish difficult things. Celibates who have distorted notions that they should not have sexual feelings or that they are "bad celibates" if they find themselves romantically attracted to another may defend against, and therefore lack awareness of, their sexual or romantic impulses. Recognized or not, emotions motivate our behaviors, and we are more likely to make appropriate choices about how to behave when we are aware of the motives behind our actions, including the emotional motives.

Beyond situational factors, there are also longer-term personality traits associated with poor emotional awareness. Overly rational individuals who rely more on intellectual knowledge and experience may see little value in or lack the skills needed to engage their emotions when processing the world around them. At a pathological level, some individuals are characterized by what mental health professionals call schizoid personality disorder. These men and women appear emotionally aloof, detached, and indifferent from situation to situation and across most or all of their relationships.

As a skill, normal emotional awareness begins developing early on when our parents and caregivers point out and label our emotions for us. "Gosh, you look really angry. What's wrong?" a parent might say to a young son or daughter. Or, "I know you are going to be upset about this, but Katie is not going to be able to come over to play this afternoon." Simple interactions such as these result in the development of insight: "Oh, this is what 'upset' feels like," or, "This is called anger—how I feel right now." Growing up in an emotionally literate and appropriately demonstrative family environment goes a long way in establishing this basic skill of being aware of one's emotional state. While efforts to remediate a total lack of awareness or to overcome a highly deficient skill in this area may be ill-fated (and not really the responsibility of a religious or priestly formation program), some candidates may need to be encouraged from time to time to pay closer attention to their feelings or increase their level of emotional awareness. Strategies such as taking time to reflect regularly on the emotional content of certain interactions or events, or stopping periodically throughout the day to monitor their internal emotional state can be helpful.

Skill 2: Skill in discerning others' emotions

The world of emotions quickly becomes two-directional, and the emotionally competent individual is able to accurately discern or read the emotional states of others. Here, a simple awareness of another's feelings is assumed, and Saarni does well to use the word "discern" to describe an activity that is data-driven. Dictionary definitions of the word "discern" include the idea that discernment involves coming to a decision about something using the information available to us. When it comes to discerning the emotions of others, we interpret not only what others are telling us (if only it were that easy!) but also what they are *not* telling us: the volume and tone of the person's speech, and all the subtle nonverbal cues such as posture, behaviors, and facial expressions. The tiniest movement of the eyebrows makes the difference between communicating sadness and anger, and a million different kinds of smiles can communicate a wide variety of emotions and intentions.

Reading the emotions of others is a highly sophisticated skill. Just as important as the ability to discern what is not stated verbally, is *not discerning* what is *not there*. Often the person opposite us is not providing enough information to allow us to interpret what he or she is feeling, and the emotionally savvy person knows when not to interpret what isn't there. How often have we thought to ourselves, "She doesn't like me" because we haven't been able read someone else's facial expressions? Or we might assume someone feels the same way we do about something in the absence of information to the contrary. When the situation is emotionally ambiguous—when there is very little information to interpret from the other person—we run the risk of "projecting" our own feelings or thoughts about how someone is feeling onto the person opposite us.

Again, the person with a high level of emotional competence (beginning with great awareness and insight into one's own emotional state) is able to recognize that there just isn't enough information to interpret and to leave it at that for now.

One other important implication worth noting is that if you are trying to discern the emotions of another person, that person is likely also engaged in interpreting and understanding your emotional state. And while it may seem obvious, the further implication is that your emotional state has an impact on other people. Your sadness brings others down. Your joy may be infectious. Your bad mood can ruin a party or cause others to wonder if they have done something wrong. This is something we all know at some level, but the emotionally skilled person is more aware of it and responds accordingly.

Skill 3: Skill in using the vocabulary of emotion

In describing this third skill, Saarni talks about the ability to use the language of one's particular culture to accurately describe how you or other people feel. As we will see, language is key to solving and coping with different emotional challenges and experiences. We have a better chance of handling and controlling all kinds of things—emotions, fears, people, illnesses, and even our pets—once we have named them. We want a diagnosis (a name for our condition) in order better to understand and cope with an illness. We use names and labels to influence and control people, for better or for worse.

When it comes to emotions, competency involves having accurate names for the myriad shades and nuances of emotional experience. When asked the question: "How are you feeling?" replying "Bad" is not a very sophisticated or helpful answer.

"Bad sad? Bad angry? Bad sick?" we follow up, hoping to point the individual in a more nuanced direction.

"Bad angry!" tells us there is more work to be done here.

Consider how many varieties of anger a person can feel: frustrated, irritated, peeved, annoyed, irate, outraged, boiling hot, disappointed in oneself, ready to punch someone! And if you think anger is complicated, think about all the feelings associated with sexuality: love, lust, attraction, desire, arousal, infatuation, loneliness, pining, obsession. Then mix in various other feelings: hurt, embarrassed, disillusioned, rejected, offended, overlooked. It's no wonder that colors are often used as metaphors or ways to name feelings. When you begin to mix and blend feelings, like colors, the spectrum is practically limitless.

The ability to discriminate between and name feelings is a skill we can develop with the assistance of others (e.g., counselors, therapists, spiritual directors, formation staff). Let us remind ourselves once more, however, that the primary work of spiritual direction and religious formation should not be psychological in nature. Close friendships and social interactions are also potential classrooms for learning how to identify and name emotions. Finally, reading novels and other forms of literature is a great way to expand affective knowledge and vocabulary. Several years ago, my mother confessed feeling that she could have been a better mother to me and my brother growing up. When I asked what she meant, she said she thought she had been a little lazy, explaining: "Often, after your dad left for work and you and your brother went to school, I would spend the entire day just reading." I was not shocked at all. I immediately thought about how fortunate I had been to be raised by a mother who devoted so much of her time to cultivating an inner life and forming herself in the ways and vocabulary of the human heart. She is one of the most emotionally competent people I know.

Skill 4: Capacity for empathic and sympathetic involvement in others' emotional experiences

Empathy is one of the ways we participate in the emotional lives of other people. It is a high-level skill associated with emotional competence, one which clearly draws on the previous three. Empathy and compassion—both words meaning to *feel with* another person—involve the ability first to identify accurately the emotional state of another; then to search one's own experience for the same or similar emotions in order ultimately to say or do something helpful for the other person.

Empathy and compassion are central to ministry and the Christian life in general, and as we have seen above, the formation documents for priesthood and religious life underline the importance of compassion and empathy as skills to be cultivated in celibate men and women. The great command to "Love your neighbor as yourself" is a commandment to be empathic or compassionate. Love by just about any definition is an expression of empathy—a laying down of one's life in response to the understood needs of others, or a placing of the interests of another above one's own.

We should briefly point out that there are also dangers and risks involved in accepting into our communities and dioceses individuals who lack the ability to empathize with others. People who lack adequate empathy are, at best, egocentric in their relationships, making them potentially problematic members of communities and organizations. Clinical narcissism, characterized by the inability or unwillingness to take another person's frame of reference into consideration—in other words, a lack of empathy—has been shown, along with a general lack of emotional awareness, to be a significant risk factor among potential clergy sex offenders.[10]

Poor empathy skills do not always lead to criminal behavior. Selfishness with one's time and possessions, reluctance to volunteer when help is needed, inconsiderate use of the community's resources, chronically avoiding work or not doing one's fair share of the work, attitudes of entitlement, and a general lack of interest in the lives of others all suggest the person is unconcerned with the needs and viewpoints of others. These further suggest the possibility of a deficit in empathy skills.

Skill 5: Skill in understanding that inner emotional state need not correspond to outer expression

Several years ago, when I led high school retreat programs for teenagers, we used to stage a skit we called "the mask skit." The general theme: that people often mask their true emotional states and that, as responsible Christians and citizens, we must always try to be sensitive to the possibility that what we say or do may affect and hold meaning for others beyond what we can readily see.

Saarni's fifth skill suggests that emotional competence involves the ability to read people more deeply—"between the lines" or in light of the circumstances of their lives—and then to respond appropriately to what we may not be able to see but know is likely to be true. "I'm doing really well," the young wife and mother says to all the concerned friends and family at her spouse's funeral. "I know you are. And I know you will be fine," you still might say, "but if or when you hit a rough patch, I am

---

10. Paul Dukro and Marc Falkenhain, "Narcissism Sets Stage for Clergy Sexual Abuse," *Human Development* 21, no. 3 (Fall 2000): 24–28.

a text away. In the meantime, I will be praying for you first thing in the morning and last thing I do before I go to bed."

Sometimes our outward emotional expressions differ from our internal state; this may be due to social convention, because of a role we are in, or because we are defending against an emotion or a threatening experience too painful to handle all at once. As mentioned previously, defense mechanisms such as denial, repression, and intellectualization can be helpful coping strategies, particularly if they allow a person to assimilate a feeling or a difficult experience in smaller, more manageable bites. If parents were to feel all the grief and worry of a child's terminal diagnosis all at once, for example, they would not be able to function.

Another thing to recognize with this fifth skill is that at times we ourselves need to produce an "outward expression" that may not be consistent with how we are feeling internally, particularly when our ministries or community obligations require us to do so. For example, a priest or chaplain stopping by the hospital to visit with the family of a dying loved one on the way home from an exciting baseball game is obviously going to need to generate an outward expression that does not communicate his or her internal state of excitement and elation. In contrast, a provincial or community leader who is worried about a significant financial crisis may still need to "put on" a celebratory face when presiding over a profession ceremony or jubilee. It happens in all walks of life. Good and effective parents find ways to avoid passing on all of their worries and fears to their children by producing emotional expressions and presentations that may be inconsistent or out of sync with how they are actually feeling.

Skill 6: Skill in adaptive coping with emotions

Adaptive coping with emotions is at the heart of emotional competence and affective maturity. Emotions animate and enrich our life experience; however, when too flattened or out of control, they may also interfere with our functioning across many different areas of our lives.

When considering how we experience our emotions, we begin by thinking about their intensity and duration. Intensity has to do with the strength or the "volume" of a particular emotional experience. Duration, of course, refers to how long the emotional response lasts. The appropriate intensity and duration depends to some degree on the type of event that provokes a particular emotion. Breaking a favorite coffee mug is likely to result in some sadness, but not the intensity of sadness that is expected upon losing a lifelong friend to cancer. A normal grief reaction in response to losing a loved one can be expected to last up to twelve or eighteen months. If feelings of sadness over the coffee mug are still consuming one's thoughts a week later, we might begin to suspect that the person's coping strategies are not terribly effective.

In general, when it comes to managing or coping with our emotions, the primary goal is to keep our emotions within a range of intensity and duration that allows them to enrich our lives, but not overtake or overwhelm us. The *Program of Priestly Formation* similarly describes a person possessing affective maturity as: "Someone whose life of feeling is in balance and integrated into thought and values; in other words, a man of feelings who is not driven by them but freely lives his life enriched by them."[11]

Cognitive psychology tells us that there is an important relationship between our thoughts and our feelings—between "cognition" and "affect"—and our emotions are often modulated (dialed up or down) by our thoughts. Certain types of thoughts can intensify and extend the duration of particular feelings. Thoughts like "I'll never be good at this"; "Why can't I ever do anything right?"; and "Nobody is ever going like me" are what cognitive psychologists call "depressogenic" thoughts because they contribute to and support depressive symptoms. They are also referred as "distorted cognitions" or faulty thoughts because they have a black-and-white quality that is rarely realistic or true (notice the use of words like *never, ever, anything,* and *nobody*). Research has shown that when people are trained to recognize and eliminate these distorted, depressogenic thoughts—in other words, change the way they think about themselves, the world, and the future—their mood improves.

Similarly, rumination or perpetually thinking or complaining about something is not helpful to improving our outlook about a situation or person we are upset with. A little venting may be helpful, but it quickly reaches a point of diminishing returns. Rehashing the event over and over intensifies and lengthens the duration of the emotional response. Individuals who are overly upset about something can try finding a way to interrupt their thoughts, perhaps by distracting themselves with some other activity to stop reinforcing the feelings of anger or frustration. Of-

11. *Program of Priestly Formation*, 31.

tentimes, once we get some physical and emotional distance from an event or situation—for example, something we are angry about, something we feel we must buy, or even the desire to engage in a morally compromising behavior—the urgency cools and our emotional state can return to a healthier or more adaptive level.

There are obvious implications here for celibacy and chastity and the skills required to avoid giving in to temptation. We will discuss this in greater depth in chapter 12 on coping with emotional and sexual attraction, but it is helpful here to speak briefly about the dynamics of emotional arousal.

At the same time that distorted thoughts can lead to and support greater intensity and duration of emotions, higher levels of emotional arousal can also result in greater levels of distorted thinking. Think of a four-year-old in the midst of a temper tantrum over being told he can't have a cookie—it is not possible to reason with him! It won't help to appeal to his rationality by telling him that it will spoil his dinner. It will not even help to show him that the cookie jar is empty. It's true with adults as well: as we become more and more emotionally aroused—whether with fear, sadness, anger, or sexual feelings—our capacity to think clearly and accurately and to use reason to modulate our emotion diminishes. There may even be a "point of no return": the point at which we become so emotionally aroused—so angry, so sad, so sexually turned on—that we are likely to do something we will later regret. Past this "point of no return," our thinking often becomes so distorted or ineffective that we are able to rationalize hurting others, harming ourselves, cheating on spouses, or breaking vows.

An important implication is that successful or adaptive coping with emotions involves early awareness and early intervention—recognizing that an emotion is becoming aroused—and employing a strategy to dial down the intensity or interrupt the duration of the emotion before it reaches a point at which it is too late for coping strategies to be effective.

One final thought relative to this critically important skill of emotional competence: Saarni describes this skill as the capacity to adaptively cope with *adverse* emotions; however, there are circumstances and contexts (and celibacy and chastity are certainly among them) when individuals are called upon to manage or cope with pleasant or enjoyable emotional experiences. Few things are more pleasant or feel greater than falling in love or being in love; and yet for celibates and for people who are married, falling in love (for married people, falling in love with someone other than one's spouse) is an emotional experience that will have to be managed and coped with in order to honor one's vows and to safeguard chastity.

Skill 7: Awareness that the structure or nature of relationships is in part defined by both the degree of emotional immediacy or genuineness of expressive display and by the degree of reciprocity or symmetry within the relationship

Although it sounds a little technical at first, Saarni's seventh skill is essentially about boundaries. We will revisit this skill in chapter 11, but let's also explore it a bit here in the context of affective maturity.

Saarni's idea is that different kinds of relationships (if they are healthy) have certain expectations with respect to how much genuine emotion we are allowed to share with another. For example, a parent-child relationship is a type of relationship. In a healthy (now we are talking "quality") parent-child relationship, we expect there to be genuine emotional exchange. If this doesn't happen, we would say that it was an unhealthy parent-child relationship. Next, we observe whether the emotional exchange is *reciprocal*—meaning does the emotional exchange travel in both directions? Yes, both the mother or father and the child express feelings with and toward one another. Finally, is the emotional exchange *symmetrical*—meaning do both parties share the same types of emotions or at the same level of depth with one another? Here the answer is no. In a parent-child relationship, the parent is not free to share emotions at the same depth as the child without compromising the quality of the relationship. Children are free, for example, to pour all of their worries, fears, and concerns out to their parents. However, their parents are not free to share with the same level of emotional honesty ("I've had a terrible day too, honey. I think your father is having an affair and I'm afraid I may lose my job!"). An emotionally competent person with good boundaries understands that "the type, nature and quality of different relationships depends, at least in part on the amount of genuine emotional exchange, and whether that exchange is reciprocal and symmetrical."[12]

We will return to this approach to conceptualizing boundaries, but we can begin thinking about the different types of relationships that come

---

12. Saarni, *Emotional Competence*, 77.

with the roles of priesthood or religious life and their accompanying expectations. In a priest-parishioner relationship, is there emotional exchange? To some degree, yes. Is that exchange reciprocal? Yes, a priest must be able to show some of his joy, his concern, his excitement with his parishioners. But is it symmetrical? No. While it is acceptable and even expected that parishioners will potentially share some very personal things with their pastor, a priest is not at liberty to share at the same level of personal and emotional depth with his parishioners. We could configure the superior–community member relationship similarly, as well as a formation director–novice relationship.

It is also very important to note that once we affiliate with a diocese or religious community and enter into a formation program, the structure of our relationship with the rest of the church changes. Like it or not, priests and religious, even seminarians and men and women in formation, become "public" people. The personal things we share about ourselves, including our emotions, opinions, and beliefs, are heard in a different way and carry a different weight than they did before. In addition, once we affiliate with a diocese or religious community in any kind of official capacity, we lose the ability to speak only for ourselves. When we do something, say something, or share something, we do so in the name of the diocese or the community and, to some degree, the church.

Being aware that our emotions play a role in the type, nature, and quality of our relationships once again presumes a basic understanding of our emotions and requires that we cope with or manage our emotions appropriately if we want those relationships to be healthy and effective. A disillusioned formation director who is angry with her community leader must be able to manage her emotional distress effectively in order not to pass on her feelings about leadership to her charges. A brother or priest who is a teacher and who finds himself attracted to one of the college students in his class must manage his emotions in order not to show them or share them with his student. Boundary keeping is a complex emotional skill that requires high levels of self-awareness, awareness and respect for the feelings of others, and effective coping skills.

Skill 8: The capacity for emotional self-efficacy

Saarni defines emotional self-efficacy as generally feeling the way we would like to feel. Self-efficacy comes through developing the rest of

Saarni's skills of emotional competence. There is probably little we need to add, except simply to point out that emotional self-efficacy, and therefore emotional competence, takes time. Although many of the seeds are sown earlier in our lives and formed in us by our parents and families, the skills of identifying, naming, coping, generating, and using our emotions does not develop overnight.

Emotional efficacy and affective maturity also take time, as all of the skills discussed here require time and attention to be practiced well. If our lives are overcrowded with commitments and distractions, we risk not allowing ourselves the time and focus needed to thoughtfully consider the emotional content of our experiences and relationships. When this is the case, we are prone to simply reacting rather than reflecting first on what emotions are motivating our reactions, what the people around us may be feeling and needing, what our particular role requires relative to how we express or manage the emotions, and what decisions or actions on our part are likely to lead to a positive emotional outcome for ourselves and others.

It is easy for priests and religious to become overextended. There are fewer and fewer of us and the demands on our time and energies are greater than ever. Still, as we have noted before, a responsible living out of our call to love more generously also requires that we spend the time and attention needed for recollection and critical self-reflection. It is tempting to say that it gets easier and will require less attention over time; however, new emotional and relational challenges will arise throughout the course of our lifetime, and affective maturity, like love and charity, will be a lifetime's work.

Summary and Conclusions

Pope John Paul has identified affective maturity as a "significant and decisive factor in the formation of candidates for the priesthood," and this emphasis is easily applied to the formation of candidates for religious life. Consequently, affective maturity has been identified as the first skill for the celibate life warranting special attention within our model for celibacy formation.

The bishops have suggested that affective maturity is evidenced by the following qualities and skills: "prudence, vigilance over body and spirit, compassion and care for others, ability to express and acknowledge emotions, and a capacity to esteem and respect interpersonal relationships between men and women."[13] In this chapter, we have reviewed Carolyn Saarni's eight skills associated with emotional competence, and we see how beautifully Saarni's work complements the list of indicators of affective maturity suggested by the bishops.

Having established some helpful benchmarks against which to evaluate the affective maturity of candidates for priesthood and religious life, let's entertain some important questions. To what degree should we expect these skills and qualities to already be in place before a man or woman enters a seminary or religious formation program, and to what degree can we expect candidates to acquire these skills in the process of formation? Because many of these skills are rudimentary and develop fairly early in our lives (e.g., awareness of one's emotions, the ability to discern the emotional states of others, the ability to empathize), candidates should, for the most part, come into formation programs with these skills basically in place. It is not, and *should* not, be the responsibility of a seminary or formation program to teach an individual how to empathize or how to be sensitive to the feelings of others. Consequently, vocation directors should also have a good understanding of these or similar benchmarks for affective maturity in order to effectively screen candidates for formation.

Having said this, we can expect the formation process to help candidates build on their basic emotional competencies and to learn how to apply these skills to a life of celibacy, ministry, and other aspects of priestly and community life. In other words, the goals of religious formation should not be to teach candidates how to empathize, but rather to help them better understand how and when empathy is necessary and important to the consecrated life. Similarly, seminary formation is not expected to teach seminarians how to identify their feelings, but rather to help them better understand how being aware of emotions is important to living as a celibate, to ministry to others, and to one's relationship with God.

At times, formation directors may be called upon to guide their charges through the process of applying the skills of affective maturity to challenging or novel situations. By reminding individuals to review their

---

13. *Program of Priestly Formation*, 38.

emotional reaction to a situation or to consider someone else's point of view, or by cuing them to use a coping strategy for dealing with a particular challenge, formation directors and spiritual directors assist their charges in mobilizing and further developing their emotional competencies. In the course of formation, whether initial or ongoing, we hope to see progress in candidates' ability to guide themselves through the process of accessing, applying, and developing their skills in the area of affective maturity.

In his Rule for monks, St. Benedict refers to the monastery as the "school of the Lord's service," and whether the environment in which we live our celibate commitment is a monastery, an apostolic community, a parish, or a school, we are reminded that our communities and the relationships that comprise them are schools for our continuing education in the affairs of the heart and in our capacities to love.

CHAPTER 10

COMMUNITY:
SUPPORT AND ACCOUNTABILITY

I t is difficult to overstate the importance of community in the life of
the celibate. If indeed conversion to Christ, the model of love, is the
aim of any priestly or religious life, then community is the crucible in
which that transformation most often takes place. One could point to the
example of hermits as an instance of the celibate "going it alone"; however,
even the Desert Fathers and Mothers of the early church sought out the
encouragement and counsel of elders to direct and support their efforts
to seek God. And although St. Benedict acknowledges the possibility of
the eremitic (solitary) life in his Rule for cenobites (community-dwelling
monks), he clearly states that the hermitage is for the exceptional few who
have already graduated from the school of community living.

We have countless ways of saying it: *No man is an island. I've got your
back. Lean on me. There is strength in numbers. I'm here for you.* In every
walk of life, there is practically universal recognition that we are healthiest,
strongest, most successful, and perhaps happiest when we are joined with
others. But why? What is it about affiliation that strengthens and protects us?

Praesidium is a child safety accreditation agency that helps religious
communities practice ethical ministry with minors. One of the standards
Praesidium (working with the Conference of Major Superiors of Men)
has established for promoting safe and healthy communities states: "The
institute will identify and utilize systems of *support and accountability* for
its Members" [emphasis added].[1]

---

1. Praesidium, "2012 Standards for Accreditation," last accessed June 9, 2017, https://
website.praesidiuminc.com/wp/wp-content/uploads/2013/05/2012_Standards_for
_Accreditation_and_Glossary.pdf.

Although this idea of "systems of support and accountability" is articulated in the specific context of child safety, these two constructs—support and accountability—are also essential for perseverance and fruitfulness in the lives of celibate men and women. Let's look at each of these in greater detail.

Support

Recent research shows that whether or not one feels interpersonally supported is one of the strongest predictors of perseverance in a religious or priestly vocation within the first five to ten years. Dean Hoge looked at diocesan priests and found two major factors that contributed to men leaving priesthood within five years of ordination. Summarizing his results, Hoge writes: "We found that most resignees had two levels of motivation: one, a feeling of loneliness or being unappreciated; two, an additional situation or event that precipitated a crisis of commitment."[2] By "crisis of commitment," Hoge cites events such as falling in love, coming to terms with one's sexuality, or experiencing a conflict with the bishop or a diocesan administrator. But what was perhaps most impressive among Hoge's findings was that *both* of these factors—feeling lonely or unappreciated and a "crisis of commitment"—had to be present in order for the individual to leave. In other words, if celibates fall in love or experience a crisis around sexuality at a time when they are feeling adequately supported and appreciated in their ministry and vocation, they will probably not leave but will work through the crisis and persevere in their celibate vocation.

Sr. Jane Becker, OSB, and I found something very similar when we were invited to explore factors related to men leaving monastic life within ten years of solemn profession. Again, what stood out was that experiences of feeling isolated, overworked, and under-supported were common within the first years of final profession. Further, these experiences, along with particular challenges to celibacy (e.g., falling in love, dealing with issues related to sexuality), were significant factors contributing to a desire to leave.[3]

2. Dean R. Hoge, *The First Five Years of the Priesthood: A Study of Newly Ordained Catholic Priests* (Collegeville, MN: Liturgical Press, 2002), 63.

3. John Mark Falkenhain and Jane Becker, "The First Ten Years of Solemn Vows: Benedictine Monks on Reasons for Leaving and Remaining in Monastic Life," *The American Benedictine Review* 59, no. 2 (June 2008): 184–97.

The importance of social and emotional support in predicting perseverance should not surprise us. A recent collaborative study on religious vocations by the National Religious Vocation Conference and the Center for Applied Research in the Apostolate indicated that one of the primary factors attracting young women and men to religious life is the opportunity to live in community.[4] The study showed that those joining religious communities were drawn to opportunities to work together, pray together, and share meals together, preferably in larger-sized communities. An especially striking finding was the inverse relationship between the number of members a congregation had living independently outside the community and the congregation's likelihood of attracting new members. Simply put, young women and men are motivated to religious life—a celibate life—largely by the opportunity to live communally. They are most vulnerable to abandoning their commitment when, even after a few years of final profession, they find themselves feeling isolated and distanced from the formation community from which they once drew much support.

Nor should we be surprised by the finding that young priests and religious often feel unsupported and isolated in the years immediately following ordination or profession. The realities of diminishing numbers and aging members in dioceses and religious communities often result in greater responsibility shouldered by fewer and fewer members. No longer, for example, can a priest expect to be one of two or three priests assigned to a single parish, living together in a rectory. Now he is more likely to be living alone and assigned to a two- or three-parish cluster. In a community of sisters whose membership has declined to half of what it was fifty years ago, it is not uncommon for members to have multiple roles and responsibilities, the result of redistributing the original work of many among the remaining few.

In diocesan and religious life alike, the gradual decline in able-bodied members has meant that, only a few years out of formation or ordination, a priest or religious is likely to have multiple jobs. Oftentimes this leaves little time for recreation with others, marginalizes important systems of support such as spiritual direction, private prayer, and devotion, and even

---

4. Mary E. Bendyna and Mary L. Gautier, "2009 Vocations Study—Executive Summary," last accessed June 9, 2017, https://nrvc.net/247/publication/913/article/1022-executive -summary-english.

hinders the ability to pray the Liturgy of the Hours. Hoge's follow-up on research with priests five to ten years post-ordination found that only 37% of diocesan priests were attending spiritual direction at least once a month (42% of religious priests) and only 62% of diocesan priests (59% of religious priests) were saying the Liturgy of the Hours on a daily basis.[5]

Interestingly, when Sr. Jane Becker and I asked recently professed religious to predict how they would cope with a serious desire to leave religious life, the most frequently named strategies were talk to someone (a superior, a friend, a confrere); "give it time"; and pray. The irony is that it is the very *lack* of these "systems of support" (especially supportive relationships and time for prayer) that motivates people to leave their commitments in the first place. The major implication is that if celibate priests and religious are going to persevere in the celibate life they have chosen, especially when crises arise, they must be proactive in identifying and utilizing their systems of support from the very beginning.

Accountability

In addition to support, another primary benefit afforded by community is accountability. Accountability is the experience, either real or perceived, of being held responsible for what one says or does.

There is a reason that ordinations and vows—even marriage vows—take place in the context of public ceremonies. Vows are made in front of the larger church so that when the commitment becomes difficult, there are many witnesses who can remind the celibates what they have promised to do and hold them accountable for keeping those promises: "No, I heard you say you would do this perpetually. Now you have to honor that vow and see what God has in store for you beyond this struggle." From time to time, we all need to be held accountable for what we have said or done.

Accountability also comes in more subtle and indirect forms, especially the accountability that accompanies daily life in a community. When our lives are connected and open to others, we are automatically prone to thinking beyond our own point of view. We see or hear our own actions and words from the perspective of another. This means we are less

5. Dean R. Hoge, *Experiences of Priests Ordained Five to Nine Years: A Study of Recently Ordained Catholic Priests* (Washington, DC: National Catholic Educational Association, 2006).

likely to do or say something questionable if we know that other people are watching or listening. We are less likely to visit questionable websites when using computers that are in public spaces. We are less likely to make off-color or suggestive remarks if we think a superior or even another community member is within hearing distance.

Oddly enough, when finally professed monks in our research were asked what they struggled most with in the first years after making solemn vows, several stated that they had a difficult time handling new levels of freedom. One religious told me before leaving his community that he was disappointed and hurt that none of his fellow community members challenged him when he began drifting away from common prayer and common meals. Strange as it may seem, not only do we *need* accountability in order stay faithful to our priestly and religious commitments, including celibacy, but often enough we *desire* accountability. We find security and comfort in knowing that if we begin to drift dangerously close to the edge of the road, there will be guardrails in place to give us the nudge we need to get back on track.

Interestingly, the research on sexual misconduct also suggests that the accountability found in community is a mitigating factor against sexual impropriety. The John Jay Report on clergy sex offenders found the incidence of sexual offense against minors among religious priests to be almost half of that among diocesan clergy (2.7 % vs 5.0% respectively).[6] While this finding also points to the potential value of emotional and psychosocial support that comes with community, it clearly suggests that living with others offers at least the perception of accountability for potentially problematic behavior, whether it be drinking, gambling, or exercising poor boundaries with adults or minors. When we live closely with others, we are more likely to have someone say, "You need to be careful in that relationship." We are also more likely to monitor our own actions more carefully: "I probably shouldn't do this. It might look a little inappropriate to members of my community."

Because it brings potentially greater levels of accountability, community also serves as an antidote to narcissism. Narcissism can be thought of extreme egocentricity or selfishness. The cardinal feature of narcissism

---

6. John Jay College of Criminal Justice, *The Nature and Scope of Sexual Abuse of Minors by Catholic Priests and Deacons in the United States 1950–2002* (Washington, DC: United States Conference of Catholic Bishops), 4.

is the inability, unwillingness, or simple neglect to take the perspective of others into account when making decisions, especially decisions that affect other people's lives. In other words, narcissism involves operating solely out of one's own frame of reference or point of view. I frequently warn the young men and women with whom I work that celibacy, especially when lived outside of the context of community, increases our risk of becoming narcissistic. Why? Because when we live on our own, we easily get out of the practice of considering the needs and wants of others in so many of the ordinary decisions we make. When you live alone, for example, who decides what time you will eat? Who decides what you will eat? Who decides what you will watch on television, what music you will listen to, which car to buy, when to go on vacation, where you will go on vacation? You, you, and only you!

Unless we are careful, unless we proactively "identify and utilize sources of support and accountability," we place ourselves at greater risk for self-centeredness and, in the extreme, narcissism—both of which undermine celibacy, which is ultimately about living and dying to self for others.

Special Systems of Support and Accountability: Internal and External Forum

It is frequently pointed out in religious life that formation is the work of the entire community. New members are formed by the example and feedback of all of the members (both peers and seniors alike) and by the daily exercises, interactions, and experiences that make up the everyday life of the community. The *Program of Priestly Formation* similarly highlights that one way human formation (which includes formation in the celibate life) is conducted is through a seminarian's "application to the tasks of seminary life." It says: "Human formation develops through interaction with others in the course of the seminary program. This growth happens, for example, when seminarians learn to accept the authority of superiors, develop the habit of using freedom with discretion, learn to act on their own initiation and do so energetically, and learn to work harmoniously with confreres and laity."[7]

7. *Program of Priestly Formation,* 5th ed. (Washington, DC: United States Conference of Catholic Bishops, 2006), 34.

Although formation is everyone's job, specific relationships and designated personnel within the larger formation community are responsible for teaching the way of life and providing the support and accountability necessary for seminarians or candidates for religious life to be formed for their specific role in the church. These personnel include formation directors, vocation directors, religious superiors, spiritual directors, confessors, and sometimes counselors or psychologists. In differing degrees and situations, men and women in formation receive instruction, support, and accountability from these various individuals identified to assist in their formation.

Canon law helps us to sort out these various relationships by classifying them as occurring in either the "internal forum" or the "external forum." Relationships in the internal forum include spiritual direction and confession and afford the candidate particular levels of confidentiality—this means that spiritual directors and confessors are prohibited from participating in the evaluations of their directees or confessees. Although they do not fall under the jurisdiction of canon law, counseling or psychologist-client relationships are also guaranteed confidentiality (within certain limits) by civil law. Consequently, information shared in counseling or psychotherapy cannot be used as part of the candidate's evaluation without the candidate's written permission.

Internal forum and counseling relationships are important in the formation process because they can offer support as well as a safe space in which to explore often threatening and messy issues, including those related to celibacy and sexuality (e.g., sexual identity, sexual and romantic attraction, dealing with temptation). These relationships are also rich in their capacity to offer a certain level of accountability—for example, by pressing candidates to address issues that are problematic or contrary to a commitment to celibate chastity (e.g., sexual naïveté, pornography use, engaging in genital sexual activity).

By comparison, relationships in the external forum are entered into with personnel who are responsible for representing not only the interest of the individual candidate, but also (and one might say, *primarily*) the interest of the entire church or the larger community. Consequently, personnel and relationships defined by canon law as falling in the external forum (e.g., rectors, formation directors, religious superiors) must be free to use acquired information in the public evaluation of candidates, such as yearly seminary evaluations, reports to diocesan vocation directors or bishops, and chapter or community meetings where members are presented and voted upon for profession or continuance in formation. Because discernment of a religious or priestly vocation always involves two parties (i.e., the candidate and the diocese or the community), the community or diocese must have adequate knowledge about the character and suitability of candidates in order to freely choose whether to accept them for profession or ordination.

Support and accountability can be similarly found in both external and internal forum relationships. It is worth acknowledging, however, that external forum relationships carry more weight in their capacity to offer accountability since individuals in the external forum have greater influence over the candidate's future with the community or diocese.

"Utilizing" Community as a Skill for the Celibate Life

In the preceding pages we described the importance of community as a source of both the support and accountability needed for a fruitful and enduring life of celibate chastity. But what *skill* is involved in having a community that offers these benefits? The needed skill relates to how one draws upon or utilizes the community in order to live a celibate life that is healthy, fruitful, and consistent with the church's vision.

It should be pointed out that the skill of utilizing the benefits that community offers is cultivated across the entire span of the celibate's life. Celibates should anticipate that this skill will become not only more *critical* as time goes on, but also more their personal responsibility once the years of initial formation are completed. It would be nice, of course, if the bishop or the local superior were regularly and perpetually to ask individual members of the community or presbyterate about their spiritual direction, private prayer, supportive relationships, and use of the sacrament of penance; however, a newly ordained or professed celibate shouldn't count on this.

Newly ordained priests and newly professed religious often struggle with the transition from initial formation to ordained priesthood or to life as a finally professed member of the community. Consequently, it is strongly recommended that as men and women approach the conclusion of their initial formation that they clearly and specifically identify who their sources of support and accountability will be once they leave the more structured, supportive environment of the seminary or formation community.

In terms of what it means to *utilize* these systems of support and accountability, some specific aspects are especially worth attending to. Spiritual direction, the sacrament of reconciliation, and counseling are all practices that must be approached with an attitude of transparency and faith in order for them truly to benefit the individual and foster transformation and conversion. Similarly, celibates must be willing to make themselves appropriately vulnerable in relationships from which they hope to draw support and accountability. Individuals cannot expect to receive the support they need, when they need it, if they don't allow their fellow priests or religious, community members, and trusted others to see their struggles and then to ask for their help. Unfortunately, men and women in helping professions (including ministry) often struggle to admit when they need help. They often feel inhibited to display their vulnerability for fear that if they appear weak or needy, others will judge them as unfit for ministry or community life. The opposite is true, however, and research on impaired professionals suggests that caregivers are most at risk of being ineffective and even harmful to others when they deny their limitations or try to keep the vulnerabilities they are experiencing to themselves.

There is also skill involved in correctly distinguishing between internal and external forum relationships, and knowing when to use them accordingly. Occasionally, individuals limit their handling of an important or personal issue to internal forum relationships only. This is not necessarily an inappropriate strategy, especially if in the course of spiritual direction, confession, or counseling, they are able to appropriately resolve the issue or make satisfactory progress in addressing a problematic behavior or relationship. This strategy can become problematic, however, in a number of situations: when an issue cannot or is not being adequately addressed or resolved in the internal forum; when there are clear implications for the well-being of the larger community or church; or when critical information is needed by personnel in the external forum in order to adequately discern the community's or diocese's interests in the ongoing relationship with the candidate. Let's explore some of these points.

Case study 1: Sr. Julia

> *Sr. Julia is a twenty-seven-year-old sister in her second year of temporary vows. For the last two years, since the completion of her novitiate, she has been living in a smaller community with three other*

sisters (all of whom are at least twenty years older than she) and teaching at a local Catholic elementary school. One of only two sisters on faculty at the school, Sr. Julia befriends several lay teachers closer to her age and eventually develops an intimate friendship with one of them in particular. After several months, the relationship becomes physical and romantic. Sr. Julia brings this to her spiritual director, with whom she meets once a month. Her spiritual director is supportive, helping her to understand her loneliness and vulnerability to falling in love, especially in light of her living situation and the limited support she receives from her community as a result of the busy and conflicting schedules of the other sisters with whom she lives. Julia's spiritual director also challenges her by pointing out the inconsistency of the romantic relationship with her vows and recommends taking the matter to confession. Julia complies with this recommendation, but continues hiding the relationship from her fellow community members and her superiors. Julia justifies her silence by convincing herself that she is "working out the issue in spiritual direction and confession."

Case study 2: Paul

Paul is a third-year seminarian preparing for his ordination to the deaconate. He has a history of using internet pornography and was confronted by his seminary rector during his first year of theological studies when the seminary's internet filter detected that Paul was visiting inappropriate websites. At that time, Paul was referred for counseling and was also encouraged to address these concerns in confession and spiritual direction. Paul complied with these requests and has continued in psychotherapy for the last two years. In that time, despite ongoing treatment, Paul's internet pornography use has escalated, but he has also become more sophisticated at finding ways around the institutional filters so he does not get caught by seminary officials. Paul frequently states that he wants to quit using pornography; however, his longest period of sobriety has lasted only three weeks. As he approaches ordination, Paul continues to use internet pornography several times a week and has become involved in pornography sites where he has had to pay fees for use as well as fees to hide his involvement.

Paul's spiritual director and therapist have challenged him several times to consider whether he is really called to celibacy and the priesthood. Paul minimizes these concerns, reminding himself that he knows other seminarians who have struggled with online pornography at one time or another. Paul is also convinced that he is called to be a priest because he receives excellent feedback about his preaching and pastoral skills at his supervised ministry sites. He is making excellent progress in his coursework and has been encouraged by one of his professors to consider doctoral work in the future. In spiritual direction and counseling, Paul continues to state that he would like to quit using pornography, but he tells his director and therapist that he suspects that "like my patron, St. Paul, I am probably just going to have accept this 'thorn in the flesh' and learn to live with it." He feels that as long as he is talking to his spiritual director and counselor, and taking the issue to confession regularly, he is "doing all [he] can to address the problem."

On his yearly self-evaluation for the seminary, on the question about his progress in the celibate life, Paul crafts a careful response that, although not technically false, is also not fully truthful: "My seminary formation has helped me to grow in my understanding of myself as a sexual person. Temptations in the past have helped me learn to recognize my limitations and understand that being a good celibate does not mean that I will never be tempted, but that I will have to continue to be vigilant and hone my skills at recognizing temptations and coping with them with the support of friends, spiritual direction, and the sacraments."

In both cases, Julia and Paul have limited their discussion of celibacy-related challenges to the internal forum. Both are drawing support and some level of accountability from spiritual direction, confession, and, in Paul's case, counseling; however, as time goes on, the limits of the support and accountability these relationships can offer become more pronounced. In Julia's case, for example, her superiors and formation directors might be able to help her explore a more satisfactory living situation as well as assist her in better staying connected to her peers in the community (i.e., increased support). But Julia's strong hesitation to share her concerns with these external forum personnel prevents this from happening. She is likely fearful that if her superiors find out about the relationship, she will be forced either to give it up right away or leave the community (i.e., increased accountability).

Paul's situation is similar to Julia's in that he doesn't face any "real" and immediate consequences for his problematic behavior as long as discussion of it is confined to the internal forum. A spiritual director, confessor, or counselor might appropriately suggest to Paul that his escalating and intractable pornography use may mean he is not ready for a lifelong commitment to celibate chastity and therefore recommend that he not move forward with ordination. Ultimately the spiritual director has no power to prevent Paul's ordination or even to raise his concerns to the formation staff or diocese due to the limits of confidentiality characterizing this internal forum relationship. Paul's spiritual director might appeal to Paul's theological sense and remind him that his suitability for ordination must be discerned by both parties—Paul himself and the diocese—and that by withholding pertinent information, he is not allowing the church to make a free choice in the matter. Still, he cannot force Paul to disclose this information.

Paul's or Julia's spiritual director or counselor might raise the level of accountability by asking hypothetical questions, such as "If your rector/ superior knew about this, what would he say about your continuing in formation?" and "What rationale legitimately justifies not telling your formation director about this at this time?" A spiritual director or counselor might also be able to move candidates closer to sharing the information needed in the external forum by inviting them to make an agreement stipulating concrete signs of progress (or lack thereof). For example, Julia's spiritual director or counselor might ask, "Could you agree that if you have not taken steps to end the relationship before our next appointment that we will ask to meet together with your formation director and ask for her assistance in deciding where to go from here?" Or in Paul's case, his spiritual director or counselor might suggest generating a schedule of concrete goals for ending his use of pornography and suggest that he tell his rector, vocation director, or bishop if any of these are not met according to the agreed-upon schedule.

In the end, candidates must be assisted in judging when and how to move issues from the internal forum to the external forum. This is particularly important for accessing greater levels of needed support and accountability and for maximizing the freedom of both parties to discern the candidate's call to a life of celibacy.

Summary and Conclusions

In this chapter, we have explored the importance of being able to draw on community and, specifically, one's sources of support and accountability as important skills for persevering in the celibate life in a meaningful and fruitful way. The types and availability of different kinds of support systems will vary from vocation to vocation, but may include the following:

- close relationships

- living with others

- common meals and prayer

- priest support groups

- common recreation

- mentoring

- sacramental life

- adequate time and support for prayer

- the good example and witness of other priests or community members

- spiritual direction

- counseling

Sources or systems of accountability may vary depending on the type of vocation, but are also likely to include the following:

- close relationships

- living with others

- spiritual direction

- counseling

- sacrament of reconciliation

- community culpa services

- yearly evaluations

- ◆ regular meetings with superiors or formation directors

- ◆ cell/room visitations

These lists include more general sources of support and accountability; however, certain issues or concerns may warrant more specific types. When dealing with internet pornography, substance abuse, or other types of addictions or compulsions, the following may be important sources of support and accountability: website tracking software; "sponsors" or accountability partners; twelve-step groups; or specialized medical support.

Identifying sources of support and accountability should be an early goal for formation. New community members or first-year seminarians may need some initial assistance and direction in identifying these. As candidates progress in initial formation, they should be able to recognize how their systems of support and accountability have changed over time, and identify upon what and whom they are currently relying. Ultimately, prior to ordination or final profession, we should expect candidates to be able to articulate particular instances in which they have utilized specific sources of support and accountability to help them grow in holiness and perseverance in the celibate life.

CHAPTER 11

Establishing and Maintaining
Effective Boundaries

The previous chapter on sources of support and accountability
provides a nice segue into a discussion of establishing and maintaining effective boundaries as an essential skill for living the celibate life. Most often, discussions on boundaries focus on the dangers of
having inadequate or overly porous interpersonal boundaries. You know
the type: the man or woman who shares too much personal information
with virtual strangers, or the person who is disrespectful of others' pri-
vacy and personal space. Because people with these boundary types are
easy to spot and because they can be socially disruptive in obvious ways,
we tend to focus on them. But there is also the equally potent danger of
establishing boundaries that are too forbidding and impermeable. Here
we're talking about the man who isolates himself and keeps everything
inside, or the woman who never lets anyone see her vulnerabilities and
never opens herself up to receiving the support or feedback she needs but
doesn't really desire. We'll name these two extreme boundary types "Too
Much Information (TMI) Tammy/Tommy" and "Brick," and proceed to
spend a little time with each of them on the way to considering what it
means to maintain healthy boundaries.

TMI Tammys/Tommys

One morning several years ago, I took a confrere to the doctor's office
for a minor medical procedure. When we arrived for the appointment, we
were the only ones in the fairly large waiting room, and after my brother was

taken back for the procedure, I remained alone in the waiting area looking through the smorgasbord of available magazines. After a few minutes, a woman whom I didn't know entered and passed up about twenty empty chairs before choosing the chair right next to mine. A red flag went up!

"I'm so worried," she began. (Don't make eye contact, I thought.)

"It's my daughter," she continued. "She's in there and I have no idea how she's going to handle this. She's really not well, you know. She suffers terribly from nerves and headaches, and she barely sleeps at all. She gets that from me. I never sleep. I just can't. I lie awake all night and think about things and remember things. My doctor says it's anxiety and it probably is. Mental health problems run through our whole family. I have a history of abuse—I'm sure that's where it came from—and nervous breakdowns run in my husband's family. Of course, we divorced a few years ago, but still . . ."

Mind you, I was not wearing my habit, nor did I have my "Talk to me: I'm a psychologist" T-shirt on. We had never met, and I didn't even learn her name. But I am going to call her "Tammy."

Tammy (or Tommy—this type is found among men too) is a stereotype, though such individuals certainly do exist. Tammys and Tommys tend to be very social. More than prefer, they *need* other people to help define them, to give them feedback, to support them and tell them they are okay. Beyond needing other people, they need to *be needed* by other people. They are very suggestible and susceptible to cues from others to tell them how to act, what to believe, what to like, and what is acceptable.

Tammys and Tommys are very sensitive to being liked or disliked, and they don't tolerate being left alone for too long. With limited capacity for introspection, Tammys and Tommys have ravenous appetites for social reinforcement, filling moments of quiet, and fighting off solitude or boredom with text messages, Facebook posts, emails, and telephone calls.

Tammys and Tommys have inadequate filters. They have a poor sense of what not to share and when not to share it. Their friends and associates constantly give them this feedback: TMI! (too much information!). Because Tammys and Tommys are outgoing and open with others, they sometimes make great first impressions, especially if the first encounter is brief. But with additional exposure, these folks quickly become overwhelming.

In ministry, Tammys and Tommys are complicated. They may be drawn to ministry because they feel strongly that they want to help others; however, they are at high risk of confusing "helping others" with getting their own social and emotional needs met. They may experience their sensitivity to people and their ability to make quick emotional connections as gifts for ministry; however, they often lack the discretion needed to keep them from overidentifying with their parishioners, clients, or students. They assume the person with whom they are interacting feels exactly what they feel (or have felt) and may respond with anger, hurt, rejection, or even a desire to retaliate if the other person backs off, asks for space, or tries in some other way to set a boundary.

When it comes to celibacy, Tammys and Tommys are prone to misinterpreting the meaning of others' gestures or emotional displays, as well as misjudging their own actions. Because she has a difficult time separating her emotional experience from another's, a Tammy may assume that if she is feeling romantically or sexually attracted to somebody, the other person also feels the same thing. Based on the same inability to separate feelings, a Tommy may miss the sexual or romantic valence in another person's actions or communications, simply because he (Tommy) does not feel a sexual or romantic attraction himself. As a result, he may even flirt or make suggestive comments, thinking "It doesn't mean anything" when actually the other person is interpreting his actions seriously and feeling led on by him.

Celibacy is also likely to be a challenge for individuals with poorly developed boundaries due to the difficulty they have with tolerating aloneness. In religious life in particular, Tammys and Tommys may struggle to figure out how to live in close proximity to others without becoming too emotionally involved. In such cases, the issue is not necessarily how to avoid romantic or sexual involvement, but rather how not to be overly affected by the emotions of others and how to be sensitive to the effects of their own emotional displays on the people with whom they live. I often explain to candidates with whom I work that living in a religious community is like living on a small island with a large number of people. We have to learn how to manage our personalities (including our emotions) in such a way that they take up a little less interpersonal space.

Bricks

Bricks (named after the metaphorical brick wall they surround themselves with) are at the opposite end of the boundary spectrum. I always know a Brick when, at a reception, a meeting, or in an interview with a potential candidate, I feel like I am playing a game of interpersonal catch with a padded wall. You keep tossing questions in an effort to make conversation—Oh, where are you from? Have you lived there long? What do you do there? Do you enjoy it? Do you have family around?—only to get single-word answers and a conversation that is never tossed back in your direction with questions such as: How about yourself? How did you get into this line of work? Does your family live around here?

In contrast to Tammys and Tommys, Bricks let very few people, if anyone, into their emotional world. Sometimes there is a veneer of sociability, but one's knowledge of a Brick (who he or she *really* is) rarely grows over time. They let us see very little, and the type of emotional exchange that signifies intimacy in most relationships (i.e., occasional revelations of vulnerability or disclosures of a personal nature) seldom happens. Whether it is because they are unable or unwilling, or adhering to some notion that it is unacceptable, Bricks show little interest in or need for social reinforcement or emotional support. They prefer to deal with challenges, problems, and crises alone.

Bricks are sometimes interested in priestly or religious life because they perceive celibacy as a perfect way to meet their desire to be left alone. They may also interpret their minimal social interests as a clear sign they are called to celibacy. This latter notion, of course, should be challenged. As we have already established, celibacy requires the ability to draw support and accountability from community, not the ability to get along without needing others.

In ministry, Bricks are often wooden, inaccessible, and problem-focused at the expense of being warm, welcoming, and pastoral. If Tommys tend to overidentify with the emotions of a grieving spouse or an angry parishioner, Bricks more often appear unmoved by others' plights and jump quickly to offering solutions without expressing genuine sympathy for the parishioner's grief or anger. When it comes to working with others, collaboration is too messy for them; consequently, Bricks are prone to either under-delegating or over-delegating—anything to avoid having to deal with others too long or too closely.

In an effort to keep interested parties away, Bricks can either put on a glossy but never-changing expression of pleasant politeness, or discourage interaction altogether with an affect that is perpetually sullen and unapproachable. Either way, metaphorically speaking, Bricks shutter the windows of their house, dig moats around the perimeter of their property, and open the door only wide enough to slip in and out, in order to make sure that nobody gets a peek inside their highly protected domain.

Probably the greatest tragedy in my own community's history was the suicide of one of our brightest and most talented members several years ago. A canon lawyer and a gifted teacher who had served in many leadership positions in our community, including formation director and academic dean, this confrere struggled mightily but privately with depression, perfectionism, and loneliness, turning increasingly to alcohol to help him cope. Sadly, few of us knew of his struggles, and although he suffered intensely in private, he put on a brave face in public and performed his duties without any external indication that anything was terribly wrong. He finally revealed his unbearable distress, anger, and suffering in his suicide note.

Healthy Boundaries

Examining extreme boundary types like Tammys or Tommys and Bricks can help us to define healthy and effective boundaries. To this end, it might also be helpful to back up and give some thought to other types of boundaries—those that exist outside the context of interpersonal relationships.

In the concrete, practical world, boundaries include fences, borders, walls, lines on basketball courts and playing fields, and lines on roads and crosswalks. In whatever form, boundaries serve a number of important functions. They define a person's property and distinguish between what is yours and what is mine. They protect—sometimes by keeping things in, sometimes by keeping things out—and they can indicate zones of safety and zones of danger. Boundaries on ball fields and tennis courts facilitate play and cooperation, making clear what is foul territory and what is fair game. Efforts are undertaken to mark boundaries more clearly when there is doubt, and players can take a time-out or be sidelined when rest is needed or the game becomes too intense. Where boundaries have been trespassed, fences are often built higher and walls are fortified. Where war and violence have occurred, borders are oftentimes altered, and the distinction between what was mine and what was yours no longer applies.

Interpersonal boundaries operate in many of these same ways and serve all of the same functions. People with healthy or effective boundaries have a clear sense (or definition) of who they are and are generally able to establish which feelings, which experiences, how much of the blame, how much credit, and how much of the world's attention belong to them. "It's not *all* about you," we like to say. But *some* of it is.

Men and women with healthy boundaries are able to protect their vulnerability from being freely trampled on by others. But the same walls that define and protect must also have doors through which people can invite appropriate others in so they can share joys, sorrows, fears, and accomplishments.

Robert Frost famously wrote: "Good fences make good neighbors," but what exactly do we mean by "good"? Walls that are too low or too unstable may offer very little protection and prove ineffective at keeping those who have a bulldog of a temper from wreaking havoc all over their neighbor's feelings and rights. On the other hand, personal walls that are too tall and too thick result in a stagnant interior wherein ferocious tempers never get aired out and run the risk of turning on the owners themselves.

What accounts for boundary styles like those of Bricks and Tammys/Tommys? Experiences of hurt or trauma often cause individuals to develop extreme boundary types. Individuals with histories of being sexually abused, for example, may respond to the forced violation of their boundaries by building fortresses around themselves in an effort to guarantee that no one will ever harm them again. Others respond to such violations by giving up on boundaries altogether, assuming that all that was valuable about themselves has already been taken and that there is nothing left worth protecting (if it were even possible to protect it).

Revisiting Emotional Competence

Carolyn Saarni offers an excellent description of effective boundaries in her work on emotional competence. Recall Saarni's seventh skill for emotional competence from our previous chapter on affective maturity: "Awareness that the structure or nature of relationships is in part defined by both the degree of emotional immediacy or genuineness of expressive display and by the degree of reciprocity or symmetry within the relationship."[1] It's a mouthful, but Saarni's point is that different kinds of relationships carry different expectations with regard to how much and what kind of personal and emotional information is shared. This is

1. Carolyn Saarni, "Emotional Competence: A Developmental Perspective," In *The Handbook of Emotional Intelligence*, ed. Reuven Bar-On and James D. A. Parker (San Francisco, CA: Jossey-Bass, 2000), 77.

basic to an understanding of boundaries as well as to our capacity for establishing and maintaining them effectively.

When we recognize that other people have exercised poor boundaries, we can see that they have shared too much with the wrong person—in other words, they have allowed a "degree of emotional immediacy or genuineness of expressive display" in a relationship where such sharing was either (a) not supposed to go both ways ("reciprocity") and/or (b) was not supposed to occur on an equal level of depth ("symmetry"). To use a concrete example, we would say that a therapist had exercised poor boundaries with her patient if, in response to the patient's expressing grief over his marital difficulties, the therapist also broke down, crying and sharing everything that was going wrong in her own marriage. In contrast, a close friendship allows for both reciprocity *and* symmetry of genuine emotional exchange.

This concept is complex, though, and there are lots of subtleties. This is why many people often struggle with boundaries. Back to the therapist: we do expect therapists to show *some* emotional display; if not, they would come off as too wooden and seem unsympathetic. At the same time, if the therapeutic relationship is going to be an effective one, therapists can't show too much or share too often. They must recognize that their sharing should be less frequent and not at the same depth as what their patients share.

Below is a chart that maps out the dynamics of emotional display or exchange for a number of different types of *healthy* relationships:

Type of Relationship	Is emotional exchange expected?	Is the exchange reciprocal?	Is the exchange symmetrical?
Best Friends	Yes	Yes	Yes
Husband-Wife	Yes	Yes	Yes
Teacher-Student	Yes	Yes	No
Accountant-Client	Yes	No	No

Now, how would you categorize the following, assuming the relationships are healthy and good boundaries are in place?

Type of Relationship	Expectation of emotional display?	Is the exchange reciprocal?	Is the exchange symmetrical?
Priest-Parishioner			
Formation Director–Candidate			
Religious Sister–Sister Relationship			
Community Member– Vocation Guest			
Superior–Community Member			
Religious Sister–Coworker			

Power Differentials and Dual Relationships

When determining how much personal or emotional information should be shared between two people (and therefore what the boundaries will look like), it's important to consider the power dynamics involved in the relationship. The phrase "power differential" is used to describe a relationship in which one of the participants has more power to influence the life of the other. The practice laws and ethics codes of mental health providers, for example, consider sexual relationships between therapists and their clients to be illegal because it is universally recognized that the therapist has more power to influence the patient than the patient has to influence the therapist. This is also one of the primary premises upon which we agree that sex between an adult and a minor is illegal.

In most of the relationships listed in the charts above, there is a recognized inequality of influence (or power differential) that leads us to conclude that there cannot always be symmetry when it comes to depth of personal or emotional exchange. It is not fair for college professors to unload all of their frustrations about the university or discuss their sexual feelings with individual students because professors have more power than students. If, for example, a professor shared information that made a student uncomfortable (and it likely would), the student may not feel comfortable or free to complain or tell the professor to stop, fearing that doing so might negatively affect his or her grade or academic standing.

Sometimes power differentials are not as obvious. A sister who works in the same department and at the same level of employment as a lay coworker in an institution sponsored by the sister's community may not realize a power differential even exists. Yet, as a result of her affiliation with the community, she is not as free to develop the type of friendship with her colleague that includes a completely symmetrical level of personal sharing and emotional exchange. Even if the sister has no direct authority over the work of her colleague, the lay coworker is still likely to be aware that she works for and therefore is dependent on the sister's community for her livelihood. The coworker may be mindful, for example, that if she were to complain about her work or the institution (even if the sister shared those frustrations), it could come back to haunt her—especially if the sister ever decided to share the coworker's complaints at home with one of the others sisters in administration. Because power differentials can be very subtle, they are often overlooked or forgotten. Also, the person with the greater amount of power is often more likely to overlook or forget about the power differential. People with less influence are almost always aware that they hold less power in the relationship.

Finally, the possibility of dual relationships is another important factor to consider in determining whether personal sharing and emotional displays are appropriate. As the name suggests, dual relationships occur when two people are involved in more than one type of relationship with one another. This becomes especially problematic when the rules of one relationship are different from those of the other, or when the distribution of power in one of the relationships is different from that in the other. We could all probably agree, for example, that it is problematic for a seminary rector to relate to one of his seminarians as a close personal friend. It is a dual relationship: a friendship on the one hand, and an authority-subordinate relationship on the other. The problem lies in the fact that rules of friendship (which allow for reciprocal and symmetrical emotional exchange) are different from the rules of an authority-subordinate relationship (where there is not freedom for reciprocal and symmetrical emotional display because there is not an equal distribution of power). What would happen, for example, if the seminarian (operating out the *friendship* role) told the rector about personal information that the rector (operating out of the *rector* role) determines must be shared with the seminarian's vocation director or bishop? Confusion, a sense of betrayal, and possible ethical complaints would likely ensue.

Many priests and religious function in situations in which dual relationships are unavoidable or, at best, very difficult to avoid, especially over time:

- A confrere who was once your peer and close friend is now appointed prior of your community. Can he still be your friend?

- A lay employee in a school run by your community complains to you about one of your confreres with whom you live and who also happens to be your local religious superior. You are caught in the middle.

- A priest in a very rural diocese is assigned to a parish a hundred miles from the next priest and any of his family. Should he develop a close friendship with one of his parishioners?

We should work to avoid dual or multiple relationships wherever we can; however, the realities of parish and community life often makes this impossible. When this is the case, we must proceed with extreme care, frequent self-reflection, openness to the input of others, and sensitivity to the needs and experience of all parties involved.

Public Persona

Newcomers to religious and priestly formation are often unaware that their affiliation with a community or a diocese brings with it a degree of power and an official role in relation to the larger church. Priests, sisters, brothers—even seminarians and novices—have a canonical status in the church and are perceived by many as representing the church in official ways. A certain degree of influence (or power) comes with this affiliation and, as a result, men and women in religious and priestly formation are no longer free to express personal opinions, values, and experiences without representing their community, diocese, and, to some degree, the institutional church. Seminarian and candidates for religious life enter into a specific kind of relationship with the rest of the church, and as Saarni has pointed out, that relationship (if it is going to be an appropriate and healthy relationship) is partially defined by certain demands with respect to what, how, and with whom the candidates share personal information, including their thoughts, feelings, experiences, opinions, and frustrations.

Like it or not, priests and religious are "public people." This means that others take particular interest in and pay special attention to what priests, seminarians, religious men and women, and candidates for religious life do and say. It takes a little getting used to, and the young monks in my community are always caught off guard the first time someone they don't know approaches them and says, "You're Brother Matthew! I read about you in the newsletter. I'm from Iowa too, and I really love that you decided to become a monk. How did you come to decide to join a monastery?" When young members or seminarians complain about this kind of unexpected interest, they must be reminded that they have invited this attention by answering God's call to be a witness to his kingdom. As priests and religious, we no longer belong entirely to ourselves; we belong to the larger church. And while our vocation affords us a greater degree of power to witness to a love much greater than our own, it also brings with it a greater capacity to mislead or scandalize others when what we say or do is contrary to that witness.

Boundaries with Things and Activities

While the focus of this chapter is primarily on establishing and maintaining interpersonal boundaries as a critical skill for living the celibate life, we would be remiss not to point out, at least briefly, that much of what we have had to say about interpersonal boundaries can also be applied to our relationship with things, activities, technology, and non-human beings such as pets.

Several years ago, I was asked to give some talks to a group of religious sisters about substance abuse and addictions. We discovered that by using the metaphor of relationships, we were able more clearly and decisively to determine when certain kinds of activities and the use of particular things become problematic. We began with this question: How would you know if one of your seminarian's or candidate's relationship with another person was unhealthy? The answers were unanimous: when he is spending most of his time with the other person and withdrawing from community life; when aspects of her relationship with the other person is inconsistent with her vows or promises; or when the relationship is a source of potential scandal to others.

These same criteria apply to our relationship with activities and objects. If a monk is spending so much time working that he is increasingly skipping out on prayer or community exercises such as meals and recreation, then we might say he has an unhealthy relationship (or ineffective boundaries) with his work. Similarly, a sister who increasingly uses community recreation time or time designated for private prayer to catch up on Facebook, to shop online, or to read political blogs might be falling into an unhealthy relationship with technology. Finally, a priest who reports that his dog is his primary source of support and emotional satisfaction may need to be challenged regarding the correct prioritization of his relationships. Pets are wonderful and can be a great source of joy in our lives; however, they are a not a substitute for investing in close and appropriate human relationships. From time to time, I hear pet owners say that they prefer animals to people because they are more consistently loving and easier to relate to. It is probably true—pets are *easier* to relate to in that they aren't ever petty, sarcastic, inconsiderate, or confusing in the messages they send. On the other hand, pets are not capable of providing the type of community support and accountability that leads to conversion: calling us on our faults and negligence, reminding us to be more polite to others, challenging us to pray more often, inquiring about our loneliness, helping us cope with difficulties in ministry.

Finally, the ways celibates relate to and set boundaries with the many competing demands for our time, attention, and affection must always be examined in relation to the primary relationship we have committed ourselves to as priests, sisters, and brothers: a relationship with God and his people. When our relationships with things, activities, or individuals take priority over our particular commitment to love, then we need to revisit our boundaries in order to more effectively protect, define, and facilitate the charism of our vocation.

Summary and Conclusions

In this chapter, we have explored two different extreme boundary styles—"Tammys/Tommys" and "Bricks"—to help us think about what heathy and effective boundaries look like and how they function. We have also discussed concepts of power differentials, dual relationships, and public persona when considering what kind of emotional and personal sharing is appropriate within different kinds of relationships.

Most of us like to think we have strong, healthy boundaries, and you may have even been congratulating yourself on not being a "Tammy/Tommy" or a "Brick." Still, keeping a constant eye on how we relate to others is an especially important practice and skill in the pursuit of the celibate life. We are constantly forming new relationships, and our existing relationships within our communities, workplaces, and parishes shift and change over time. It is rare for any of us to occupy—especially at *all* times and in *every* situation—the sweet spot of having good, solid, and effective boundaries.

Part of having a healthy and adaptive personality style when it comes to boundaries involves developing insight about your own boundary tendencies (i.e., do you tend to develop too-loose or too-rigid boundaries?) and under what situational variables your style becomes more extreme. If you are uncertain whether you are more of a Tammy/Tommy or more of Brick, consider spending a little time listening to yourself and to the feedback you receive from your peers, friends, and family. People often try to give us feedback about our personalities through their teasing and pointed comments. If in response to your sharing, friends or colleagues laughingly, but frequently say, "Uh . . . too much information!" or "We didn't really need to hear that!" chances are good that your boundaries are too loose. Similarly, if you catch yourself prefacing comments with the phrase, "I probably shouldn't share this, but . . . ," you are probably a bit of a Tammy/Tommy and you really shouldn't share this! On the other hand, if you rarely ask a friend for advice, hardly ever lean on another for emotional support, or have never really considered what other people think of you, you may be living behind a bit of a "Brick" wall.

In the life of a celibate, establishing and maintaining effective boundaries are critical skills. Not only do healthy boundaries help to safeguard celibate chastity, but they are also crucial to our fulfilling the end to which our celibacy is aimed: to preach boldly and credibly the love of God and the coming of his kingdom in our very midst.

CHAPTER 12

COPING WITH ROMANTIC
AND SEXUAL ATTRACTION

In her book *The Cloister Walk*, Kathleen Norris, a married laywoman writing about Benedictine spirituality, includes a chapter entitled "Learning to Love: Benedictine Women on Celibacy and Relationship." In what turns out to be an engaging and occasionally humorous discussion of celibacy, Norris recounts her interview with an elderly sister who tells a story of falling in love as a young sister while still in formation. The sister communicates what she had learned from the experience: that infatuation is a part of her, that she enjoyed the feeling of being in love, and that falling in love was probably going to be an occasional if not regular part of pursuing a relationship with God as a celibate. Accepting the inevitability of romantic and even sexual attraction to others, the sister ultimately comes to understand that the critical issue is not whether one falls in love, but rather how one responds in the face of the experience. She tells the author: "I finally realized . . . that I had to keep in mind that my primary relationship is with God. And all of my decisions about love had to be made in the light of that person."[1]

This personal account beautifully parallels Pope John Paul's remarks about celibacy in *Pastores Dabo Vobis*, his document on priestly formation: "Since the charism of celibacy, even when it is genuine and has proved itself, leaves man's affections and his instinctive impulses intact, candidates to the priesthood need an affective maturity which is prudent,

1. Kathleen Norris, *The Cloister Walk* (New York: Riverhead Books, 1996), 251.

able to renounce anything that is a threat to it, vigilant over both body and spirit, and capable of esteem and respect in interpersonal relationships between men and women."[2]

In our naiveté, we sometimes imagine that the safest path to celibate chastity is either to try to rid ourselves of our sexual and romantic desires completely, or to carefully avoid any situation in which we might be sexually tempted or romantically stimulated. With this mind-set, celibates try to go about life meticulously guarding their eyes, ears, and mind from any books, magazines, movies, conversations, or billboards that could stir sexual feelings or excite the romantic imagination. But in a world as highly sexualized as ours, and one peopled with so many beautiful men and women, celibates adopting this approach would ultimately have to place themselves in the solitary confinement of a windowless room to avoid any and all temptations! And even there, memories of beauty and desire-driven fantasies would inevitably arise, leading the poor soul to temptation in the end.

As Pope John Paul reminds us, the true charism of celibacy doesn't take as its aim the amelioration of our romantic and sexual desires, but rather leaves our "affections and . . . instinctive impulses intact." He focuses instead on the development of skills for coping with such desires, as well as a healthy degree of trust in our ability to make the proper decisions when we do find ourselves sexually tempted or falling in love. Recall how even in our recitation of the act of contrition we promise to avoid the *near* occasion of sin, not *every* occasion of sin. Were we to attempt the latter, we again would have to close ourselves entirely off to others. Even if we could succeed at such a feat, we would probably still end up sinning, having eliminated in the process most occasions to love.

What *Pastores Dabo Vobis* recommends instead of denial of our human impulses and desires, then, is to cultivate certain tools for coping with temptations and attractions. These include affective maturity, renunciation, vigilance, and esteem for relationships. With these in mind, let's outline some strategies for coping with sexual and romantic temptation.

2. John Paul II, *Pastores Dabo Vobis: On the Formation of Priests in the Circumstances of the Present Day* (Washington, DC: United States Catholic Conference, 1999), 44.

Affective Maturity

In our discussion of affective maturity in chapter 9, we used the constructs of emotional intelligence and emotional competence to establish a fundamental relationship between simple awareness of one's emotions and the ability to cope adaptively with them. It may be perfectly obvious (and therefore easily overlooked) that individuals increase their chances of making good and proper decisions regarding romantic and sexual attraction when they recognize the emotional experience early and honestly—not once it is far advanced. I often tell parents of two-year-olds that if they want to avoid meltdowns or extreme tantrums with their toddlers, they have to recognize the early signs that they are getting upset and intervene quickly with an effective strategy. Dealing with temptation and attraction is no different: it is best to intervene before it is too late. This is vigilance.

But what is "too late" when it comes to sexual and romantic arousal? Let's consider two different definitions or indicators of "too late." The first we will call "too far," and the second we will call the "point of no return."

We would say that people have gone too far in response to a sexual urge or a romantic attraction if they have acted in a way that is sinful or morally wrong. Informed by Catholic moral teaching, "too far" for celibates is the point at which they engage in an action that is inconsistent with their promise to remain celibate and chaste. For celibates, having a sexual relationship with someone, masturbation, and the use of internet pornography are examples of "too far." So is becoming so emotionally engaged or attached to another single person that they overlook or ignore the needs and considerations of the larger community.

But before we reach the point of having gone too far, we encounter the "point of no return" (PONR)—a point at which our romantic or sexual emotions become so greatly aroused that we are not likely to be able to turn ourselves around. It is the point beyond which the inevitability of going too far is a foregone conclusion. To illustrate this concept, let's consider two people who are sexually attracted to one another. If these individuals are on a date and are now alone together, undressed, and kissing passionately, they are probably at or beyond the point of no return. There is very little chance that they will refrain from sexual intercourse. We can't imagine that, suddenly, one or both of them will stop the proceedings and say, "Okay. That's good. Let's stop here and get dressed. What do you think about getting some lunch? Shall we get something to eat?" At some point our emotions gain a critical amount of momentum such that we are unable to use what little capacity we have left for reasoning to keep from running full throttle toward "too far." Let's see if we can illustrate this with a diagram.

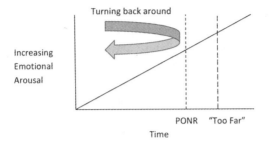

In contrast to the point of too far, which is fairly fixed (the church clearly defines the parameters of celibate chastity as refraining from genital sexual expression and marriage or exclusivity in relationships), the point of no return is less predictable, varying from person to person and even varying over time within a single person. For example, depending on an individual's level of impulsivity and reactivity to sexual or romantic stimuli, the PONR may be reached more quickly or slowly. Within a single person, the point of no return may shift in response to a number of factors. Alcohol use, for example, decreases inhibitions and diminishes rational problem-solving skills, thereby moving the PONR to the left on our graphic representation below. Stress, loneliness, and experiences of feeling underappreciated and unsupported can also cause us to be overcome by our emotions much more quickly. On the other hand, a general satisfaction with one's vocation, including satisfaction in ministry and a strong sense of connectedness in community life, can increase our tolerance for emotional arousal and decrease our susceptibility to being carried away by romantic or sexual feelings.

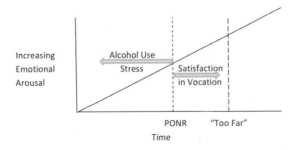

One clear implication to be taken from all of this, then, is that if celibates hope to cope adaptively with the inevitable experiences of romantic attraction and sexual arousal, they must be aware early on of the attraction or emotional arousal, be able to evaluate their proximity to the point of no return, and finally intervene with proper decisions and coping strategies before being overcome by emotions (i.e., before "passing the point of no return").

Indications of Sexual and Romantic Arousal

It may seem odd, but it is possible to be romantically attracted to someone or even be sexually aroused without knowing it. We often talk about people "falling in love" or hear people say, "I just woke up one morning and suddenly realized I was I love with him." These expressions make romance seem quite unpredictable and impossible to prevent. But as with the tantrum-throwing toddler, there are almost always early signs that the attraction is developing.

People do not usually progress from not being in love to being involved in a sexual or romantic relationship overnight. Where the *recognition* of the attraction or arousal might seem rather sudden, early signs of romance or a person's vulnerability to falling in love or acting out have probably been overlooked, misinterpreted, or perhaps even denied or repressed. When this happens, people may experience a fairly advanced state of arousal or degree of romantic valence within a relationship before they ever recognize or admit it. They may even be pretty far along the trajectory and quickly approaching—if not beyond—their point of no return.

Early (and not so early) signs

If you were asked to list the signs of sexual and romantic arousal, you might include some of the following, which are listed below roughly in the order of early to late or more obvious signs:

- noticing someone

- taking a second look

- smiling

- staring

- feelings of warmth—a flushed face

- wondering what kind of person he or she is

- increased heart rate

- fantasizing about how you might introduce yourself to him or her

- taking steps to meet the person

- exchanging basic information about yourself with one another

- sharing personal information about yourself

- developing a shared history, which includes shared jokes and experiences

- greater sense of self-confidence and possible pride in the association

- sitting and standing more closely to one another

- spending time alone together

- increased physical touches—hugging, patting, leaning in

- verbal expressions of affection

- sexual and romantic fantasies involving the other person

- physiological signs of sexual arousal (e.g., erection, flushing)

- verbal expressions of sexual attraction

- kissing, sexual touching

- feelings of euphoria, well-being, and power

- disrobing

- genital sexual activities: intercourse, mutual masturbation, etc.

If space permitted, we would arrange these signs along the horizontal or bottom axis of our diagram above, placing the earliest sign (noticing someone) on the far left and the later ones (genital sexual activity) at the far right. (You could do this on a large sheet of paper or a blackboard.) Once we lined them up, we would mark the point of "too far," and then ask where to put the "point of no return."

Creating such a chart and including the concrete markers of arousal is an excellent tool for increasing self-awareness and self-observation or vigilance, and it can help us better understand the importance of taking preventive measures once we recognize that we are moving along the trajectory of sexual temptation or romantic attraction. One of my favorite exercises when working with young celibates is to assign them to watch a film in which the characters fall in love—a romantic comedy or a drama. It is always helpful to discuss the characters' trajectory of romantic attraction: What were the first signs he was falling in love? Did he realize it at the time? When did she first realize she was in love? What kept her from recognizing it earlier? Given his state in life, did he make the right decisions once he recognized his feelings for her? Did there seem to be a "point of no return" for either of them?

So far we have been discussing these dynamics of attraction and arousal as applied to romantic relationships with others. But it is also worth noting that these same dynamics and strategies of identifying and monitoring progressive signs of arousal can also be used to deal with the temptation to engage in solitary sexual behaviors, such as masturbation and pornography use. The aim is the same: to learn from past experiences of vulnerability what our environmental triggers and early signs of arousal are, and then learn to recognize them early and intervene before we get too carried away. For many men and women, environmental triggers and early signs include specific times of the day or week; particular emotional states (such as loneliness, boredom, or sadness); periods of extended and purposeless internet use; and patterns of drift from non-tempting internet sites to mildly provocative ones and eventually more explicit sexual images and content. Like sexual activity involving other people, pornography use and masturbation do not occur without warning signs, catching us by surprise. Consequently, we should work to cultivate a reasonable vigilance for the things that tempt us and trigger our arousal (many of which we encounter in our ordinary, everyday lives) and aim to respond early and mindfully, increasing the likelihood that we will conduct ourselves in ways that are healthy, respectful of the gift of our sexuality, and consistent with the demands of celibate chastity.

Imaginary Problem-Solving: Practice for Real Life

Beyond recognizing the attraction, one must be able to identify appropriate strategies for coping with romantic and sexual feelings, particularly as we get closer to the point of no return. Candidates for celibacy will be much better equipped to make good decisions in the face of real-life sexual temptation or romantic attraction if they have given previous thought to how they would respond, and perhaps even rehearsed strategies they might use to cope with temptation. A helpful formation exercise—one that is especially effective in group settings—is to practice problem-solving with hypothetical scenarios. The advantages of group problem-solving include hearing how others think through similar situations as well as normalizing situations that celibates think will either never happen to them or have happened only to them. Solving imaginary challenges as a group also increases the chance that candidates will feel comfortable seeking out assistance from peers and formation staff when these situations occur in real life.

In presenting hypothetical scenarios, I prefer to begin with simple situations and proceed with progressively more challenging scenarios. Here are some examples:

Scenario 1: As a priest/sister/brother, you are involved in campus ministry at a local university. One of the students asks to meet with you for spiritual direction. In the middle of your first meeting, you notice how attractive the student is. What should you do?

Scenario 2: (Building on scenario 1.) As a priest/sister/brother, you are involved in campus ministry at a local university. An especially attractive student asks to meet with you for spiritual direction. One night, after one of your appointments with him or her, you wake up from an erotic or romantic dream involving the student.

Scenario 3: You have agreed to be a spiritual director for someone close to your age whom you increasingly find attractive. During one session, your directee breaks down crying over the loss of his or her parents in a tragic car accident. You find yourself feeling compelled to move closer and put your arm around the person. What do you do? Would your response be different if this was someone you had not previously felt attracted to?

Scenario 4: In your ministry as a spiritual director to someone close to your age whom you find attractive, you find yourself, in the middle of one of your sessions, thinking, "Had I known I could feel this attracted to someone, I'm not sure I would have ever decided to be a priest/sister/ brother." The morning of your next appointment with this person, you give extra thought to what you are going to wear.

Scenario 5: (Building on scenario 4.) In one of your spiritual direction appointments with the person above (with whom you have never shared your feelings), your directee pauses, appears very nervous, then timidly tells you that he or she has feelings for you.

Scenario 6: You have "hit it off" with one of your lay colleagues at the parish (or other ministry) where you are assigned. You consider the colleague to be a close friend. One day, a fellow priest or community members asks if "something is going on" between you and the lay colleague. When you defensively ask what the person is suggesting, he or she describes noticing the two of you sharing private jokes, hanging out in one another's offices, and behaving flirtatiously with one another. After some initial anger at the accusation, you realize this person is correct: you have been falling in love with your friend and colleague. What do you do?

There is, of course, a range of possible responses to each of these scenarios. Extended discussions about what to do and what might have prevented some of these situations from developing can help prepare candidates for these or similar situations when they inevitably arise. When is it advisable to discontinue the ministerial relationship? How do you end the ministerial relationship without telling the person about your attraction? Is it ever appropriate to share your romantic feelings with someone to whom you are ministering? What should you do once you see that you have already crossed a boundary?

Sometimes when discussing these types of scenarios, seminarians and candidates will quickly jump to the conclusion that if they are feeling attracted to someone in ministry, they need to discontinue the relationship immediately and refer the person to someone else. This of course is not a very practical solution. Throughout our lives, we will have to work with, minister to, and socialize with attractive people. Sometimes, simply noting the attraction and reminding yourself to be vigilant is enough. In cases where the attraction continues to grow, an appropriate response is to disclose the attraction to someone you trust, such as a spiritual director or close friend. This person can provide support and accountability by asking you about the relationship in the future, giving you feedback on how you are handling the situation, and reminding you of the vows and promises you have made as a celibate man or woman.

When the romantic attraction is mutual, it will be important to think carefully about power differentials and the other boundary issues we have discussed in the previous chapter when deciding how to respond and whether to acknowledge your own feelings. It will be especially important to have told a spiritual director, trusted friend, or even counselor with whom you can discuss the situation and decide how best to respond. As we have already mentioned, the clarity and quality of our thinking is often affected by higher states of emotional arousal. Consequently, involving an objective person can help to challenge our distortions, allow us to see the situation from someone else's point of view, and even raise possible solutions we had not considered.

When a boundary has already been crossed, it is especially important to bring a superior (i.e., formation director, religious superior, vicar for clergy) on board and proceed with transparency. When there is a power differential, regardless of who initiated the relationship and whether or not the relationship was consensual, the interests of the parishioner, student, or directee (the person with less power) must take priority. In these situations, legal considerations can compete with pastoral responsibilities. One of the many difficult lessons we have learned from the sexual abuse crisis is that the primary response to boundary crossings must be pastoral, not defensive. When the church has responded by taking responsibility for mistakes, wounds heal more quickly and with a lesser likelihood of protracted anger and the need for retaliation on the part of victims and their families.

Being the Object of Affection

It is not unusual in ministry and in other helping professions for clients, parishioners, and even students to become attracted to or even fall in love with their minister, teacher, or religious professional. Ministry often places us in situations in which we appear strong, supportive, caring, and effective at listening. In their vulnerability, grieving parishioners, lonely singles, battered spouses, and struggling directees may develop strong feelings for a priest or a religious sister or brother who listens and supports them in ways that no one else in their life currently does.

Some may find it fun or amusing to tease or flirt with a celibate man or woman, thinking that everyone recognizes their actions as a safe joke since the target is a celibate. Rarer is the man or woman who delights in the challenge of tempting a celibate man or woman to abandon his or her commitment to chastity. In all of these cases, celibates must not be naive, and they must take special care not to play into the joke or lead the other on inadvertently. False accusations and emotional traps are relatively rare, but they do occur and we can do our best to avoid falling prey to them by exercising reasonable precautions and maintaining effective boundaries with everyone.

Here are a few more scenarios to illustrate these points:

Scenario 7: At a parish council (or school advisory board) meeting, one of the council members approaches you and makes what could be interpreted as a suggestive comment about what you are wearing ("Nice pants, Father" or "That sweater really shows off your figure, Sister"). How should you respond?

Scenario 8: (Building on scenario 7.) At subsequent meetings, this same member of the parish council makes a point of always sitting next to you and interacts in ways that seem too familiar without any basis for the familiarity (e.g., calling you by your first name, asking what you had for lunch, suggesting that you "broke lots of hearts" when you decided to enter the seminary/religious life).

Scenario 9: (Continuing to build on previous scenarios.) This individual has overheard you telling others how much you enjoy learning about differing kinds of wine. At Christmas, he or she gives you a $250 bottle of wine, finding a way to leave it on your desk while you are out of the office.

Scenario 10: (Building on scenario 9.) There is a card with the $250 bottle of wine that reads: "You bring the wine. I'll bring the mistletoe. —Pat"

It can be very tricky dealing with situations in which you suspect someone has romantic feelings for you. In some fairly innocuous situations, it may be advisable simply to ignore the flirtation or suggestive remark and avoid being alone with the person. If you decide to confront someone whom you think has feelings for you, you run the risk of embarrassing or offending the person if you have misinterpreted the situation. The other person may even respond angrily or respond to your confrontation by telling others that you came on to him or her. On the other hand, passing off a suggestive remark as a joke, teasing back, or ignoring too many advances can also sends the wrong message—that you enjoy the banter or that you are comfortable with the direction the relationship is heading.

When remarks or advances are clearly inappropriate, the person may need to be confronted, and here the celibate must proceed with extreme caution and counsel. Individuals who exercise very poor boundaries and terrible judgment (scenario 10) may also have very poor emotional functioning or even personality deficits that can quickly lead to a gross distortion of the situation and high levels of conflict and blaming. "Pat" may claim that you have entirely misunderstood his or her intentions, accuse you of making advances, and threaten to sue or file a sexual harassment complaint with the diocese or order.

In every one of these situations, it is advisable that you share your concerns and consult with someone whose judgment you trust in deciding how best to respond. In addition to getting another objective opinion on the situation, sharing your concern with someone also serves to establish a witness to your concerns. This will be helpful in the unfortunate case that the situation gets out of hand and you end up being accused of something untoward.

When romantic feelings are expressed in the course of a close ministerial relationship, you may need to make very clear the limits of the relationship and perhaps even remind the other person that you are committed to living a celibate life in the church. It is not advisable to share your own personal feelings for the person (if you have them). In the person's vulnerability, he or she may interpret your admission as a sign of hope for a relationship in the future. After pastorally clarifying the boundaries of the relationship, it may be appropriate to ask the person to whom you are ministering if he or she would prefer that you help find an alternate spiritual director, pastoral counselor, etc.

Summary and Conclusions

Celibates fall in love. It could even be true that good celibates are at *greater* risk of falling in love than ineffective celibates because they make themselves available to others in moments of vulnerability. It is important to remember that few things increase a person's attractiveness like vulnerability. When we are allowed to see other people's weakness, fears, and limitations, we feel closer to them, and they may become somewhat dependent on us, even if momentarily. These experiences arouse our own desires to care for and wish the best for another. Consequently, we should not be surprised to find ourselves occasionally attracted to men or women who make themselves vulnerable to us in ministerial settings.

Making the right decisions in the face of romantic attraction and sexual temptation (not total avoidance of these experiences) is one of the primary goals of celibacy formation. As we have described above, responding correctly begins with awareness and is further facilitated by our ongoing cultivation of friendships and formative relationships (e.g., spiritual direction, confession, and counseling) that can offer us the support, feedback, and accountability needed to remain faithful to our commitment to celibate chastity.

As members of official church institutions who occupy a position of perceived power and authority, we must always remember that when romantic feelings enter the dynamics of the relationship, we need to prioritize the interests of the other person and take responsibility for establishing and maintaining the boundaries. In situations where boundaries have already been crossed (by you or the other), it is again critically important to involve a trusted advisor who can offer objective advice, provide a witness to your concerns, or (in the case of your having crossed a boundary) advocate for the best interests of the other person involved.

Practicing problem-solving with hypothetical scenarios can be an excellent way to sharpen skills for dealing with romantic attraction and sexual temptation. Because relationships are complex, it is helpful to hear how others might approach a similar situation and what aspects of the situation they might focus on in particular. As the title of this book suggests, the goal of celibacy is not to avoid love, but rather to increase our capacity to love in a particular way. While a careless celibate can do great harm, a responsible and chaste celibate is a great gift of love to the world and to the church.

CHAPTER 13

SOLITUDE

At the gate of the Trappist Abbey of Gethsemani, a sign above the entrance to the monastery reads: "God Alone." I suspect that most people who encounter this sign read it to mean that the men within the enclosure are seeking *only* God—"It is God alone whom I seek." But this sign can be read another way, and probably is by the monks who are living inside and cultivating a life of solitude. The key to solitude—and as we will see, to contemplation—is to read the word "alone" not as describing God ("It is God alone whom I seek") but rather as an adverb describing *how* the seeker seeks God. I seek Him *alone*—not with others, not mediated by others, but alone, by myself.

One final skill for the celibate life that we will explore in some depth is the capacity for solitude. Initially, this chapter was called "Coping with Loneliness," but focusing solely on loneliness tells only part of the story. As celibate men and women, we will certainly encounter periods of loneliness, and we will need to know how to deal with them. However, our goal should be not simply to avoid or eradicate the uncomfortable feeling of loneliness, but rather to pass through the doorway of loneliness into solitude.

In this chapter, we will take a closer look at solitude as the transformed experience of loneliness and as a means of journeying toward a deeper and more personal relationship with God—the ultimate goal of our celibate commitment.

Distinguishing between Loneliness and Solitude

Loneliness and solitude are two ways we experience the external, physical reality of being alone. While doing a little online research into the meaning of the words "loneliness" and "solitude," I stumbled on a fascinating feature of Google. For many if not most words, Google provides a graphic display of the frequency with which a word is used in books over the course of the last two hundred years. What I was intrigued to learn is that, relative to other words in the English language, the use of the word "solitude" has dropped off dramatically, decreasing nearly 300% over the last two centuries. The slow downward slope of the graph reflects that, over time, we appear to be sidelining the whole notion of solitude.

Compare that to "loneliness." While "solitude" has gradually become less and less important in our written vocabulary, the word "loneliness" has taken off, occurring in books approximately *seventeen* times more often in 2007 than in the year 1800—an increase of 1,700%! Sociologists could have a field day interpreting this finding, especially in light of social networking and the explosion of technologies keeping us connected to others every waking hour.

What do we make of this? The stark difference in the use of these two words over time suggests that, when it comes to the experience of being alone, we have come to focus increasingly on the negative aspect (i.e., loneliness) while losing sight of the importance and potential benefits of choosing to spend time by ourselves (solitude). To place this in the context of celibacy formation, let's assert that an important skill for celibates to develop is the ability to move through and beyond loneliness to an experience of solitude.

Loneliness Reconsidered

A quick survey of dictionary definitions for loneliness leaves us without doubt that loneliness is universally considered an unpleasant emotional state. Two key components are common to almost every definition: (1) feelings of sadness, depression, or dejection associated with (2) the state of being alone. But does this really adequately describe loneliness?

Consider that most people can identify with the experience of loneliness even when in the presence of others. It is possible, many say, to feel lonely in a crowded room. A little closer to home, we celibates frequently hear from our married friends and family that even they get lonely. This suggests that the experience of loneliness is not limited to—or even dependent upon—the condition of being by oneself or not having other people physically in our lives.

Loneliness might better be defined in relation to the presence or absence of *intimacy*. The best definition of intimacy I can think of is *being known*. We feel close to or intimate with other people to the degree that they know us and we know them. If two people are emotionally intimate, they know one another's deep emotions. If two people are physically intimate, they know one another's bodies. In fact, in some places, Scripture uses the word "know" to connote sexual intimacy between two persons.

Knowing and being known by another person is deeply gratifying. But when we have lost the person who knows us best—a spouse or a best friend—we grieve, we feel lost, and we even wonder who we are. It is the lack of intimacy, therefore, not merely the physical absence of others, that best explains loneliness and helps us to understand why indeed it is possible to feel lonely even in the presence of others.

One of the deeply gratifying things about intimacy, about being known, is the measure of personal reassurance that it brings. We have pointed out in previous chapters that, to a large degree, self-acceptance results from being known deeply by others and then being loved and accepted by them for who we are and for whom they know us to be. We all want to be known, to be understood, and then to be accepted and loved—warts and all.

But why do married couples still feel lonely at times? The answer lies in the fact that no one—not even a spouse—can ever know us or understand us as deeply and completely as we desire. No matter how strong and healthy the relationship, husbands and wives still hurt each other and disappoint one another. After twenty years of marriage, a wife may still say an inconsiderate thing from time to time, or the husband may still embarrass his wife in front of others. It can even come down to an unrinsed ice-cream bowl—especially if one spouse has begged the other countless times not to leave dirty dishes in the sink. While these may seem like little things (and there are larger ones for sure), they nonetheless lead to feelings of not being understood or appreciated: "After all these years, why can't she still understand how this upsets me?" Or, "I wonder if he will ever know just how much it hurts my feelings when he teases me about that in front of other people?" The result is loneliness, even in the best of relationships.

Therefore, whether we are single, happily married, or celibate—whatever our state in life—loneliness is inevitable. When those whom we rely on to know us and care for us end up disappointing us, we feel lonely, misunderstood, and still unknown.

Celibacy: A Fast Track to Loneliness

I am fond of saying that celibate men and women take a fast track to loneliness. And they do so by design. By agreeing not to marry, by choosing to refrain from an exclusive relationship with another person, celibates reach a state of loneliness sooner than others. Because there is no one person to buffer it, no one who has taken on the responsibility and desire to know them more deeply, celibates go unknown for a greater part of their life. They feel ultimately unknown sooner. They feel lonely more often.

This surely doesn't sound very appealing, but (and it is crucial that celibates recognize this) loneliness is actually what the celibate hopes to cultivate. As celibates, we invite loneliness in. We welcome it through the front door. And why? In order, all the sooner and more frequently, to have the experience of knowing God and being known by God, the only one who can and who truly does know us as deeply and completely as we desire.

Allow me to put a more personal spin on it. For my first several years in the monastery, I avoided any acknowledgment that I might be lonely. I considered loneliness to be a symptom that something must be wrong in my life as a celibate. Occasionally, while speaking to my parents over the phone, my mother would ask if I ever felt lonely and I would always be quick to reassure her that I did not. "Lonely? How could I ever get lonely? I live with seventy other monks! There are always people around," I would say. My denial was more an effort to protect myself than to protect her from any worries that I might be lonely, and therefore maybe unhappy.

Eventually, during a very difficult time when I was feeling unsuccessful in my work in the monastery and particularly hurt by a number of my confreres, I could no longer deny my loneliness. I had been living with the expectation that my community would meet my needs for intimacy and keep me from feeling lonely. But when they disappointed me and left me confounded in this expectation, I had to choose between two possibilities: that either (1) community and the celibate life really do not work and therefore I had made a mistake in choosing them; or (2) that I was entering into the next phase of my life as a celibate, that I was being pulled deeper into the uncomfortable mystery of God's design, and hopefully not without his grace.

I decided to put my faith in the second possibility and began spending more time in theological reflection, more time with the question: How could this loneliness (assuming it is God's providence) be drawing me closer to him? I recalled the theological understanding of celibacy as an unmediated relationship with God, and begged for such intimacy with him. I began getting up a little earlier in the morning, carving out a little extra time to pray alone, to be with God alone, to write about and reflect more on this "unmediated relationship" with God—the kind of relationship that is suggested to us in the Song of Songs, in the mystical poetry of John of the Cross, in the writings of Therese of Lisieux, Teresa of Avila, and Hildegard, and in the preaching of Bernard of Clairvaux.

One morning soon after—don't think me crazy!—upon kissing the altar while processing into Mass with my confreres, I had the sense that I had been kissed back! The hymns that followed became love songs, my petitions became personal favors, and my silent early mornings with God came increasingly to remind me of the countless evenings I had seen my parents share, still sitting together in the living room after fifty years of marriage, reading and occasionally rising to get a drink of water and quietly asking the other, "Is there anything I can get you while I am up?"

On one of these mornings, I composed this poem:

Solitude

I sowed a corner of my field in loneliness.
It's not a weed. I put it there.
Now and then, I pull up the self-pity and doubt
that creep in around it.
It has taken hold,
and next year I may plant another acre or two.
The neighbors think I'm crazy:
"We spray against that," they say,
laughing and shaking their heads
as they walk away.
But they don't see its bloom in the middle of the night,
or taste its fruit in the earliest hours of the morning.

Fruits of Solitude

Perhaps we can think of solitude as the chamber we enter after passing through the doorway of loneliness. Solitude is the space in which we meet God alone and come to understand just how deeply we are known by him and how completely we are loved by him.

Solitude is closely associated with contemplation, and although we are not all called to be Carthusians or Trappists, we are each called at least in part, by nature of our baptism, to a contemplative life in Christ—to develop a deeply intimate, one-on-one relationship with God. In his accessible and practical book on contemplation, Martin Laird, OMI, explores contemplation as cultivating a relationship with God who dwells within.[1] While time spent with others draws us out of ourselves (often for great good), choosing to spend quiet time by ourselves draws us inward, toward God who dwells at the very core of our Christian identity. We may have to drill down through layers of poor self-concept, self-deceit, and sin in order tap into it, but in solitude we have the opportunity to discover and explore a relationship with God that has existed from the beginning and continues to exist whether we choose to access it or not. Solitude affords us the time and the space to embark upon this essential work of contemplation, of relating to the indwelling God, and celibacy—our cultivated loneliness—widens the door to this chamber.

In many ways, solitude is the state in which so much of what we do in the rest of our liturgical and devotional life comes to fruition. Why else do we pray the Liturgy of the Hours, engage in the slow and careful reading of Scripture (*lectio divina*), or even consume Christ in the Eucharist if not, continually, to internalize Christ? In reading and reciting Scripture over and over again, we steep ourselves in Christ, the Word made flesh. Over time the Word is pressed into the very pores of our being so that we become flesh-made-Word. In other words, we allow God's Word to get inside of us until it becomes part of our very makeup. Then, when all else is quiet, in our solitude, the Word has a chance to resound or echo, like a song you have heard over and over again on the radio, so often that you end up humming it to yourself when all is quiet.

---

1. Martin Laird, *Into the Silent Land: A Guide to the Christian Practice of Contemplation* (New York: Oxford University Press, 2006).

In his book on solitude, which he has subtitled *A Return to the Self*, Anthony Storr emphasizes that "the capacity to be alone thus becomes linked with self-discovery and self-realization; with becoming aware of one's deepest needs, feelings and impulses."[2] We Christians would say that it is Christ whom we discover at the core of our being. And it is God, in whose image and likeness we have been made, whom we aspire to realize or actualize—to make real and make present—in the world. Christ is our deepest need, our most profound impulse. And we come to know this fully when we create the time and the space—the solitude—to turn inward and attend to the indwelling God. I am reminded time and time again of a snippet from T. S. Eliot's poem *Ash-Wednesday*:

> *Where shall the word be found, where will the word*
> *Resound? Not here, there is not enough silence*[3]

Once we have welcomed loneliness and crossed its threshold to solitude, we discover that we are never entirely alone and recognize that we have already been, and continue to be, fully known:

> *My frame was not hidden from you,*
> *when I was being made in secret,*
>   *intricately woven in the depths of the earth.*
> *Your eyes beheld my unformed substance.*
> *In your book were written*
>   *all the days that were formed for me*
>   *when none of them as yet existed.* (Ps 139:15-16)

And because grace must eventually extrovert itself, the joy we experience in our solitude, upon the discovery that we are fully known and loved by God, spills over into our relationships with those who share our lives and to whom we minister.

In my own Benedictine tradition, humility and hospitality take pride of place among the many virtues we are to cultivate. And we should not wonder why. Humility, an inward disposition of complete and radical

---

2. Anthony Storr, *Solitude: A Return to the Self* (New York: The Free Press, 1988), 21.

3. T. S. Eliot, "Ash-Wednesday," in *The Complete Poems and Plays 1909–1950* (New York: Harcourt, Brace and Company, 1958), 65.

honesty before God, not only leads to an acceptance of ourselves as we currently are, but further enables us to accept and love others—*all* others—as they present themselves to us in all of their imperfection. This is hospitality—the reception of all guests as Christ—as St. Benedict demands of us in his Rule.

Solitude as a Skill

The skill of cultivating solitude in our lives as celibate men and women begins with increasing our tolerance for time spent alone. This may seem to contradict our earlier insistence on being people who embrace community and draw support and accountability from close relationships. But these two realities—community and solitude—are not mutually exclusive; rather, they are complementary, best held in balance with one another. True, our natural predispositions often leave us inclined more toward one or the other—introversion or extroversion—but both are needed and we must develop the capacity for both.

Beyond cultivating time alone, we must also learn to tolerate silence and stillness. Noise and activity are just as powerful distractions as calling up acquaintances on the phone or knocking on our neighbor's door when we are lonely. Even when enjoyed alone or in private, surfing the web, playing solitaire, listening to music, or watching movies is not solitude. As countless mystics have suggested, solitude requires that we still our bodies and minds and dial down the noise in our environment long enough to make resting in the Lord a possibility.

Cultivating solitude takes discipline and intention. It is often best to set realistic goals and slowly build time for solitude into one's schedule. Commit to turning off all devices (including the access to email, Facebook, or whatever social media platform is trending at the time) for the last thirty minutes of the day. Eventually increase the time to sixty minutes. You might find that sleep comes more quickly and that moods and problems sort themselves out more naturally when we give our minds time to rest and our souls time to re-center. As you commute to or from work, choose not to use the time to listen to music or to catch up with friends on the phone. Commit yourself to quarterly days of recollection or monthly tech-free Saturdays. But again, don't expect it to be easy. You'll quickly discover that thirty minutes of real silence and solitude can be a long time. A day without technology can even seem unwise, if not impossible. But solitude is possible and it is wise. We may just need to tolerate its discomfort as we work to stop distracting ourselves from who we really are.

Finally, be willing to accept suffering as part of your life as a celibate and as a Christian. The particular suffering we are talking about here is the grief and sadness that accompanies loneliness and being alone. Without wallowing in it, aim to encounter loneliness with an air of resignation and the reminder that you have invited upon yourself a greater portion of loneliness by accepting the call to celibacy. And try to adopt a disposition of sincere gratitude for the opportunity that loneliness brings to seek God and be found by him alone.

In many respects, and most of the time, celibacy is not difficult. But when it is difficult—when we are experiencing a season of loneliness or having to say "no" to a relationship with a truly beautiful person—celibacy can bring much suffering. *Passio*—the root of passion—not only connotes love, but also suffering and patience. Solitude, the chamber in which we come to understand God's deep and abiding love for us, often requires patience and suffering. If we turn away from the suffering of loneliness and look for some other temporary distraction or relationship to fill our need to be known or appreciated, we may very well be depriving ourselves of a new and surprising relationship with God that lies just beyond the suffering. "But as it is written: 'What eye has not seen, and ear has not heard, and what has not entered the human heart, what God has prepared for those who love him'" (1 Cor 2:9).

Formation programs—particularly those for diocesan priesthood and apostolic religious communities—have often come under criticism for being too "monastic" in style, not preparing candidates for the realities of a busier and more active life beyond ordination or final profession. While there may be some merit to this argument, it is also important to consider that young priests and religious may need some assistance, especially early in their formation, in developing habits of recollection and solitude—habits which, as we have argued above, will be crucial in their ability to persevere joyfully, meaningfully, and fruitfully in their lives as celibate men and women. As with most types of formation, the ultimate goal is for candidates to internalize the necessary knowledge, skills, and values so they may carry them out into the field and practice them with a certain degree of independence. Still, skills and habits are internalized only after they have been introduced, modeled, and practiced with some degree of externally imposed assistance and expectation. Parents help infants and toddlers learn the crucial skill of self-soothing gradually: first, by first rocking them back to sleep; then helping them grab their blanket; then making sure the blanket is nearby; and then withdrawing the support once their children have demonstrated some success in being able to calm themselves down.

In formation programs, it is helpful to establish clearly designated times and places for solitude and recollection. Developing good habits in this area early in formation will be important, and as candidates gradually become less dependent on the structures of earlier formation stages, formation directors and candidates alike should be able to discern whether they not only have the capacity for being alone, but also the skills to transform their experiences of loneliness into solitude that nourishes their celibate vocation and draws them closer to God.

SECTION VI

FOR FORMATION PERSONNEL

CHAPTER 14

PUTTING IT TOGETHER: CONTINUING TO BUILD A PROGRAM FOR CELIBACY FORMATION

The prospect of preparing young men and women for a life of celibate chastity is an awesome and daunting responsibility. Formation work can be compared on many fronts to parenting. Like parents, formation directors tend to draw heavily on their own experience of being in formation in their work as formation directors. As we have already said, this is not always a bad thing. Traditions and wisdom are passed on when we teach our children or charges what our parents or mentors have taught us. On the other hand, just as wisdom is passed on through generations, so are limitations and areas of inadequacy or uncertainty. If, as we have learned from our formal and informal surveys of recently ordained and professed men and women, many feel that their preparation for celibacy was inadequate or limited, it is likely because many men and women charged with conducting formation for celibate chastity had relatively little formation themselves as young priests or religious. This reality, along with the fairly frequent turnover in formation personnel in both seminaries and religious communities, helps to account for our finding that, especially among religious communities, there is a fairly wide range in the level of structure reported for celibacy programs across the United States. As formation personnel change, so do levels of expertise, availability of resources, and ideas about how formation should be approached. The result is often a formation program that is continuously under construction.

This book aims to help formation directors build, organize, and bring greater stability to their celibacy formation programs in seminaries and religious communities. Drawing from various areas of research and theological writings, I have presented a program of formation centered on four major content areas: motives for celibacy; theological dimensions of celibate chastity; sexual identity; and skills necessary for the celibate life. An overarching goal for each of these major content areas, borrowed from the *Program of Priestly Formation*, has been for candidates to grow in self-knowledge and self-acceptance on their way to making a free and total gift of themselves to a life of celibacy as a priest or religious sister or brother. Within each of the major content areas, we have also articulated specific goals to help direct formation and monitor progress.

In this chapter, I would like to address formation directors in particular in considering what we can expect from men and women who are simultaneously in formation and discerning a permanent commitment to celibate chastity. As we explore progress in formation and readiness for ordination or final profession, it will be helpful to adopt a developmental approach that considers candidates as moving along a trajectory of maturity. Answering critical questions such as, "How much growth can be expected?" and "How quickly should candidates show signs of improvement?" can be facilitated by establishing benchmarks and formation goals. It is important to remember that while formation directors rightly work to serve the interests of the individual man or woman in formation, their primary responsibility is to represent the best interests of the community or diocese as well as the larger church in forming and especially discerning the appropriateness of the individual for priesthood or religious life.

A Developmental Approach

The word "formation" is a development-oriented word. It implies growth, movement, change, acquisition of skills, and maturation. Because individuals come to our formation programs at different places in their own personal development, formation directors are expected to meet people where they are, then provide the support, encouragement, skills, knowledge, and consequences candidates need to be considered "ready" to make a free and permanent choice of celibacy by the conclusion of their initial formation.

When considering candidates as moving along this trajectory of formation, two critical questions quickly arise: "How well-formed do we expect someone to be before entering our programs?" and "Where do we expect them to be just before final profession or ordination?" The first of these questions should ideally be addressed in coordination with the vocation director, who is responsible for determining whether a potential candidate meets the minimum criteria for readiness for formation. Sitting down with the vocation director and working out these criteria together will not only benefit the vocation director in screening candidates, but it also helps to avoid situations in which formation directors are responsible for candidates whom they would not have personally judged ready for formation. In the end, a clear and shared understanding of who is appropriate for formation serves the vocation director and the formation staff as well as the candidates themselves, who are less likely to suffer as a result of a breakdown in communication between the vocations and formation personnel.

In determining readiness for formation, it is helpful to set benchmarks in each major content area within our program for celibacy formation (i.e., motives, theological understanding, sexual identity, and skills for celibacy). For example:

Prior to entering formation, candidates should expect to demonstrate the following:

Motives: Candidates should be able to articulate a very basic understanding of their motives for considering a celibate life—even if motives are no more evolved than "It comes with the territory of priesthood/ religious life."

Theological Understanding: Candidates should be able to articulate at a very basic level how a commitment to celibate chastity facilitates the priestly or religious charism (i.e., allows one to serve or love more broadly, is necessary for community life, etc.).

Sexual Identity: Candidates should be able to freely and comfortably offer a basic description of themselves as sexual beings. For example, when interviewed, they should be able to provide, possess, or demonstrate:

- ◆ an honest account of their sexual and dating history
- ◆ a realistic statement of their sexual orientation

- a positive and healthy attitude about sexuality in general

- basic values regarding sexuality that are in line with the teaching of the Catholic Church

The vocation director should have the general sense that candidates have an age-appropriate understanding of themselves as sexual people and are not avoiding dealing with issues of sexuality.

Skills for Celibacy: Candidates should demonstrate a capacity for sexual abstinence by having refrained from sexual activity with others for period of two years before entering. Candidates should also

- report a history of having at least one close friendship

- be involved in spiritual direction

- demonstrate a capacity for introspection

- be observed to interact appropriately with similarly aged men or women in the community/diocese during vocations visits

- be able to identify experiences of strong emotion (e.g., love, anger, fear)

- be capable of communicating affection in non-physical ways

- be free from sexually compulsive behaviors (e.g., compulsive masturbation, compulsive or habitual pornography use)

- be free of a history of sexual contact with minors

Vocation directors may rely on the psychological assessment to identify some of these entry-level skills and criteria; however, when this is the case, the vocation director is responsible for educating the psychologist on what suitability for formation looks like. Thus, once the formation and vocations staff have agreed upon basic indicators of readiness for formation, the vocation director should consider meeting with the screening psychologist to discuss in concrete terms what they are looking for in candidates.

Once candidates are accepted into seminary or religious formation, their progress should be evaluated regularly throughout the formation program. Formal annual or semester evaluations can be very helpful along these lines, and including self-evaluations as well as input from peers, work supervisors, and other community members can also make tracking progress (or lack thereof) more concrete. When it comes to evaluating a candidate's progress in formation, a few pointers are worth mentioning:

1. The formation staff determines what progress looks like. At times, in our efforts to be collaborative, formation directors fall into the trap of giving candidates too much control in determining what they should be working on. Formation staff should be clear about what is expected of candidates in order for them to live a healthy, fruitful, and appropriate life of celibate chastity. While candidates may be invited to raise areas of needed growth, the formation personnel should always be prepared to articulate these for candidates so it is clear what is expected of them. Similarly, although it may be helpful to enlist the help of candidates in identifying objectives toward meeting these goals, the goals themselves should be in place prior to beginning formation.

2. Don't confuse effort with progress. There are many forces and pressures acting on formation personnel that make them eager to see progress in the men and women with whom they are working. Decreasing numbers in priestly and religious vocations, perceived pressure from the diocese to keep men in seminary, and even our own insecurities about our performance as formation directors can cause us to see progress where none or very little exists. True, effort and compliance are desirable and frequently indicate earnestness and openness to formation; however, they are not to be valued above actual progress made toward the goals of the formation program. A young man, for example, who works hard in counseling, is faithful to spiritual direction, and makes assiduous use of the sacrament of reconciliation is still not a good candidate for the celibate life if, despite all these good practices, he continues to struggle with habitual use of internet pornography or exercises poor boundaries with members of the opposite sex. Similarly, a young woman in formation who is compliant with going to counseling and who is willing to apologize after making suggestive or sexually inappropriate comments may ultimately not be an appropriate candidate for celibacy, especially if, despite her efforts and responsiveness to feedback, she continues to engage in inappropriate behaviors. It is tempting to say to ourselves about a candidate we like, "Yes, he makes bad choices, but I can see that he is really trying and the

counselor says he is beginning to see why he does these things." Still, effort and compliance do not automatically translate into progress. Particularly when evaluating the candidate's appropriateness for ordination or final profession, formation personnel must recognize that if little progress has been made in the course of initial formation—a time when there are higher levels of support and accountability—the likelihood of future progress once support and supervision decreases is even more limited.

3. Early intervention and feedback are best. Concerns should be shared with candidates as soon as the need arises. In general, correction and feedback are more easily offered and received when the candidate is new to the formation process and the formation staff has the liberty of saying, "You may not have known this . . ." or "This is a mistake that is easily made early in formation." Early intervention facilitates a number of positive outcomes. It establishes the expectation for candidates that feedback and correction are normal and helpful parts of the formation process. It also facilitates ongoing feedback and helps all parties to learn whether a candidate is capable of change. After all, people cannot be expected to make improvements in some aspect of their life if no one brings the behaviors or attitudes of concern to their attention in the first place. Waiting and hoping that candidates will develop insight and make the change on their own, or hoping that they will receive the needed feedback from their peers may be more indicative of the formation director's passivity and desire to avoid conflict. In the end, delaying intervention rarely benefits candidates or the community. Above all, early intervention helps to prevent "surprises" late in the formation process. Candidate should never arrive at the end of a formation program and learn for the first time, just before ordination or final profession, that the formation staff has serious concerns about their ability to live a chaste, celibate life.

4. "Stringing along" candidates does them no favors. Formation directors frequently point out that it becomes increasingly harder to say "no" to candidates the longer they are allowed to continue in formation. Consequently, candidates for priesthood and religious life are sometimes approved for ordination or final profession in spite of serious concerns. This is all the more likely to occur when those involved feel guilty about having allowed these candidates to spend several years of their life in formation

with little to show for it. Time is precious, particularly in young adulthood, and years spent in formation often come at the expense of potential earnings, accumulation of debt (in some cases), a loss of time and energy that may have been more appropriately invested other careers, educational opportunities or training, and even missed opportunities for relationships. These losses are minimized when formation staff, acting in the candidates' interest, shares early on with the seminarians or candidates that they do not believe that they are truly called to the priestly, religious, or celibate life. There is sure to be some disappointment, argument, and even anger on the part of candidates; however, the magnitude of their upset reaction will surely be much greater (and much more justified) if this decision is reached at the conclusion of formation rather than earlier in the process.

5. Intervention is facilitated by tying feedback to clear behavioral markers. Formation staff should work to make feedback, correction, and goals clear and concrete. To tell a seminarian that he needs to work on making his emotional reaction to events less exaggerated and more consistent with how others are reacting to the same or similar events is much more helpful than telling him you have concerns about his emotional maturity. Telling a young woman in formation that talking about her bathroom habits or sharing her sexual fantasies at supper is inappropriate is much more helpful than asking her to work on having better boundaries in her relationships in community. The more concrete the behaviors of concern are, the more easily they can be pointed to and used as indicators of progress in the more general areas of emotional maturity or boundary keeping. Clear markers also facilitate understanding on the part of the larger community or diocesan officials when it has been determined that the candidate is ill-equipped to continue in formation. In a chapter meeting, for example, voting members can easily dismiss "concerns about her emotional maturity" by rebutting, "Well, aren't we all a little emotionally immature at times?" On the other hand, it would be difficult to overlook or argue with a report that a candidate has been observed yelling at coworkers, sharing dirty jokes with parishioners, laughing inappropriately at others' misfortune, and touching coworkers in a manner that other members of the community or other priests typically do not. When working with candidates themselves, being clear and concrete about behaviors or attitudes of concern is further fortified by providing

clear consequences if these behaviors are not addressed within a finite period of time. For example, a formation director might explain: "If we are still seeing these specific or similar behaviors by the end of the year, we will have to conclude that you are not ready, at this time, to continue in formation." When such clarity is achieved, candidates are forced to assume greater responsibility not only for their actions, but also for the ultimate decision as to whether they are allowed to continue in formation.

Establishing Benchmarks for Formation

In the preceding chapters I have suggested concrete goals for formation for each of the major content areas. By arranging these goals along a four-year continuum, we can create a solid framework around which to build or further organize a program of initial celibacy formation. The schema offered below can be adapted to fit the specific needs or parameters of a particular community or seminary setting, but the example illustrates how goals can be translated into benchmarks that serve the dual purposes of guiding the formation process and adding greater objectivity to the evaluation of candidates.

Year I

Motives: Candidates are able to identify their initial motives for choosing celibacy.

Theologies: Candidates are able to articulate three different theological dimensions supporting the celibate life.

Sexual Identity: Candidates are able to describe themselves as sexual people with increasing ease with appropriate formation personnel.

Skills: Candidates demonstrate capacity to spend time alone and contribute effectively to community events and discussions.

Year II

Motives: Candidates continue to identify and evaluate the validity and health of their initial motives for choosing celibacy.

Theologies: Candidates have learned and practiced a model of theological reflection on the celibate life.

Sexual Identity: Candidates are able to articulate how their sexual or romantic identity has affected their choice of celibacy.

Skills: Candidates are able to identify their primary sources of support in the community and can identify a specific instance of utilizing support.

Year III

Motives: Candidates are able to articulate how their choice of celibacy is motivated by spiritual or theological ideals.

Theologies: Candidates are able to articulate an experience of practicing theological reflection to derive meaning from an experience of celibate life.

Sexual Identity: Candidates are able to identify a personal experience of romantic or physical attraction and describe strategies used for coping.

Skills: Candidates are able to identify primary sources of accountability and can describe an instance of transparency and accountability.

Year IV

Motives: Candidates have valid and healthy motives capable of sustaining a fruitful and generous life of celibacy.

Theologies: Candidates regularly practice theological reflection on the celibate life and can articulate how their theological understanding of celibacy has developed in formation.

Sexual Identity: Candidates recognize areas of temptation and demonstrate appropriate mastery of sexual and romantic impulses.

Skills: Candidates possess boundaries that facilitate ministry and personal spiritual growth. Candidates can articulate a plan for ongoing formation in the celibate life.

Once such a schema is in place, formation personnel can go back through each of the goals or benchmarks and determine in which arenas of formation (e.g., classroom, workshops, or spiritual direction) the work is accomplished and what personnel are needed to accomplish these goals. Recall that suggestions for systems of delivery (who is responsible and in which specific arenas of formation) have been explored in the preceding chapters.

It is recommended that once formation directors have a schema or program in place, they consider publishing it in a formation handbook to be made available for candidates and the larger community. Again, the advantages of establishing and publishing benchmarks are many. They make clear for both candidates and the formation team what is expected in order for candidates to continue their formation toward ordination or final profession. These steps also help the diocese or larger community better understand recommendations made by the formation staff to endorse or not endorse a candidate for continued formation, ordination, or profession. This may be especially helpful when the larger community or diocesan personnel have a more removed or limited experience of a seminarian's or candidate's progress in formation.

An established and published program for celibacy formation also helps stabilize and improve a formation program over time. Given the frequency with which formation personnel change in seminaries and religious communities, a formalized program for formation eliminates the need to reinvent the proverbial wheel each time there is turnover. Less time is lost while new formation directors work to better understand their responsibilities and the resources available to them. Formation directors who pass on a well-defined and implemented program of formation not only give their successors something to work from, but also promote program development, allowing time and energy to be devoted to program evaluation rather than starting over term after term or year after year.

Program Evaluation

Program evaluation refers to efforts to continuously build the effectiveness of a formation program. Having candidates complete evaluations of presenters, personnel, resources, and workshops is one concrete way that formation directors can begin to assess and build the effectiveness of their program.

Conducting occasional internal reviews or discussions with staff "successful" and "unsuccessful" graduates of the program (i.e., those who have gone on to embody or fail to embody a fruitful and well-adjusted approach to celibate living) can help to further inform what characteristics, virtues, or qualities might need to be included among the program's benchmarks and goals. Regularly soliciting feedback from program participants and recent graduates can also help identify what aspects of the program are particularly effective and which could use greater attention or refinement. Having said this, it must also be noted that participant feedback must be balanced or tempered with the judgment of the formation personnel, recognizing that the value of certain interventions is not always realized until years later or until life circumstances make them more apparent. Along these lines, the input of men and women who have persevered as celibates for decades is also a valuable resource for formation directors working to build a program that will prepare others to similarly persevere. Who better, after all, to weigh in on what would benefit newcomers than seasoned and successful practitioners of self-gift?

CHAPTER 15

ONGOING FORMATION

T he paradox of preparing and forming someone for any vocation or life commitment, including celibacy, is that despite our best efforts, so much of the learning comes from living the life itself. Many of the lessons come only several years into the commitment. Take marriage, for example. Young people may grow up watching their mothers and fathers work successfully at marriage. Their parents may even have frequently explained some of the important points: "It simply takes work. It can get very difficult at times, and you have to commit yourself to the relationship, no matter what it costs." But even with such effective modeling and constant reminders of the inevitable challenges, young men and woman are still likely to be surprised by their experience several years into their own marriage: "Oh, *this* is what my mother was talking about. She warned me it would get difficult and that I would want to call it quits, but I had no idea!" Celibacy, of course, is no different.

Part of the challenge is that our standard model for religious and priestly formation aims to squeeze a lifetime's worth of educational, practical, and other formative experiences into the first four or five *years* of what we hope will be a commitment of four or five *decades*. This is not necessarily misguided, but it is probably incomplete. How, after all, do you prepare a twenty-seven-year-old for a healthy celibate life at age forty-seven or sixty-seven? Even ten or fifteen years post-profession or ordination young men and women are, to some degree, different people. They are in a new stage of their life with new developmental tasks confronting them. The vocation itself may have even changed in some respects, with new responsibilities and a different set of realities compared to the life for which they were formed. Again, it's not that initial formation isn't necessary, but it probably isn't sufficient.

In this final chapter, we will give some thought to the necessity and practicalities of ongoing formation in the celibate life. I am careful to choose the word "in"—i.e., ongoing formation *in* the celibate life, as opposed to ongoing formation *for* the celibate life—since once we have made a final commitment as ordained or professed men and women, we are being formed by and therefore *in* the life itself. One overarching theme we will highlight, then, is that ongoing formation for celibacy must equip men and women at every new stage in their lives to weather the crises and seize the opportunities that inevitably arise and pull them ever more deeply into the paschal mystery.

Before we talk about specific goals and strategies for ongoing formation, we emphasize the importance of grounding the celibate vocation with a solid initial formation, regardless of when that initial formation takes place.

Ongoing Formation versus Overdue Initial Formation

In my work speaking to various religious communities, dioceses, and seminaries about celibacy formation, I have heard many older and middle-aged priests and religious tell me that their own formation for celibacy was very limited, if not entirely absent. When I first joined religious life and became involved in formation work, I made a point to ask some of the older men in my community what kind of formation for celibacy they had received. Many reported that they had had none at all. Some explained that they were simply told "not to think about it (sex)!"

These anecdotal accounts square with research findings that even as recent as ten years ago, newly professed monks reported receiving little to no formal training for celibacy.[1] A 1999 study published by the Ford Foundation found that, across many Christian denominations, ministers receive fairly limited, or at least unsystematic, training or formation in

---

1. John Mark Falkenhain and Jane Becker, "The First Ten Years of Solemn Vows: Benedictine Monks on Reasons for Leaving and Remaining in Monastic Life," *The American Benedictine Review* 59, no. 2 (June 2008): 184–97.

the area of sexuality relative to their ministry.[2] All of this suggests that there are many men and women among priests and religious who have pursued a life of celibacy with relatively little formation.

I bring this to light in order to say that when we talk about the need for ongoing formation—that is, formation for those who are already ordained and/or professed—what we are more likely talking about is the need for *overdue initial* formation. This is not to say that the church is peopled with priests and religious men and women who have no knowledge or skills when it comes to living the celibate life—as we have already pointed out, the life itself teaches us many lessons. Nonetheless, many priests and religious are likely to benefit from a more comprehensive and systematic exposure to celibacy formation similar to what we have outlined in this text. Such a program may help them in their ongoing efforts to persevere, derive meaning, and perhaps even for the first time, experience celibacy as a means of drawing deeper into the beauty of their celibate vocation rather than experiencing it as a required dimension of their priestly or religious life.

Recall that one of the primary goals of initial formation is to provide celibates with a framework and vocabulary to better understand their experiences and to effectively communicate themselves to others who can support them and help them to grow. These needs are present in every cohort of celibates and at every stage of our celibate lives. Therefore, even if obtained late or in the middle of a lifetime, the acquisition of a more solid grounding in motives, theology, sexual identity, and necessary skills can provide the needed framework to sort out not only current and future experiences of celibacy and sexuality, but past experiences as well. The likely result is a greater capacity for making sense of the decisions they have made and for reading the movement of God's providence in their lives. I have heard several formation directors who have studied celibacy with me along with their charges say, "I wish I had had some of this years ago. It would have helped me to make sense of so much and even avoid some mistakes." Better late than never.

2. Sarah C. Conklin, "Seminary Sexuality Education Survey: Current Efforts, Perceived Need and Readiness in Accredited Christian Institutions," *Journal of Sex Education and Therapy* 26, no. 4 (2001): 301–9.

My hope for this book is that, in addition to being a text for use in seminary and religious formation programs, it might also serve as some overdue
celibacy formation for those who are already ordained or professed. To
this end, I suggest that this book might be used in a number of ways. An
individual reading of the text would be further complemented by discussions of each chapter with a spiritual director or trusted other who might
agree to read along. This volume could also be used in group settings as a
framework around which to structure a series of priest or religious support
group meetings. Dioceses and religious communities might similarly adopt
the model used in this book to offer a semester- or year-long course for
celibacy formation to priests or members who have already completed their
initial priestly or religious formation but desire more celibacy formation.

Seminary and initial religious formation programs might contribute
to the overdue formation needs of already ordained or professed men
and women by opening celibacy formation courses or workshops to local
priests and religious. Although this would need to be done carefully so
as to prevent the needs of the two groups (newcomers and already professed or ordained) from competing with one another, there could be
some real benefits for all involved. These might include the generation
of richer discussion; opportunities for older celibates to testify to some
of the positive and challenging realities of the celibate life; opportunities
for younger members to inspire older members with their idealism and
confidence; and opportunities for seasoned celibates to demonstrate that
perseverance in celibacy is not only possible, but attractive and fruitful
for the life of the individual and the church. Finally, including some older
celibates might go a long way in building supportive relationships among
generational cohorts and possibly initiate some mentoring relationships
once the formal programs are completed.

Technology is another approach that some communities and dioceses
are using to provide their already ordained and professed members with
greater formation for celibacy. Along these lines, a video series based
on the model used in this book has been developed and produced by
Saint Luke Institute and is available for easy access via their website,
www.sliconnect.org. Similarly, some religious communities are recording
formation conferences within their formation programs to make them
available to all community members. While I am not aware of any seminaries or dioceses currently doing this, it would be a relatively inexpensive

and effective way to allow former generations of priests to benefit from formation currently being offered in seminaries.

Ongoing Formation as Post-Initial Formation

Ongoing celibacy formation is post-initial formation and should have the following goals: (1) to provide ongoing support to men and women in their efforts to lead celibate lives; (2) to refresh individuals' knowledge and skills in the area of celibate living; and (3) to provide anticipatory guidance and assistance as celibates encounter the particular challenges and opportunities that arise at later stages of the celibate life.

1. Ongoing support

Research underscores the role of ongoing support in the adjustment and perseverance of priests and religious, especially in the first five to ten years after ordination or final profession. In these first years post-initial formation, once the structures and ready-made communities of formation programs are no longer accessible, men and women may need some assistance in finding new systems of support and developing the skills needed for more independent living. Leadership and directors of ongoing formation in dioceses and religious communities can play an important role by organizing quarterly or semiannual gatherings for more recently professed or ordained members, developing mentor programs, and, in situations where in-person gatherings are not feasible, helping to establish online arenas for promoting communication, social support, and interaction among the newly professed or ordained.

As important as peer support is, it is probably even more critical that priests and religious feel supported by the leadership in their communities or dioceses. Unfortunately, a perceived lack of support and personal relationship with one's bishop or superior is often the reality. Dean Hoge found, for example, dissatisfaction with one's relationships with his bishop and other priests to be a particular area of concern for priests in the first five to nine years after ordination.[3] Although religious life, in contrast,

---

3. Dean R. Hoge, *Experiences of Priests Ordained Five to Nine Years: A Study of Recently Ordained Catholic Priests* (Washington, DC: National Catholic Educational Association, 2006), 5.

would seem to afford a greater potential for support, both from fellow community members and leadership, living with others does not necessarily lead to supportive relationships with other professed members. Abbots, provincials, and leaders in religious communities (like bishops) are often preoccupied with the more urgent concerns within their institutions. They, too, are at risk of overlooking the emerging needs and concerns among their younger members who are experiencing a sense of being "out here on my own" for the first time.

One preventative recommendation along these lines is to establish yearly or semiannual structured meetings between each newly professed or ordained member and his or her superior or bishop. If the leader of the institute or diocese cannot meet with the individual member, a delegate should be appointed to meet regularly with the newly ordained or professed. When a delegate is necessary, it is important that this person communicate clearly that the interest is coming from the bishop, provincial, or prioress. Additionally, the delegate should be clear about how potential concerns or key points of the conversation will be communicated to leadership and what kind of follow-up the members can expect. A delegate such as an assistant or a liaison for newly professed may begin a meeting with a recently professed member by stating, "The prioress is concerned about how you are adjusting to your new community assignment, community life, and your work now that you have been finally professed for six months. She asked if I could meet with you at least once or twice a year so she can know what your needs are on an ongoing basis." While delegated meetings are sometimes necessary, meetings with the bishop, provincial, or head of the institute directly are preferred, and members should feel that they have direct access to the bishop or community leader upon request.

Regularly scheduled meetings with leadership personnel can accomplish much in satisfying the ongoing formation needs of the recently ordained or professed. In addition to communicating a general sense of support and interest on behalf of leadership, they also establish an ongoing relationship to which members can bring their needs, problems, personal struggles, and mistakes as they arise. Having a relationship in place before concerns arise is key to addressing concerns early and in a proactive manner. In our research with monks one to ten years into their solemn profession, the most frequently mentioned strategy men thought they would use if they experienced a strong desire to leave would be to talk to their abbot or a fellow community member. Unfortunately, feelings of disconnection and perceived lack of support from their community were chief among the factors causing individuals to want to leave in the first place.

Yearly, semiannual, or even quarterly meetings with community or diocesan leaders are likely to be more effective when guided by a schedule of specific, purposeful inquiries into the life and well-being of priests or members. Asking about their work, health, living situation, circle of friendships, experience of celibacy, possible loneliness, and relationship with other priests or community members not only helps to surface concerns before they become significant problems, but also communicates to the finally professed or ordained that the provincial or bishop understands the important dimensions of their personal and professional lives and what kind of specific challenges they might be encountering. Appropriate personal disclosures by the bishop or community leader related to his or her own adjustment to celibacy and life after initial formation also communicate a sense of support and approachability when it comes to sharing concerns.

When establishing a relationship between bishop and priest or community leader and member, the initiative may need to come from the superior, especially in the early stages of development. Diocesan and community leaders may tell their priests or congregation members that they have an "open-door policy"; however, the newly professed or ordained may still feel hesitant to "burden" their bishop or provincial with concerns they consider not important enough or not truly problematic. Initiative on the part of leadership helps to assure the members of the community or presbyterate that they are genuinely interested in the ongoing welfare of the members and eager to learn about individual members' concerns as soon as they arise.

2. Refreshing knowledge and skills for celibate living

Priests and religious, like other helping professionals who are required to complete continuing education (i.e., doctors, psychologists, social workers, nurses), would also benefit from opportunities for ongoing formation aimed at re-sharpening their skills for effective ministry, ethical conduct, healthy community living, and personal and spiritual development. With specific respect to ongoing celibacy formation, several of the content areas and skills covered in this book are worth revisiting with some regularity throughout one's lifetime. I will highlight a few.

A periodic return to studying the various theological dimensions of celibate chastity is certain to benefit priests and religious as they negotiate new assignments, new developmental stages in life, ongoing challenges to their celibate commitment, and the inevitable transition into retirement from active ministry. At various times in their vocation, priests and religious may need to draw on a new theological dimension of celibacy to make sense of their ministry or life circumstance. This may be done in a variety of ways, including reading books and articles on the theology of celibacy or attending lectures or workshops in person or online.

In terms of refreshing or fostering skills in the area of theological reflection on the celibate life, individuals within the community or presbyterate might be invited to share some of the fruits of their own theological reflection with the rest of the community or presbyterate. This could be accomplished at community or presbyteral gatherings or via articles in newsletters, community bulletins, or other means of group communication. Seasonal theological reflection groups such as Lenten *lectio divina* groups or Advent reflection groups are other opportunities to encourage theological reflection on the celibate life, especially if proceedings incorporate questions specifically related to the celibate experience: How does your experience of celibacy relate to the themes of temptation, sacrifice, and resurrection found in this set of Lenten readings? or How does your experience of being celibate relate to the perennial Advent themes of patience, longing, and expectation? Regular reminders that one's commitment to celibacy is intended as a theological and spiritual journey are important to any and all of us who over time can grow forgetful of the potentially powerful witness and value of the celibate charism.

Due to the complexity and subtlety of personal, professional, and ministerial relationships a regular review of boundary issues, dual relationships, and power differentials is also recommended. This may be accomplished in part by yearly reviews of diocesan or institutional boundaries policies; however, more practical, experiential approaches can make this area of ongoing formation more engaging and potentially more effective. For example, a series of hypothetical scenarios or boundary vignettes along the lines of "What would you do if . . ." could be sent by email to members of the diocese or congregation on a monthly basis. Proposed solutions or key considerations might be provided in a follow-up email the next day or several days later. Inviting members to contribute challenging or complicated boundary situations they have encountered can help generate content for a project like this. The primary aim, of course, is to provide members with opportunities to practice critical thinking skills and ultimately to help them better identify potential boundary issues before or as soon as they arise.

In terms of ongoing formation in the areas of emotional intelligence and skills for dealing with loneliness, romantic attraction, and falling in love, participation in priest and community support groups are an obvious and often-tried approach, especially to the degree that they encourage appropriate self-disclosure and mutual accountability. Other perhaps less obvious approaches to growing in emotional insight and maturity include participation in book and film clubs and attending theater events with others. Art has a powerful way of tapping into our basic human experience, and participating in discussion forums encourages engaging with literature and art at deeper levels. The end result is an ongoing education in basic human processes, interpersonal relationships, and emotional dynamics. Reading not only improves the mind, but educates the heart as well. In my own work with celibates in initial formation, I often use discussion of films and literature to explore themes of motivation, attraction, emotional arousal, and moral decision-making. Discussing questions about the various characters' experiences (e.g., *How did you know he was in love? When did the character realize she was attracted to him? What kept him from acknowledging the attraction and how could he have avoided making such poor decisions?*) can be a powerful and engaging means of gaining better insight into emotionality and recognizing signs of love, distress, vulnerability, and temptation within ourselves and in others.

Finally, the faithful practice of spiritual direction and use of the sacrament of reconciliation are critical components of ongoing celibacy formation. Occasionally, celibates may also find it helpful to engage a counselor or psychotherapist to help them deal with more significant psychosexual, psychosocial, emotional, or behavioral concerns, particularly as they relate to the celibate experience. Psychotherapy can also be a helpful forum for developing social skills, learning new boundary styles, exploring appropriate ways to meet needs for intimacy, and finding effective strategies for dealing with stress and burnout.

3. Anticipatory guidance

Anticipatory guidance helps celibates prepare for some of the ordinary and predictable challenges that arise in the course of the celibate life. Assignment changes, geographical relocations, the failing health or death of a parent, and retirement from active ministry are all examples of commonly experienced events that bring higher levels of stress and can challenge a person's celibate commitment. Helping celibates anticipate these challenges and suggesting possible strategies or resources for coping are much more effective when implemented in close proximity to the need, as opposed to the more hypothetical and remote instruction men and women receive in their initial formation. Let's look at a few examples.

Priests or community members in the midst of an assignment change are likely to experience some anxiety, grief, and possible loneliness as a result of changes in their personal and work relationships. Including some anticipatory guidance around what celibacy-related challenges might arise and how to cope with them could help prevent significant crises or more serious struggles around issues of celibacy. Personnel directors or directors of ongoing formation could draft a short pamphlet highlighting some of the common stressors and challenges that often accompany assignment changes (i.e., changes in personal support structures, loss of professional relationships, feelings of isolation, increased personal freedom, decreased levels of personal oversight, doubt and uncertainty regarding new responsibilities). Normalizing these issues and discussing their possible effects on living the celibate life may help prevent personal crises and ineffective coping. The pamphlet might also suggest strategies for staying healthy and well-adjusted during the transition and identify resources available in the diocese or congregation to assist them during this time of increased stress.

Anticipating the stressors and challenges that accompany the illness or death of an aging parent may also be very helpful to a priest, brother, or religious sister who already feels heavily burdened by ministerial responsibilities and other emotional demands associated with the priestly or religious life. Although all children of aging or dying parents (not just celibates) experience feelings of worry, grief, loss, and anxiety as they try to balance their already busy lives with caretaking responsibilities, there are particular challenges for the celibate. These include the realities of not having a spouse and children of one's own to provide emotional support and dealing with the frequent misperception by married siblings that the celibate is automatically freer to assume the primary role of caretaker to an elderly parent. Dioceses or religious communities may wish to offer yearly voluntary workshops for members on dealing with the challenges of parental caretaking and coping with parent loss. These could be an effective way to promote adjustment and to deepen members' celibate commitment at an important developmental stage in their adult lives.

Elderly priests and religious may similarly need some assistance anticipating and coping with the challenges of their own retirement or withdrawal from active ministry. An ongoing formation program fostering appreciation of a more contemplative, spousal, or even ascetic outlook for understanding celibacy can be a great and very timely gift, especially for celibates whose theological model of celibacy has primarily been an apostolic one. While these various theological dimensions may have all been presented and learned years earlier in initial formation, it is an entirely different and richer experience to be formed in these models once again when one's life circumstance creates a particular opportunity and a greater need for adopting a new theological outlook.

As discussed earlier, many of the formative experiences that will deepen our understanding of celibacy occur only once we have committed ourselves to the celibate life for ten, twenty, or even fifty years. To the degree that we can foresee and prepare for these experiences, we remain open to the formation and transformative power of the life itself. When this is the case, we more effectively become collaborators with time, with our own human nature, and with God's great providence to grow ever more deeply into the mystery and gift of the celibate life.

Summary and Conclusions

A recent study of celibacy formation in the United States shows that at least among religious communities, relatively little has been done to develop stable programs for ongoing celibacy formation.[4] Child protection policies and accreditation requirements have been the impetus for

---

4. John Mark Falkenhain and Beth Owen Davis, "2015 Survey of Religious Communities' Celibacy Formation Programs," last accessed April 21, 2017, https://www.sliconnect .org/wp-content/uploads/St.-Meinrad-SLI-Survey-Summary-Report.pdf.

most dioceses and men's religious communities to write, implement, and regularly review boundaries policies and abuse reporting protocols. These have doubtless led to additional efforts to promote emotional and psychosexual health; however, the focus has likely been on the prevention of problem behaviors rather than promoting theological depth or deepening emotional and spiritual insight.

This chapter has explored the practicalities of ongoing formation for the celibate life. We began by distinguishing between overdue initial formation and ongoing or post-initial formation and suggested that for many priests and religious, the real and most pressing need is a program of initial formation such as the one we have developed here.

With respect to true ongoing or post-initial formation, I have recommended three broad goals to direct these efforts: (1) providing ongoing support; (2) refreshing and fostering knowledge and skills for celibate living; and (3) providing anticipatory guidance to assist with the ordinary and predictable challenges that arise over the course of a celibate's life. In exploring each of these goals, we have discussed some specific issues, strategies, and systems of delivery in order to spark the reader's imagination. More specific details and strategies are likely to depend on the particular context of the celibate life one is pursuing (i.e., diocesan priesthood, monastic life, apostolic religious life).

To a great extent, especially given the current state of ongoing formation programs in most dioceses and religious communities, the responsibility for ongoing celibacy formation has fallen on individual priests, sisters, or religious brothers themselves. Many of the recommendations suggested above can help individuals embark on a self-directed program of ongoing formation for the celibate life. Having said this, I would certainly encourage diocesan and religious congregation leaders to work toward implementing programs for ongoing support, the continued cultivation of skills for the celibate life, and anticipatory guidance for their ordained and finally professed members. Obvious forums for delivering ongoing celibacy formation at the diocesan or congregational level include yearly assemblies and study days; annual retreats; regularly scheduled meetings with individual members; the promotion of online seminars and courses developed by other organizations; tips, reminders, and articles in already established systems of communication (i.e., newsletters and community bulletins); and encouragement of participation in support groups.

Unlike professional organizations and licensing boards for medical health professionals that make membership or licensure dependent on completion of continuing education requirements, dioceses and religious communities cannot realistically require ongoing formation. That being said, with some creativity and knowledge of the needs and wishes of their membership, dioceses and religious congregations can find creative ways of incentivizing participation in ongoing formation programs. For example, a diocese or congregation might consider generating a list of ongoing formation opportunities with credits assigned to each. Rewards (e.g., days at the community's vacation house, gift cards, the waiving of certain diocesan fees, free or reduced cost for participation in a yearly outing) can then be assigned based on the number of accumulated ongoing formation credits. Any expense associated with ongoing formation programs are easily offset if they prevent even a single lawsuit associated with boundary crossings or other types of unprofessional behavior. But beyond the value of avoiding legal fees and monetary damages, the cost of ongoing formation efforts are a smart and excellent investment if they deepen the intentionality, meaning, and love with which the diocese's or congregation's members live out their celibate life and stand as bright, shining witnesses to the kingdom to come and the kingdom of God already rising up in our midst.

BIBLIOGRAPHY

APA (American Psychological Association). "Guidelines for Psychological Practice with Lesbian, Gay, and Bisexual Clients." *American Psychologist* 67 (2012): 10–42.

Bendyna, Mary E., and Mary L. Gautier, "2009 Vocations Study—Executive Summary." Accessed June 9, 2017. https://nrvc.net/247/publication/913 /article/1022-executive-summary-english.

Bieschke, Kathleen J., Parrish L. Paul, and Kelly A. Blasko. "Review of Empirical Research Focused on the Experience of Lesbian, Gay, and Bisexual Clients in Counseling and Psychotherapy." In *Handbook of Counseling and Psychotherapy with Lesbian, Gay, Bisexual and Transgender Clients.* 2nd ed. Edited by Kathleen J. Bieschke, Ruperto M. Perez, and Kurt A. DeBord, 293–315. Washington, DC: American Psychological Association, 2007.

Cantalamessa, Raniero. *Virginity: A Positive Approach to Celibacy for the Sake of the Kingdom of Heaven.* New York: St. Paul's Press, 1995.

Center for Applied Research in the Apostolate. "Center for Applied Research in the Apostolate, a 2015 report to the USCCB Secretariat of Clergy, Consecrated Life and Vocations." Last accessed April 21, 2017. https://www .sliconnect.org/wp-content/uploads/CARA-Survey-Summary-Report.pdf.

Congregation for Catholic Education. *Instruction Concerning the Criteria for the Discernment of Vocations with regard to Persons with Homosexual Tendencies in View of Their Admission to the Seminary and Holy Orders.* 2005.

Congregation for the Doctrine of the Faith. *Letter to the Bishops of the Catholic Church on the Pastoral Care of Homosexual Persons.* 1986.

Conklin, Sarah C. "Seminary Sexuality Education Survey: Current Efforts, Perceived Need and Readiness in Accredited Christian Institutions." *Journal of Sex Education and Therapy* 26, no. 4 (2001): 301–9.

Cozzens, Donald B. *The Changing Face of the Priesthood: A Reflection on the Priest's Crisis of Soul.* Collegeville, MN: Liturgical Press, 2000.

Diamond, Lisa M. "Gender and Same-Sex Sexuality." In *APA Handbook of Sexuality and Psychology, Volume 1: Person-Based Approaches,* edited by Deborah

L. Tolman, Lisa M. Diamond, José A. Bauermeister, William H. George, James G. Pfaus, and L. Monique Ward, 555–69. Washington, DC: American Psychological Association, 2014.

Dubay, Thomas. ". . . *And You Are Christ's*": *The Charism of Virginity and the Celibate Life.* San Francisco: Ignatius Press, 1987.

Dukro, Paul, and Marc Falkenhain. "Narcissism Sets Stage for Clergy Sexual Abuse." *Human Development* 21, no. 3 (Fall 2000): 24–28.

Eliot, T. S. "Ash-Wednesday." In *The Complete Poems and Plays 1909–1950.* New York: Harcourt, Brace and Company, 1958.

Ellis, Alan L., and Robert W. Mitchell. "Sexual Orientation." In *Psychological Perspectives on Human Sexuality*, edited by Lenore T. Szuchman and Frank Muscarella, 196–231. New York: John Wiley & Sons, 2000.

Falkenhain, John Mark, and Beth Owen Davis. "2015 Survey of Religious Communities' Celibacy Formation Programs." Accessed April 21, 2017. https://www .sliconnect.org/wp-content/uploads/St.-Meinrad-SLI-Survey-Summary -Report.pdf.

Falkenhain, John Mark, and Jane Becker. "The First Ten Years of Solemn Vows: Benedictine Monks on Reasons for Leaving and Remaining in Monastic Life." *The American Benedictine Review* 59, no. 2 (June 2008): 184–97.

Falkenhain, Marc A., Paul N. Duckro, Honore M. Hughes, Stephen J. Rossetti, and Jeffrey D. Gfeller. "Cluster Analysis of Child Sexual Offenders: A Validation with Roman Catholic Priests and Brothers." *Sexual Addiction and Compulsivity* 6, no. 3 (1999): 317–36.

Foster, Richard J. *Celebration of Discipline: The Path to Spiritual Growth.* Rev. ed. San Francisco: Harper & Row, 1988.

Fry, Timothy, Imogene Baker, Timothy Horner, Augusta Raabe, and Mark Sheridan, eds. *The Rule of St. Benedict in English.* Collegeville, MN: Liturgical Press, 1981.

Gonsiorek, John C., and James D. Weinrich. "The Definition and Scope of Sexual Orientation." In *Homosexuality: Research Implications for Public Policy*, edited by John C. Gonsiorek and James D. Weinrich, 1–12. Newbury Park, CA: Sage Publications, 1991.

Hald, Gert Martin, Christopher Seaman, and Daniel Linz. "Sexuality and Pornography." In *APA Handbook of Sexuality and Psychology, Volume 2: Contextual Approaches*, edited by Deborah L. Tolman, Lisa M. Diamond, José A. Bauermeister, William H. George, James G. Pfaus, and L. Monique Ward, 3–35. Washington, DC: American Psychological Association, 2014.

Haldeman, Douglas C. "Sexual Orientation Conversion Therapy for Gay Men and Lesbians: A Scientific Examination." In *Homosexuality: Research Implications for Public Policy*, edited by John C. Gonsiorek and James D. Weinrich, 149–60. Newbury Park, CA: Sage Publications, 1999.

Hill, Alexander K., Khytam Dawood, and David A. Puts. "Biological Foundations of Sexual Orientation." In *Handbook of Psychology and Sexual Orientation*, edited by Charlotte J. Patterson and Anthony R. D'Augelli, 55–68. New York: Oxford University Press, 2013.

Hoge, Dean R. *The First Five Years of the Priesthood: A Study of Newly Ordained Catholic Priests*. Collegeville, MN: Liturgical Press, 2002.

———. *Experiences of Priests Ordained Five to Nine Years: A Study of Recently Ordained Catholic Priests*. Washington, DC: National Catholic Educational Association, 2006.

Hopkins, Gerard Manley. "Heaven-Haven (a nun takes the veil)." In *Mortal Beauty, God's Grace*. Edited by John F. Thornton and Susan B. Varenne. New York: Random House, 2003.

John Jay College of Criminal Justice. *The Nature and Scope of Sexual Abuse of Minors by Catholic Priests and Deacons in the United States 1950–2002*. Washington, DC: United States Conference of Catholic Bishops, 2004.

John Paul II. *Pastores Dabo Vobis: On the Formation of Priests in the Circumstances of the Present Day*. Washington, DC: United States Catholic Conference, 1999.

———. *The Theology of the Body: Human Love in the Divine Plan*. Boston: Pauline Books and Media, 1997.

Kavanaugh, Kieran, and Otilio Rodriguez, eds. "Stanzas." In *The Collected Works of St. John of the Cross*. Washington, DC: Institute of Carmelite Studies, 1979.

Killen, Patricia O'Connell, and John de Beer. *The Art of Theological Reflection*. New York: Crossroad, 1994.

Krenik, Thomas W. *Formation for Priestly Celibacy: A Resource Book*. Washington, DC: National Catholic Education Association, 1999.

Laird, Martin. *Into the Silent Land: A Guide to the Christian Practice of Contemplation*. New York: Oxford University Press, 2006.

Laumann, Edward O., John H. Gagnon, Robert T. Michael, and Stuart Michaels. *The Social Organization of Sexuality: Sexual Practices in the United States*. Chicago: University of Chicago Press, 1994.

McAlpin, Kathleen. *Ministry That Transforms: A Contemplative Process of Theological Reflection*. Collegeville, MN: Liturgical Press, 2009.

Nestor, Thomas. "Intimacy and Adjustment among Catholic Priests." PhD diss., Loyola University, 1993.

Norris, Kathleen. *The Cloister Walk*. New York: Riverhead Books, 1996.

Praesidium. Standards for Accreditation. Arlington, TX: Praesidium, 2012. https://website.praesidiuminc.com/wp/wp-content/uploads/2013/05/2012_Standards_for_Accreditation_and_Glossary.pdf.

Rathus, Spencer A., Jeffrey S. Nevid, and Lois Fichner-Rathus. *Essentials of Human Sexuality*. Needham Heights, MA: Allyn and Bacon, 1998.

Rosario, Margaret, and Eric W. Schrimshaw. "Theories and Etiologies of Sexual Orientation." In *APA Handbook of Sexuality and Psychology, Volume 1: Person-Based Approaches,* edited by Deborah L. Tolman, Lisa M. Diamond, José A. Bauermeister, William H. George, James G. Pfaus, and L. Monique Ward, 555–96. Washington, DC: American Psychological Association, 2014.

Rossetti, Stephen J. *A Tragic Grace: The Catholic Church and Child Sexual Abuse.* Collegeville, MN: Liturgical Press, 1996.

Saarni, Carolyn. "Emotional Competence." In *The Handbook of Emotional Intelligence: Theory, Development, Assessment, and Application at Home, School, and in the Workplace,* edited by Reuven Bar-On and James D. A. Parker, 68–91. San Francisco: Jossey-Bass, 2000.

Saint Augustine. *Confessions.* Translated by R. S. Pine-Coffin. London: Penguin, 1961.

Schneiders, Sandra M. *Selling All: Commitment, Consecrated Celibacy, and Community in Catholic Religious Life.* New York: Paulist Press, 2001.

Shidlo, Ariel, and Michael Schroeder. "Changing Sexual Orientation: A Consumers' Report." *Professional Psychology: Research and Practice* 33, no. 3 (2002): 249–59.

Sipe, A. W. Richard. *A Secret World: Sexuality and the Search for Celibacy.* New York: Brunner/Mazel, 1990.

Spadaro, Antonio. " 'Wake Up the World!': Conversation with Pope Francis about the Religious Life." Translated by Donald Maldari (*La Civilta Cattolica,* no. I [2014]: 3–17). Accessed February 5, 2019. English translation available at http://onlineministries.creighton.edu/CollaborativeMinistry/PopeFrancis/Wake_up_the_world-2.pdf.

Storr, Anthony. *Solitude: A Return to the Self.* New York: The Free Press, 1988.

USCCB (United States Conference of Catholic Bishops). *Catechism of the Catholic Church.* 2nd ed. Washington, DC: United States Conference of Catholic Bishops, 1997.

USCCB (United States Conference of Catholic Bishops). *Program of Priestly Formation.* 5th ed. Washington, DC: United States Conference of Catholic Bishops, 2006.

Index

accountability, 36, 130, 156–166, 178, 188, 192, 210, 224
affective maturity, 9, 10, 135–152, 172, 180, 181, 182
androgens, 92, 104–105
androgyny (or psychological androgyny), 94–95
anticipatory guidance, 225, 227
attitudes (about sexuality), 18, 91, 93, 96, 109–111, 112–127

Becker, Jane, 6, 7, 67, 90, 154, 156, 217, 230
Bem, Sandra, 94–95
benchmarks for formation, 5, 84, 139, 151, 206–207, 212–215
boundaries, 6, 9, 107, 114, 129, 136, 138, 148, 157, 167–179, 190, 191, 192

Cantalamessa, Raniero, 49–53, 60, 229
Catechism of the Catholic Church, 48, 50, 62, 97–98
Center for Applied Research in the Apostolate (CARA), 2, 6, 155, 229
charism, 3, 37, 40, 47, 49, 52, 55–57, 62, 178, 180–181, 207, 223

chastity (meaning, versus celibacy), 50, 61–62
clergy sexual abuse, 5, 9, 90, 109, 113–114, 138, 144, 157
cognitive psychology, 146–147
community, 10, 11, 153–166, 170, 176–177, 183, 200, 221
compassion (see also empathy), 137–138, 143–144, 151
compulsive behavior, 27, 28, 37–38, 109, 128, 208
contemplation, 193, 198
conversion therapy, 102–103
counseling (psychotherapy), 10, 34, 36, 103, 128, 159, 161, 192
Cozzens, Donald, 100, 229

Davis, Beth Owen, 6, 226, 230
de Beer, John, 65, 67, 231
"deep-seated homosexual tendencies," 98–99
defense mechanisms (e.g., denial, repression, rationalization), 36, 119, 140, 145
developmental approach, 206–207
discernment, 16, 23, 32–33, 37, 39–40, 62, 91, 99, 109, 141, 160, 161, 164, 206
dual relationships, 174–176

narcissism, 144, 157–158

Nestor, Thomas, 6, 231

Norris, Kathleen, 180, 231

ongoing formation, 9, 12, 18, 213, 216–228

Pastores Dabo Vobis, 7, 12, 32, 60–61, 89, 115, 136, 137, 180–181, 231

perseverance in priesthood or religious life, 6, 11, 29, 31, 154–155, 219, 220

Pope John Paul II (see *Pastores Dabo Vobis*)

power differential, 174–175, 189, 223

Praesidium, 153, 231

program evaluation, 214–215

Program for Priestly Formation, 10, 12, 15, 58, 113, 136, 137, 146, 150–151, 158, 206, 232

retirement, 223, 225, 226

Rossetti, Stephen, 109, 113–114, 230

Saarni, Carolyn, 139–150, 172–173, 176–177, 232

Saint Benedict, 36, 59–60, 152, 153, 200

Saint John of the Cross, 49, 56, 197

Schneiders, Sr. Sandra, 24–26, 30, 55, 57, 84, 232

Schroeder, Michael, 102–103, 232

sex (i.e., male versus female), 92–93, 116

sexual abuse (history of), 27, 29, 107, 126, 128, 172

sexual history, 106–111, 117–120

sexual orientation (homosexuality, same-sex attraction), 10, 27, 96–106, 113–114, 116–121, 126–127, 207

determining factors, 101–106

church teaching, 97–100

prevalence, 100–101

Shidlo, Ariel, 102–103, 232

Sipe, A. W. Richard, 100, 232

solitude, 10, 11, 70, 193–202

spiritual direction, 10, 33, 34, 36, 83–84, 128, 129, 155–156, 159–166, 192, 208, 224

Storr, Anthony, 199, 232

support, 6, 11, 67, 126, 129, 130, 136, 153–166, 170, 178, 183, 192

ongoing, 220–222

groups, 224, 227

theological reflection, 64–85, 135, 197, 223

theology of celibacy, 3, 9–10, 45–63, 72–74

ascetic, 58–60

apostolic/missionary, 52–54

eschatological, 50–52

in persona Christi, 60–61

spousal, 54–57

Theology of the Body, 48, 62

transgender, 116

unmediated love of God, 54–57, 75, 78, 197

vigilance, 10, 137, 150, 181, 182, 185, 186

vocation director, 29, 34, 90, 124, 135–136, 151, 159–160, 207–208